SUSTAINABILITY, *the* ENVIRONMENT *and* URBANIZATION

This book is dedicated to disabled scholars and to the disabled poor in the developing countries

SUSTAINABILITY,

the Environment and Urbanization

Edited by
Cedric Pugh

from Routledge

First published by Earthscan in the UK and USA in 1996

For a full list of publications please contact:

Earthscan
2 Park Square, Milton Park, Abingdon, Oxon OX14 4RN
Simultaneously published in the USA and Canada by Earthscan
711 Third Avenue, New York, NY 10017

Earthscan is an imprint of the Taylor & Francis Group, an informa business

A catalogue record for this book is available from the British Library

ISBN: 978-1-85383-357-1 (pbk)

Copy-edited and typeset by Selro Publishing Services, Oxford

Contents

Preface

To engage discussion on 'sustainable development' is to be open to a diverse range of concepts, meanings and relevant applications. Nevertheless, an editor of a book should have some purposes, some boundaries and some directions. The boundaries were related to urbanization and especially to developing countries, though these boundaries necessarily had to have some contact with recent histories of environmentalism, with selected aspects of economic development, and with a new and growing literature which addresses the idea of sustainability. Purposes and directions for the book have very much been influenced by a mid-1990s context in which the urbanization aspects of research in sustainable development are surprisingly thin. Nevertheless, a number of urban specialists had commenced empirical studies in cities in developing countries or had started to develop some interesting conceptualizations and interpretations. A few urban specialists had a continuity of experience in environmentalism, dating from the 1970s. Thus the purposes and directions were set as drawing together the new research, and placing it within reflective characteristics of writing. The empirical content would primarily cover environmental conditions in large cities in developing countries, supported by review and evaluation chapters on infrastructure and developments in international health programmes. Conceptualization and interpretation were selected in application to broad structural economic changes in cities, to the changing nature of sustainability, and to the dependence of sustainable development upon institutional, social and political conditions.

At the outset it was clear that the researchers had earlier given thought to meaning and interpretation in the idea of sustainability and its relationship to development. However, as with the case in the wider literature, the authors had differing perspectives and arguments. My role as editor was not to compress thinking into any prescriptive definition, but care was taken to exchange some ideas on 'ecological', 'economic' and 'social' sustainability. The book has some bias in selection, mainly reflecting the present availability of good urban environmental research. Good arguments could be presented that the urban-relevant evaluations of greenhouse gases and of environment law should be included among the chapters. However, specialist urban research in these spheres is currently quite thin and elaborated treatment of these topics will have to wait on future work, though some authors in this volume do refer to these matters.

A book should do more than report progress in research. In a subject such as urban sustainable development interests and concerns for policy should have some thematic awareness and treatment. Policy issues are strongly to the fore in most chapters. Also, new research should be examined for its contribution to the development of knowledge in this emerging subject specialism. The final chapter has a commentary on the development of knowledge.

The production of a book such as this one owes much to collaboration. I have been grateful to the contributing authors who had to work to tight deadlines, to my secretary, Lynn Fox, and to Jonathan Sinclair Wilson and Jo O'Driscoll at Earthscan.

Cedric Pugh
April 1996

Foreword

One of the major themes in the book is the interrelatedness of many problems in urban environments. For example, the reduction of childhood health risks depends upon the education of mothers and carers. In its turn, better health induces improved attendance at school, and, in the longer term, this can increase GDP and reduce the incidence of poverty. The authors in the book give emphasis to the multi-faceted nature of sustainable urban environments, and, at the time of first publication, sometimes anticipated that ideas for the environment and development would change in due course.

Some important policies changed at the World Bank during the years 1997 to 2000, with new strategic policies joining together development, urban and poverty reduction policies. The World Development Report 1999–2000, *Entering the 21st Century*, brought urban agglomeration economics into the centre of development policies. Next, the urban strategic report *Cities in Transition* revealed the theory and statistics indicating the characteristics of cities as engines of growth. It also advocated poverty reduction, improved governance and sustainability as the major guiding principles for 'liveable' cities. All of this was consolidated and, again, joined together, in the World Development Report 2000–2001, *Attacking Poverty*.

This book continues to have significance for intellectuals and practitioners who wish to have an interrelated view of environmentalism, poverty and development.

Cedric Pugh,
January 2001

Notes on Contributors

Charles Choguill is Professor of Town and Regional Planning at the University of Sheffield, UK. In addition, he is director of the University's Centre for Development Planning Studies and editor of the journal *Habitat International*. He has had extensive consulting experience with the Asian Development Bank, the United Nations Development Programme, the International Civil Aviation Organization and the Arab Planning Institute, Kuwait. He is author of, among other books, *New Communities for Urban Squatters: Lessons from the Plan that Failed in Dhaka, Bangladesh* and co-editor of the Asian Development Bank's *Urban Policy Issues*. Charles Choguill's correspondence address is: University of Sheffield, Centre for Development Planning Studies, Sheffield, S10 2TN, UK.

Marisa Choguill is an architect who also holds Master's and PhD degrees in Urban Planning. She has taught architecture, landscape architecture, urban design and urban planning for more than 15 years in Brazil. Since coming to the United Kingdom in 1988, she has been a research officer at the University of Sheffield Centre for Development Planning Studies and taught at Sheffield Hallam University. A number of her papers have been published in *Habitat International* and *Third World Planning Review*. In 1993, she won the Otto Koenigsberger prize for the best paper in *Habitat International*. Marisa Choguill's correspondence address is: University of Sheffield, Centre for Development Planning Studies, Sheffield, S10 2TN, UK.

Trudy Harpham PhD is Professor of Urban Development and Policy at South Bank University, London, UK. She was previously the Head of the Urban Health Research Programme at the London School of Hygiene and Tropical Medicine. Her publications include two main texts on urban health, *In the Shadow of the City* (Oxford University Press, 1988) and *Urban Health in Developing Countries* (Earthscan, 1995). She has advised the Overseas Development Administration UK, UNICEF, the World Bank the World Health Organization and OXFAM on urban health development. Professor Harpham currently directs research projects in Brazil, Zambia, South Africa, India and Pakistan and manages a PhD programme at South Bank University. Together with

Edmundo Werna and Ilona Blue she is working with the WHO on 'Healthy City' projects in Egypt, Bangladesh, Pakistan and Burma. Trudy Harpham's correspondence address is: School of Urban Development and Policy, South Bank University, London, SW8 2JZ, UK.

Ernie Jowsey is a graduate of Sheffield University with a masters degree in economics from Nottingham Trent University. Currently a senior lecturer in the School of Urban and Regional Studies at Sheffield Hallam University, he specializes in minerals and environmental economics and his current research interests are in the fields of sustainable use of resources, the economics of renewable resources and methods of appraisal for environmental goods and services. Ernie Jowsey's correspondence address is: Sheffield Hallam University, School of Urban and Regional Studies, Pond Street, Sheffield, UK, S1 1WB.

Jon Kellett is a chartered town planner and senior lecturer in the School of Urban and Regional Studies at Sheffield Hallam University. His specialist interests are environmental issues, renewable energy developments, minerals and natural resource exploitation and techniques for assessing the impact of both existing and new projects on the environment. He has published extensively on these issues, and is responsible for the MSc Environmental Management for Business and Commerce course at Sheffield Hallam University. Jon Kellett's correspondence address is: Sheffield Hallam University, School of Urban and Regional Studies, Pond Street, Sheffield, UK, S1 1WB.

Marianne Kjellén is Research Fellow at the Stockholm Environment Institute (SEI). She is an economist with publication in the urban environmental research reports of the SEI. Marianne Kjellén's correspondence address is: Stockholm Environment Institute, Box 2142, 10314 Stockholm, Sweden.

Gordon McGranahan is Senior Research Fellow in the Urban Environment at the Stockholm Environment Institute. He has doctorate qualifications in development economics from University Wisconsin, Madison. Recent publications on urban sustainability are in the international journals *Habitat International* and *Environment*. Gordon McGranahan's correspondence address is: Stockholm Environment Institute, Box 2142, 10314 Stockholm, Sweden.

Diana Mitlin is Senior Research Assistant at the International Institute of Environment and Development (IIED). She is a development economist with postgraduate qualifications, and with extensive publication in the journal literature and in books on the subject of urban sustainable development. Diana Mitlin's major book is (with Jorge Hardoy and David Satterthwaite), *Environmental Problems in Third World Cities*, Earthscan, London, 1992. Diana Mitlin's correspondence address is: IIED, 3 Endsleigh Street, London, UK, WC1H 0DD.

Cedric Pugh is Reader in Urban Economic Development at Sheffield Hallam University. He is a development economist who has lived and researched in Europe, Australasia and Asia. Cedric Pugh has undertaken UN research contracts and he has written for international journals since the early 1970s: his major book on developing countries is *Housing and Urbanization: A Study of India*, Sage, New Delhi, 1990. Cedric Pugh's address for correspondence is: Sheffield Hallam University, School of Urban and Regional Studies, Pond Street, Sheffield, S1 1WB, UK.

David Satterthwaite is Director of Human Settlements at the International Institute of Environment and Development (IIED). His research work has been closely associated with Barbara Ward, in the years 1974 to 1979, and Jorge Hardoy, all developing leading international publications in sustainable development. David Satterthwaite's major publications are (with Jorge Hardoy), *Squatter Citizen: Life in the Urban Third World*, Earthscan, London, 1989, and (with Jorge Hardoy and Sandy Cairncross), *The Poor Die Young: Housing and Health in Third World Cities*, Earthscan, London. The journal *Environment and Urbanization* is edited by David Satterthwaite and published by IIED. David Satterthwaite's correspondence address is: IIED, 3 Endsleigh Street, London, UK, WC1H ODD.

Jacob Songsore is Associate Professor of Urban and Regional Development in the Department of Geography at the University of Ghana. He has doctorate qualifications, and has published on urban sustainability in the international journals *World Health Statistics Quarterly* and *Environment and Urbanization*. Jacob Songsore's correspondence address is: University of Ghana, Department of Geography and Resource Development, Box 59, Legon-Accra, Ghana.

Peter Townroe is Director of the School of Urban and Regional Studies (and Professor) at the Sheffield Hallam University. His work on urban economic sustainability dates from 1987, expanding from a research base in urban locational economics in industrial and developing countries. Peter Townroe is author of books and journal articles in the international literature, and he has held visiting fellowships in overseas universities. Research consultancies have been undertaken for the World

Bank and UN agencies. Peter Townroe's correspondence address is: Sheffield Hallam University, School of Urban and Regional Studies, Pond Street, Sheffield, S1 1WB, UK.

Edmundo Werna is an urbanist with a PhD from the University of London and a master's degree from the Institute of Development Studies (University of Sussex). He works as a researcher and consultant in urban development, and has wide experience in low- and middle-income countries. His special interests include urban management, the environment, health and housing. Dr Werna has also published extensively about urban development issues; his latest work includes the books *Urban Health Research: Implications for Policy* (co-edited with S Atkinson and J Songsore) and *Business as Usual: small-scale contractors and the production of low-cost housing in developing countries*. Previously at the Urban Health Programme of the London School of Hygiene and Tropical Medicine, he now has a joint research fellowship at the South Bank University (UK) and the University of São Paulo (Brazil). Edmundo Werna's correspondence address is: School of Urban Development and Policy, South Bank University, Wandsworth Road, London, SW8 2JZ, UK.

Introduction

Cedric Pugh

The idea of sustainability has a number of dimensions. In terms of definition it can be taken from official international reports which seek to establish new understandings of the relationship between the environment and development. For example, the World Commission on Environment and Development (1987:43) defined sustainable development as 'development that meets the needs of present generations without compromising the ability of future generations to meet their own needs'. Since the late 1980s much refinement and elaboration has occurred in the further conceptual analysis and definition of the idea of sustainability. Some approaches (for example, Munasinghe, 1993; Munasinghe and Cruz, 1995) distinguish 'economic', 'social' and 'environmental' sustainability. Thus, economic sustainability is understood as generating a maximum flow of economic welfare whilst maintaining the stock of assets, including environmental assets; social sustainability is people oriented, identified with the stability and cultural diversity of social systems; and environmental sustainability refers to the preservation, the resilience and the adaptation of physical and biological systems. Such approaches are insightful, but raise to relevance the problems of balance, reconciliation, and the values to be placed upon economic, social and environmental dimensions.

From some perspectives, the idea of sustainability is not simply a matter of appropriate scientific or analytical definition and conceptualization. It is related to general and operating principles of political economy, to spheres of application including 'green' and 'brown' agendas, and to processes of social and intellectual change. In considering the general level of political economy Dobson (1995) distinguishes 'ecologism' from 'environmentalism'. Ecologism is concerned with radical critiques of social, economic and political practices, adopting an appropriate social thought relevant for a postindustrial, environmental future. It takes seriously some propositions about the finitude of the

1

planet, and the advocates of ecologism believe in extensive interference in economic, social and political institutions. In this context, sustainability requires a new (environmental) political ideology because it cannot, according to the advocates of ecologism, be accommodated within the inherited ideologies of capitalist liberalism, state socialism or their compromised variants. The new political ideology would have biocentrism as its significant stance, in contrast to a damaging anthropomorphism. By contrast, 'environmentalism' can be set within existing political ideologies. It is reformist in a pragmatic way, centring upon concerns of institutionalizing environmentally relevant adaptations. Some examples of application would include conservation, pollution control, waste recycling, and improvements to squatter settlements in developing countries. Most of the issues and topics discussed in this book are within environmentalism rather than ecologism. They are relevant to brown agenda matters in developing countries.

Although it is possible to identify the general context of this book as towards environmentalism rather than ecologism, this does not mean that the political economy of brown agenda issues is straightforward and without some basic dilemmas. The brown agenda issues (for example, pollution, healthy urban living areas) overlap with the green agenda issues (for example, conservation of species). Also, in formulating and implementing environmental policies it is sometimes necessary to consider elements of the reformist and the radical simultaneously. Some reformist policies such as the regulation of motor vehicle emissions imply profound economic and technological changes in markets, firms and the activities of government agencies (see the discussions below on reform programmes in Los Angeles). Often in the advocacies and processes of reform, positions have to be adopted on the extent to which change is politically or technologically feasible and what consideration should be accorded to potentially self-defeating strategies. This is particularly relevant in developing countries because some conflicts exist between the alleviation of mass poverty and the implementation of wide ranging and comprehensive programmes of rapid and extensive environmental improvement. Nevertheless, the environmentalism rather than the ecologism approach rests on the basis that some genuine grounds exist for some reconciliation between sustainability and patterns of economic growth which can be societally progressive. Although some commentators take the position that economic growth and the cause for the environment are incompatible, various theoretical and empirical studies of growth and environmental issues (Goldin and Winters, 1995) argue circumspectly that the idea of incompatibility is exaggerated. It is suggested that specific changes in technical means of production, in environmental maintenance and in policies can have positive results for both growth and the environment. The overall costs of improved environments are not unduly high in relation to the capacity of the world economy, though they are of course significant in poor, national, economies.

THE 1980S RETHINKING ON ENVIRONMENTAL SUSTAINABILITY

Sustainability, as suggested above, is not simply an intellectually abstracted concept or scientific definition: it is closely associated to wider social processes and to its historical context. Historically it can be related to some fundamentally changed thinking about environmental issues and their relationship to society in the 1980s. The flavour of the rethinking has been well captured in reviews by Dasgupta and Maler (1994), Munasinghe (1993) and Pezzey (1992). As social causes, development and the environment were no longer to be understood as mutually exclusive. Instead, they are understood to have significant elements of complementarity. For example, environmental health programmes could improve work-related production and productivity. And, within appropriate institutional and resource conditions some negative aspects of the nexus between poverty and increased environmental degradation could be broken and reversed. In the rethinking, more significance was placed upon the medium- and long-term attributes of environmental assets as essential contributory resources in economic and social development. In economics wider ranges of concepts and principles were brought within the specialization of environmental economics. Historically, environmental economics had depended heavily upon theories of social costs and social benefits (for example, in explaining and correcting such things as pollution). The broadening range in environmental economics introduced economy-wide (macroeconomic) effects, aspects of institutional development and governance, problems associated with incomplete property rights in environmental issues, and the qualities of information available to policy makers, government agencies, non-government organizations (NGOs) and to citizens generally. Some of the broadened content had association to sociopolitical subjects. With the growing significance of the qualities of governance and institutions it became relevant to think of social and cultural capital and whether this was in harmony or conflict with environmental reform.

The rethinking on sustainability and the relationship between development and the environment had further historically-associated relevance. First, the rethinking came at a time when many countries were experiencing economic reform, especially in policies for macroeconomic stabilization and structural adjustment. Such policies often comprised elements of monetary and fiscal austerity, along with the deregulation and liberalization of markets. Such policies were widespread in sub-Saharan Africa, in Latin America, in countries transforming from state socialism to market orientations, and they also influenced economic policies in some advanced industrial countries. In one immediate perspective the economic reforms had some incompatibilities for the new rethinking and significance of environmental issues. For example, some public policy programmes in environmental infrastructure were curbed in government budget reform. However, the cause for the social development aspects of the environment also had a growing significance, reflected, for example, in the UN Conference on the Environment and Development (UNCED), Rio de Janeiro, 1992. Thus, the environmental cause, along with some return to appreciation of international poverty, led development economists towards reforming the content and approach in economic reform programmes. One example of this is research by Munasinghe and Cruz (1995) which evaluates the impact of macroeconomic reform upon environmental conditions. These authors reveal that some normal economic reform is conducive to sustainability, but contingently so, depending upon the way policies are formulated and the characteristics of institutional frameworks in which the reform is situated. In effect, reform for greater efficiency can reduce some environmental costs, but institutional conditions (for example, laws, administrative provisions) have to be in place to counter adverse social costs of environmental impact in market economies.

The second main aspect of historically-associated relevance is the general state and characteristic of development economics in the 1980s and 1990s. This becomes significant because ideas and practices in development economics, especially for developing countries, have influence in the way sustainability is understood and practised as a political economy. The range of theories, political economies and ideas in development economics is wide and characterized with controversy. It thus becomes a question of relevance and selection for the period covering the 1980s and 1990s. Selection here is related to the Earth Summit, that is the Rio de Janeiro UNCED meeting in 1992, and to two world development reports by the World Bank (1992; 1994). These three items have affinities with each other and reflect an orthodoxy of the period. Their relevance is also because they have impacts in the World Bank's loan and technical assistance programmes, also with added relevance to international policy development among various UN agencies (see the discussions below). The Bank's world development report of 1992 was devoted to a research-based review of the environment and development. In broad terms the report accepted some possible harmony between the environment and development in their two-way causal and consequential relationships. The political economy of the report emphasized an 'enabling', 'market friendly', policy development, but with some carefully selected government roles in policy formulation, regulation, tax-subsidy (dis)incentives, and institutional reform. Good policies were seen as developing 'win–win' outcomes for development and the environment, and breaking important negative development–environment relationships.

The 1992 world development report was set in a context of some 1.0 billion population experiencing inadequate sanitation, some 1.3 billion suffering unsafe air pollution conditions of soot, smoke and motor vehicle emissions, and some 700 million children and women living in housing where air was polluted from cooking fires. The brown agenda issues were given more elaborated and specialized review in the 1994 world development report, covering brown and green agenda issues related to infrastructure. The consequently favoured elements of policy development and implementation were complex, involved multi-institutional relevance (ie government agencies, markets, NGOs, community-based organizations (CBOs) and the empowerment of households in participatory programmes). Some of the selected language and discourse of the reports provide insights into the favoured political economy of development. For example, standards were to be 'realistic' and 'enforceable'; policy and institutional arrangements were to emphasize 'prioritizing' and 'monitoring'; political climates were seen as useful when steps were taken to develop a 'constituency for change'; and the organization of brown agenda infrastructure was to be reformed to achieve 'efficiency', 'decentralization', 'accountability' and 'well-targeted' subsidization. Overall, within multi-institutional conditions and policy frameworks, markets and the private sector were seen to have central roles. This has set the context for post-1992 programmes and technical aid development by the World Bank and other international organizations (see Munasinghe, 1993; Munasinghe and Cruz, 1995; Pezzey, 1992; Williams, 1995).

INSTITUTIONS AND THE URBAN ENVIRONMENT

From the foregoing it is clear that some of the orthodoxies in development economics will have a varied success–failure experience in practice and require adjustment of principle and policy. It is not simply that there are actual and potential conflicts between government agencies, markets, NGOs, CBOs and households. In further relevance, much depends upon finding solutions to creating and operating multi-institutional frameworks. The creation and operation of multi-institutional frameworks have several spheres of relevance. First, it is important to understand the principles and justifications for multi-institutional frameworks in modern political economy and in environmentalism. Second, institutional frameworks are relevant at a variety of levels, including international organizations, national governments with roles in environmental and urban action plans, and in the governance and division of labour in urban areas. Third, having in mind the inherent complexity of operating multi-institutional frameworks, it is useful to discern the prospective realities in terms of success–failure perspectives. Examples exist of good environmental reform, but there is also evidence that unwieldy and inappropriate institutions have inhibited progress in urban and environmental reform.

Institutional frameworks and policy making are related. Especially in environmentalism and urban policy development, governments have important roles in creating and formulating institutional frameworks. For example, in various applications of environmental policy it may be necessary to coordinate government agencies, to develop partnerships between infrastructure authorities and firms or organized households, or to introduce regulations for controlling motor vehicle emissions. The institutional frameworks can also have widescale effects upon incentive and disincentive structures which can operate for environmental protection, or, if inappropriate, for adversity. Institutions can be understood in several perspectives, each influencing ways of doing things. First, they are central in social bonding, in social functioning and in influencing the relationships among organizations. Also, they give organizations their characteristics and influence their (in)ability to carry out their organizational functions. In this perspective, institutions can be regarded as part of the social capital of society. Essentially, from the sociopolitical perspective, institutions create norms, rules, and legal systems. As suggested above, the resultant institutions can be useful or, sometimes, they can be obsolescent and not in harmony with social change, including, for example, with changing environmental needs.

In a second perspective, institutions have possibilities to express comparative advantage and to have major impact upon social and economic development. Coase (1960) notes that institutions arise in addition to markets when high transaction costs impede market development. Transaction costs are the costs of formulating, monitoring and enforcing agreements: they are centrally relevant to urban water and sanitation systems, to the control of air pollution, and to other brown agenda issues. For Coase, various institutions – for example, firms, government agencies, NGOs, CBOs and households – each have their characteristic comparative advantage. Firms have comparative advantage in entrepreneurship, including in the development of environmental technology; governments have comparative advantage in policy making, in setting property rights and in institutional reform; NGOs and CBOs have comparative advantage in mobilizing household effort for pro-environmental purposes; and households have comparative advantage in some aspects of personal and social development. In the circumstances of economic and social complexity in environmental conditions, it is frequently the case that multi-institutional development is relevant, enabling an appropriate combination of comparative advantages.

Multi-institutional combination has significance beyond a simple application to project-based environmental initiatives. As reasoned by North (1990), institutional frameworks have long-term consequences upon rates of economic and social development. For example, North reveals that higher standards of living in the USA relative to Mexico are largely attributable to differences in the incentive structures for productivity which are provided in the institutional and cultural conditions. The argument can be extended into environmental relevance. Long-term progress with sustainability and brown agenda issues will depend upon the quality and the social innovation in creating and implementing environmentally friendly institutions. This, of course, is far from being a straightforward task. Institutions such as markets, government agencies and households have some inherent conflicts of interest in economic, political and environmental dimensions.

In view of the foregoing, it becomes relevant as a third perspective to consider the appropriate nature of institutional combination in urban environmental contexts. In a prescriptive advocacy vein Ostrom and her coauthors suggest that 'multiple, nested institutions' are necessary in brown agenda matters because 'in many urban policy spheres private and social benefits are mixed together defying attempts at pure market or pure government classifications for the provision of services' (Ostrom et al, 1993:21).

In other words, multiple institutions, 'appropriately nested' can correct either gross market or state failure when single rather than multiple institutional provisions are applied. The idea of 'appropriate nested' multiple institutions can be elaborated further in their urban context. For example, in localized infrastructure improvement for sanitary purposes, economic and situational paradoxes and impediments arise, as explained in various chapters in this volume. Although the incomes of low-income households may increase and affordable technologies exist, without 'appropriate nesting' of institutional arrangements among government agencies, firms and households, the potential improvements will not be realized. Additionally, with special relevance for developing countries, it should be appreciated that it is not just the formulation of policies and institutions that is relevant: the qualities and commitments to implementation are also significant. Implementation can fall down owing to institutional incapacity and to opposition organized by sectional interests to restrict policy development and to undermine the intended results. This is all the more relevant in environmental contexts because wide multi-institutional possibilities require subtle political, institutional and legal structures, not simply either state provided or *laissez-faire* conditions. Accordingly, it is appropriate to review some relevant policy and institutional conditions in environmental frameworks.

INTERNATIONAL POLICY AND INSTITUTIONAL CONDITIONS IN THE 1990S

Since the mid-1980s there has been a fundamental review of international urban policy and urban environmental conditions by international organizations and independent commentators (see Williams, 1995; World Bank, 1991). The scope includes the relationships between urban policy development, economic growth and the environment, and the general condition of relevant institutions, ranging from international to local levels. The reviewing has not been limited to arguments and principles for prescriptive ideals in policy making and institutional frameworks: it also includes useful evaluations of success–failure perspectives in both developing and industrialized countries. The success–failure perspectives are important because they can provide intelligence in discerning the conditions under which good practice is generated and improved in real social, political and economic conditions.

Williams (1995) sets out the comparative strengths and weaknesses of those international organizations that have responsibilities in post-Earth Summit, Rio de Janeiro, environmental development. The major international organizations with responsibilities are the World Bank and various agencies of the United Nations including, the UN Development Programme (UNDP), the UN Environment Programme (UNEP), and in the human settlements sphere the UN Centre for Human Settlements (Habitat) (UNCHS). In general political economy roles, international organizations operate as 'regimes'. That is to say, they develop association and norms with their clients (ie national and other levels of government), they arrange meetings for exchanges of information, they promote their research and advisory programmes, and they persuade in favour of their preferred policies. As institutions, the international organizations have their respective attributes and limitations in developing their roles and influence. For relevance to the urban environmental agenda, as noted by Williams (1995), the following points can be made:

- The World Bank has the power and impact of loan finance to persuade change and national action plan development for environmental progress. The Bank gave the environment central significance only after 1987 in response to criticism and agitation by reviewers of its projects and by environmental lobby groups. However, since the late-1980s the Bank has developed its experience, its research and its technical advisory services. Compared with other international organizations (see below) it has been centralized in organization and is somewhat associated with its technocratic economic orthodoxies of the period 1980–95. Nevertheless, the Bank has the capacity to influence a course of international response, providing it finds appropriate institutional and policy conditions at the levels of national and local government in countries where it could extend loans and technical advice.

- The UNDP is the agent of the UN which is responsible for developing technical advice and related services for member countries. It has developed an interest in environmental and urban policy issues, but its capacity is limited in resources, in research capacity and in the quality of its consultant services. Meanwhile, the UNEP has pursued its environmental roles mainly along the lines of developing awareness among nations and creating monitoring and information systems for international environmental relevance. It does not have the resource capacity of the World Bank or the fieldwork contacts of the UNDP. The UNCHS entered the urban environmental field rather later than the other UN agencies, dating its involvement from the late 1980s, and bringing the environment to significance for the UN Habitat II conference, Istanbul, June 1996. The UNCHS collaborates with the World Bank and UNDP in the post-1988 Urban Management Programme (UMP), a technical advisory programme for urban policy development, including the urban environment and infrastructure services.

The increased significance of environmental agendas in international organizations raises issues of their relations with each other. As argued by Williams (1995), they will need to develop their own set of collaborative relationships and their respective comparative advantages. Much will depend upon the roles and development of the World Bank because this organization has the capacity in resources, in financial influence and in research development. But it will find it necessary to work more closely with UN agencies, including UNDP, UNEP, UNCHS, and WHO. The Bank's finances for the poorest developing countries are subject to political vulnerability. Although the Bank's basic finances are raised on world capital markets, the subsidized funds for the poorest developing countries are raised through the leading industrialized countries contributing to the special International Development Association (IDA). In 1995 the US Congress experienced conflict with President Clinton on the size and allocation of federal government budgets, with Congress favouring a reduction in American contributions to the IDA. All of this came in a context of critical review of World Bank organization and roles as it came to its fiftieth anniversary in 1994. Thus, development finance for developing countries has become entangled in the cause for reform of the Bank.

The brown agenda issues also have reference in the 'new agenda' reforms at the levels of urban governance and urban economic development. The new agenda reforms are elaborated and stated in the World Bank's strategic urban policy review (World Bank, 1991). The new agenda had a number of thrusts to persuade a cause for fundamental change. Notwithstanding progress in general urban social and economic development, along with some positive impact from the Bank's loan programmes, conditions in squatter settlements, in water and sanitation services, in the high volume of poverty and in environmental degradation remained extensive and significant. Urban demographic and economic growth portended a medium-term continuation of significant poverty and some environmental deterioration. Approaches to urban policies should, according to the Bank, be switched from project-by-project approval to urban-wide contexts. These urban-wide contexts had two main elements. First, urban development was understood to be contributory to the growth of productivity and general society-wide economic development. In other words, the (co-location) efficiencies in urban agglomeration economies were important in sustainable economic development, as a central element in development economics. Second, in recognition that urban development depended upon multi-institutional roles from markets, government agencies, NGOs, CBOs and households, this raised issues about qualities in policy making and institutional development. These two elements had particular significance for the environment and poverty, and the interdependence between poverty and the urban environment. Bringing issues of poverty and the environment together has raised the relevance of the 'social' in economic development and added importance to state roles in institutional reform.

The new agenda had implications for the political economy of urban development and the brown agenda. Political economy had relevance at both general levels of principle and at levels of operational reality. At levels of general principle, as suggested earlier, the favoured political economy fell into the advocacy of 'enablement' liberalism. That is to say, economic development, sustainability, and the environment in the 1990s were associated with market-led growth, with associated institutional development and with orthodox economic reform (see earlier discussions). Governments nevertheless had important roles: these were in policy making, in linking urban and macroeconomic policies, in creating and enforcing property rights, and in well-directed regulatory and anti-poverty initiatives. As I have argued elsewhere (Pugh, 1994) 'enablement' liberalism is characterized with the development of late twentieth-century liberalism and it has some excessive optimism in reconciling efficiency, social equity and democratic functioning. Consequently, reform is not free of dilemmas, trade-offs and political choice.

At the level of operations and from experience with policy applications, the new agenda has some real-world political economy. This can be ascertained from commentaries and reviews by the World Bank and from the coordinator of the joint World Bank–UNDP–UNCHS Urban Management Programme. Once the new agendas were set on course in the Bank it became necessary to develop its significance for loan allocations and the realities of urban circumstances in developing countries (Buckley and Heller, 1992). Bank officials recognized that earlier shortcomings in some 20 years of experience arose from policy and institutional shortcomings in many Third World cities. Actual shortcomings included failures in cost recovery, general managerial slippage in monitoring and executing projects, attempted application through insolvent institutions, and lack of institutional sustainability. The Bank also acknowledged that its own appraisal criteria were exclusively related to conventional rates of return analyses, rather than also including broad sector-wide and institutional capacity evaluations. Reform in operations was becoming urgent because modern urban loan programmes were vast, at an annual average volume of US$ 400 million per approved scheme in 1992 compared with US$ 20 million in 1972. The potential for failure had higher stakes and greater complexity, especially given that modern schemes had deep sector-wide intended relevance. As would be expected, the World Bank directed its attention to a package of reforms, including its own assessment criteria, reviews of institutional capacity, analyses of private–public sector interaction in urban programmes, the removal of inappropriate regulatory constraints, and establishing clearer definition to 'enablement' in programme development.

The officials' responsible for the UMP have also been giving reflection to the nature of the new agenda (see Wegelin and Borgman, 1995). Their main issue of relevance is the deconcentration and decentralization of authority and governance implied in the new agenda. This is especially significant for the role of municipal authorities and for community participation. The inherited qualities of local government in some developing countries have been inadequate. Inadequacies include weaknesses in public finance, managerial incapacity, and various forms of corruption and preferment for sectional political and economic interests. Historical inertia has also been evident. The inertia includes excessively high building and development control standards, along with gaps in standard setting in environmental conditions. More generally, the general orientation in urban planning in many developing countries has been towards the interests of higher income groups rather than for coming to terms with the realities of mass poverty and the alleviation of urban poverty.

In elaboration of the foregoing, Wegelin and Borgman (1995) indicated the disparity in access to water, sanitation and other services among income groups. Very often the poor are dependent upon high-cost private vendor services in water provision. Public sector services are characterized by regressive subsidization and, in the case of sanitation services, by large gaps in installation in the living areas of low-income groups. Opportunities for developing intricate informal sector–public agency relationships in solid waste disposal have also been neglected. Such opportunities include commercial scavenging and waste processing. In the most general of urban perspectives, Wegelin and Borgman (1995) emphasize the basic interdependence between policies on health, employment, education and brown agenda improvement. It is from this basis of interdependence at localized levels that Wegelin and Borgman argue for improving the resource and institutional capacity of municipal government. Various roles are envisaged. Some are people related, for example in association with community development in squatter settlements. And some have technical and professional relevance, for example in developing monitoring and localized informational bases on poverty and urban environmental conditions. In actual practice, notwithstanding economic austerity packages in the 1970s and 1980s, Chile formulated anti-poverty and social programmes within the reform of municipal government (Casteñada, 1992). Chile's approach was carefully thought out, developed on the basis of deepening institutionally-loaded reform, and largely effective in anti-poverty results, even though the economic burdens fell upon moderate- and middle-income groups.

EXAMPLES OF PROGRESS

What have been the general principles of success in brown agenda policy and programme development? Recourse can be had to examples in both developing and industrial countries. As would be expected from earlier discussions, much depends upon creating and developing appropriate institutional conditions that further the cause of sustainability. The institutional conditions usually involve the bringing together of reforms and development in markets, in government, in research organizations, in NGOs, in CBOs and in households. Examples are drawn from brown agenda policy developments in neighbourhood infrastructure services, in the reduction of motor vehicle emissions, and in developing the social culture and social capital for environmental improvement.

Orangi is a squatter settlement in the suburbs of Karachi, Pakistan. In 1980 it faced some dismal prospects in respect to water, sanitation and environmental services. Disease was rife; government agencies were unable to provide installations and services in the medium term; and private sector alternatives were variously unaffordable and ineffective. However, under the leadership of Hameen Khan a series of initiatives were taken to organize the community and to develop the necessary services (Orangi River Project, Research and Training Institute, 1995). Programmes commenced with low-cost sanitation services and health and family planning provisions at neighbourhood levels. They subsequently extended to credit facilities for small-scale economic development, to upgrading schools, and to the creation of a women's work centre. The approach was to engage the confidence and support of the community, with special regard for locally expressed needs and cultural acceptance in gender and family considerations. Progress was made through 'learning by doing' experience, and by associating affordable (low-cost) technology with the physical improvements to the local environments. In institutional perspective, community-based organization mobilized and trained households, and the improvements were demonstrated to public authorities for wider application in urban low-income living areas.

Air pollution from motor vehicle emissions first appeared in industrial countries, but has now become a widespread health threatening problem in developing countries. Research by Hall (1995) describes and evaluates the substantial progress achieved in Los Angeles, USA. Smog, ozone and health problems attracted public concern in the 1940s. Over a period of some four decades substantial air quality improvements have been achieved with policy reform and institutional development. The full package of necessary reforms was extensive. Legislation for regulation of technical standards in vehicles and oil refineries had to be passed. However, the specification and elaboration of standards had to wait upon the development of research and experimentation in the applied science of pollution. The consequent regulatory changes had to be assessed for their impact upon the management and economics of the motor vehicle and oil refining industries. Additionally, regard had to be made to the comparative economic growth and sustainability of California, ensuring no significant vulnerability. Political and community support needed to be nurtured and persuaded where regulations had some potential conflicts of interest among households, firms and political lobby groups. In a continual process of publicity, negotiation and review California succeeded in reform. Thus, an example of good progress (and its necessary social, political and economic conditions) is now available for wider assessment and emulation. Of course, cities in developing countries face sharper trade-offs in economic development than does Los Angeles and have less experience in reforming institutions. As indicated in modern statistical research (Dasgupta et al, 1995), environmental regulation and policy tend to deepen with national per capita income growth. Progression is from protection of natural resources, then to the regulation of water quality and finally to the control of air pollution. However, in the light of post-Earth Summit experience, issues such as carbon emissions and global warming are beginning to receive an internationalized response linking industrial and developing countries. For example, since 1992 UNCTAD has undertaken research and proposed a CO_2 emission allowances market. This envisages the creation of a multilaterally agreed emissions trading system, deliberately biased in favour of poorer countries in order to allow continuing industrialization. Additionally the World Bank and UNEP have promoted conferences and projects to develop international mutual aid in controlling greenhouse gas emissions.

As a final example, recognition is given to the relevance of developing social capital in environmental improvement. Social capital comprises the improvement in education and information in environmental matters, the development of environmentally useful products and technologies, and closely associating public policy reform with community-based commitments. All of this has been occurring in the 1980s and 1990s in Ontario, Canada (Henderson, 1995). Environmental goods and services generate some 3 per cent of Ontario's GDP, with further growth likely in the medium term. The Ministry of Environment promotes community initiatives with grants. This has led to the development of 'Home Green Up', in which trained visitors arrange meetings and home visits to improve energy and water efficiency. Consequently, home renovation for environmental improvement has spread among some 19 cities. This example demonstrates approaches to the relevant development of social capital on environmental issues. Again, it would not be expected that the prevailing conditions of civic association and sociopolitical experience which prevail in Canada would exist in many developing countries. Nevertheless, as the foregoing Orangi scheme and subsequent examples in other chapters in the book reveal, some good practice in developing countries has occurred.

The foregoing examples consolidate some themes and issues which have been brought to relevance in this introductory chapter. 'Sustainability' is about interdependence between social, economic and environmental sustainabilities. The interdependence occurs in broad social, political and economic processes. In urban brown agenda issues the inherent characteristics are complex and relevant to multi-institutional conditions. Thus, there are respective comparative advantage roles for government, markets, NGOs, CBOs and households. These become clearly evident in the good practice examples of infrastructure services in Orangi, of motor vehicle emission control in Los Angeles, and in deepening environmental social capital in Ontario. In these examples, progress is long term and developmental with learning by doing features. Institutional sustainability is the hallmark rather than quick fix approaches. All of this means that advocacy and understanding for the environment has to go beyond narrow physical improvements to include societal conditions in economic, social and political processes.

THE SCOPE AND THEMES OF THE FOLLOWING CHAPTERS

Although the opening paragraph to this chapter established the interdependence between matters developmental and matters environmental as being brought to the fore in official international reports (for example, the 1987 Brundtland Report) since the late 1980s, in fact relevant histories and analyses can be taken back to the 1970s. Barbara Ward wrote eloquently and persuasively during the 1970s on the basic situational interdependence between economic growth, human development, mass poverty, the living conditions in low-income residential areas, and everyday environmental problems. For example, Barbara Ward (1976) wrote about the 'inner' and 'outer' limits of development in developing countries, indicating acceptance of the development imperative, but with significant regard to environmental impact. Her ideas had international policy and institutional significance. She wrote influential documents for the Habitat I UN Conference at Vancouver in 1976, and the Cocoyoc Declaration adopted by UNEP and UNCTAD for their 1974 symposium, Pattern of Resource Use: Environment and Development Strategies. Although it is the case that under the pens of some authors who specialize in matters environmental in industrial countries, it is conservationist aims that are emphasized for developing countries, as reasoned by Barbara Ward, matters developmental, matters urban, matters to do with poverty, and matters environmental are in fact and in principle all of one piece. This is the thrust of the term 'urban sustainable development' for developing countries. It is also the general mission of the International

Institute for Environment and Development (IIED), founded in 1971.

Barbara Ward's influence, along with some 25 years of research and experience in the IIED, and the interdependence of matters developmental and matters environmental come within the scope and content of this book. David Satterthwaite was research assistant to Barbara Ward during the 1970s, and he, along with his coauthor Diana Mitlin in Chapter 1, are leading researchers in the IIED. Their chapter advances themes and ideas, historically connecting the UN's Habitat I Conference in Vancouver in 1976 and its Habitat II Conference for Istanbul in 1996. Diana Mitlin and David Satterthwaite enter discourse on the meaning and application of 'sustainable development', and from the basis of their reasonings they provide useful guidance and warnings. Readers are cautioned against a too ready acceptance of harmonies between multiple developmental and environmental objectives: also, they are persuaded that dilemmas and sometimes policy failures can occur in context because social processes and professional practices are inadequate. Chapter 1 ranges widely, providing interpretation and discussion of such physical environmental conditions as climatic change, resource depletion, the 'sink' capacity of the planet and so on. But none of this discussion loses the connection to such relevant living conditions as housing and income generation. Significantly, the developmental-environmental agenda is brought within the relevance of qualities and institutions of governance, including accountability, transparency and participation. David Satterthwaite and Diana Mitlin have a wide-ranging scope, appropriate to the idea of 'sustainable urban development'. Width becomes a characteristic of other chapters in the book, though some have focus on particular aspects such as infrastructure and health.

Brown agenda issues are closely related to improvements in health. This means that the relative significance of health has increased within urban policies, including international initiatives by the WHO. In Chapter 2 Trudy Harpham and Edmundo Werna provide exposition and evaluation of the recently inaugurated Healthy Cities Project. The project is based upon a very broad conceptualization of 'health', and the authors discuss this in relation to ideas of sustainability. Chapter 3, authored by Charles and Marisa Choguill, has close affinities with health, being centred upon neighbourhood infrastructure. Matters to do with infrastructure in developing countries are always linked to dilemmas of affordability in a context of mass poverty in unserviced settlements. Charles and Marisa Choguill deal with these dilemmas by proposing approaches that are low cost, but have the flexibility for improvement as urban economies develop. They also argue that their 'incremental' approach can provide an important element in giving practical effect to urban sustainability. One useful way of establishing general principles in neighbourhood environmental issues among the living areas of the poor is by undertaking wide ranging empirical studies in large cities in various global regions. Chapter 4 accomplishes this, reporting current research programmes among low-income living areas in São Paulo, Jakarta and Accra. The authors, Gordon McGranahan, Jacob Songsore, and Mari-anne Kjellén, are associated with international research programmes in the Stockholm Environmental Institute. Their research indicates some of the miserable realities of urban poverty, and one of their conclusions reveals the internal conflicts in setting environmental agendas. The poor prefer basic sanitation and service improvements rather than attention to the more remote global concerns such as global warming. Also, the authors interpret their empirical findings by reference to the idea of an 'environmental transition' which relates specific classes of urban environ-mental problems to affluence and stages of development.

In discussions of sustainability it is, of course, important to go beyond specific matters such as neighbourhood and environmental health. The idea of sustainability and the way it is being practised in the late twen-tieth century merits evaluation. This is done in Chapter 5, authored by Cedric Pugh. The chapter assesses Agenda 21 and subsequent develop-ments from the Rio de Janeiro 'Earth Summit'. This evaluation includes the ways certain subjects such as economics have been adapting their concepts and theories for environmentalism. Chapter 6, written by Peter Townroe, also draws upon economics and its connection with issues of social exclusion and institutional adaptability in rapidly changing cities. A major feature of Peter Townroe's chapter is the setting of urbanization in rapid spatial-structural changes in cities. Environmental dilemmas vary according to whether cities are relatively dynamic and responsive to economic change or remain static. Processes of social exclusion and social inclusion are shown to have implications for environmental needs and the patterning of economic change. Finally, the book includes a review of methods, techniques and principles in urban environmental appraisal. This review is undertaken by Ernie Jowsey and Jon Kellett in Chapter 7. They show that appraisal can be developed in a set of purposes, ranging from city-wide monitoring and auditing to the analysis of the environmental impact of specific development projects. An overall discussion of conclusions is written by Cedric Pugh, with emphasis to the intellectual and professional development of 'sustainability'.

The scope and themes of the book fall within a general conceptual framework of development. This framework is expressed in the 'demo-graphic transition' and its associated economic conditions among developing countries. Developing countries have been experiencing an explosive growth in population and urbanization. Whereas in 1950 some 30 per cent of the world's population was urbanized at 737 million, by

1995 some 45 per cent was urbanized at 2.5 billion. During the last 50 years the urban population of developing countries has increased by 600 per cent. The pattern of urban growth commenced in Latin America, followed more recently in Asia and Africa. Another urban feature has been the growth in the number of cities of over 1 million. In 1950 there were some 31 cities of over 1 million, and by 1995 this had grown to 196 cities, with most of this increase occurring in developing countries.

The foregoing is explained by the processes that are inherent in the 'demographic transition' and by extensive rural-to-urban migration in developing countries. The 'demographic transition' explains high rates of population growth over long periods of time. It can be understood in terms of a series of successive phases. In phase one population is generally stable, though punctuated with the effects of some famine: birth and mortality rates are both high. Phase two is characterized by some reduction in mortality rates with some subsequent slower decrease in birth rates. This leaves a growing number of women in the fertile stage of their life cycles, with consequences for medium-term high rates of population growth. In the later phases, birth rates fall further and overall population tends to be stable. Most developing countries are experiencing the phases characterized by high rates of population growth, but some (for example, Singapore) are at a stage of low birth rates and stable population.

The 'demographic transition' comes into conjunction with economic and developmental factors. One approach to understanding the consequences is to focus upon the new entrants to the labour market. In developing countries some 35 million new entrants annually expand the labour market supply. Their prospects for work and their levels of income largely depend upon whether the rates of saving and investment are at sufficient levels to add capital to the increased supplies of labour. Where capital is insufficient or of low technological characteristic, millions are added to the lowly-productive informal sectors. This tends to increase volumes or poverty, slum generation and squatter settlement, and it adds severe burdens to the provision of basic urban services. In other words, it heightens the significance of problems in brown agenda environmental conditions in neighbourhood disamenity. These sorts of environmental problems are clearly associated with the conjunction of the 'demographic transition', poverty and rates of saving and investment. They will also be influenced by whether suitable environmental, housing, social and health policies have been instituted. Policy responses are highly variable in quality and effectiveness.

The foregoing can be elaborated further and turned more emphatically to urban significance. In developing countries, although (calorific) poverty has been predominantly a rural phenomenon, in recent decades and for projected futures it is becoming increasingly an urban problem. It is estimated that some 430 million poor in developing countries live in urban areas; in the period 1970 to 1985 poverty in developing countries increased by some 22 per cent, 11 per cent of which was rural and 73 per cent urban; and to the year 2025 the world's poverty level is estimated to reach 4 billion, increasing from 3 billion currently. As indicated above, this poverty is set to increase pressures on housing, infrastructure and environmental conditions. In broader terms, bringing together the effects of the 'demographic transition' and urban poverty, it is useful to conceive of an 'urban transition'. As revealed by Hall (1987), some general patterns of urbanization have occurred over periods of a century or more in modernizing industrial countries. In the first phases, urban concentration occurs as settlement becomes increasingly urban and decreasingly rural. This is a phase of rapid and strong urban growth, this characterizing the present urban situation in most developing countries. Later phases have much slower demographic growth, and eventually some city regions may lose population to small- and medium-sized towns.

Clearly, in their urban setting, many modern environmental and developmental issues occur within rapidly growing cities in developing countries. What do we know about the nature and characteristics of rapidly growing cities in developing countries? Obviously there will be some variations in developmental and settlement profiles in accordance with differences in economic, geographical and other circumstances. Mohan (1994) details some characteristics of market dominated development in Latin American contexts. The dynamics of rapidly growing cities have spatial, environmental and income consequences. City centres have concentrated economic intensity, but much housing, industry and commerce decentralizes to the suburbs. Often the incidence of poverty decreases, though its volume may increase, and backlogs in services to low-income living areas are common. As suggested above, poverty is much associated with low productivity rather than mass unemployment, and this often originates in the informal sectors. Labour markets tend to be fluid and reasonably efficient in the circumstances. Although rapidly growing cities are beset with developmental problems, they cope over medium-term periods. However, the increasing significance of the environment adds to organizational, institutional and economic burdens.

Some countries have achieved high levels of saving and productive investment, leading to high rates of growth. This often means that although their volumes of urban poverty are still significant, their longer term trends are towards decreasing their incidences and volumes of poverty. In other words, these countries have been experiencing a 'poverty and wage transition' in which the absolute and relative distributions of income have improved in the bottom 40 per cent of households. Such has been the experience of countries such as Hong Kong, Taiwan, South Korea and Singapore. These countries have pursued economic development policies which relied upon export-led growth and the educational upgrading of the masses, in contrast to protectionist development policies which occurred widely in Latin America and sub-Saharan Africa. However, since the early 1980s protectionist policies have been abandoned under widespread economic reform. Consquently it can be expected that increasing numbers of developing countries will make progress in their 'poverty and wage transition' during the next two decades. Such progress does not imply that environmental difficulties will diminish. On the contrary, in many instances environmental problems will heighten and be characterized by developmental change. For example, air pollution from industrial particulates and from carbon dioxide and other greenhouse gases can increase, although in time, with growth to affluent and modernized standards, some environmental problems may be abated. It is possible to conceive of an 'environmental transition' in parallel and in association with the 'poverty and wage' and the 'demographic' transitions. This is further discussed in subsequent chapters by Gordon McGranahan and his coauthors and by Cedric Pugh. Thus, the idea of 'sustainable development' has a variety of relevant meanings in developing countries, including the underlying association to 'demographic', 'urban' and 'poverty and wage' transitions. Much of the global drama of environmental change in the coming decades will occur in developing countries. Environmentalism is not just an issue of living and health standards for future generations. Millions in developing countries from the current generation will experience childhood, their youth, adulthood and old age set in contexts of severe environmental problems.

References

Buckley, R and M Heller (1992) *Implementing the Urban Agenda of the 1990s*, Urban Development Division, Infrastructure and Urban Development Department, World Bank, Washington DC

Casteñada, T (1992) *Combating Poverty: Innovative Social Reforms in Chile During the 1980s*, ICS Press, San Francisco

Coase, R (1960) 'The Problem of Social Cost', *Journal of Law and Economics*, 3 (1), pp 1–44

Dasgupta, P and K Maler (1994) *Poverty, Institutions and the Environmental Resource Base*, World Bank, Washington DC

Dasgupta, S, A Mody, S Roy and D Wheeler (1995) *Environmental Regulation and Development: A Cross-Country Empirical Analysis*, Policy Research Paper 1448, Environment, Infrastructure and Agricultural Division, World Bank, Washington DC

Dobson, A (1995) *Green Political Thought*, second edition, Routledge, London

Goldin, I and L Winters (eds) (1995) *The Economics of Sustainable Development*, Cambridge University Press, Cambridge

Hall, J (1995) *The Automobile, Air Pollution Regulation and the Economy of Southern California, 1965–1990*, Institute of Economic and Environmental Studies, California State University, Fullerton, California

Hall, P (1987) 'Metropolitan Settlement Strategies', in L Rodwin (ed), *Shelter, Settlement and Development*, Allen and Unwin, Boston

Henderson, C (1995) 'The Green Household', *Financial Times*, 1 November 1995, p 10

Mohan, R (1994) *Understanding the Developing Metropolis: Lessons from the City Study of Bogatá and Cali, Colombia*, Oxford University Press, Oxford

Munasinghe, M (1993) *Environmental Economics and Sustainable Development*, World Bank Environment Paper Number 3, World Bank, Washington DC

Munasinghe, M and W Cruz (1995) *Economywide Policies and the Environment: Lessons from Experience*, World Bank Environment Paper Number 10, World Bank, Washington DC

North, D (1990) *Institutions, Institutional Change and Economic Performance*, Cambridge University Press, Cambridge

Orangi Pilot Project, Research and Training Unit (1995) Orangi Pilot Project, *Environment and Urbanization*, 7 (2), pp 227–36

Ostrom, E, L Schroeder and S Wynne (1993) *Institutional Incentives and Sustainable Development: Infrastructure Policies in Perspective*, Westview Press, Boulder, Colorado

Pezzey, J (1992) *Sustainable Development Concepts: An Economic Analysis*, World Bank Environment Paper, Number 2, World Bank, Washington DC

Pugh, C (1994) 'The Idea of Enablement in Housing Sector Development: The Political Economy of Housing for Developing Countries', *Cities*, 11 (6), pp 357–71

Ward, B (1976) 'The Inner and Outer Limits', *Canadian Public Administration*, 19 (3), pp 385–416

Wegelin, E and K Borgman (1995) 'Options for Municipal Interventions in Urban Poverty Alleviation', *Environment and Urbanization*, 7 (2), pp 131–51

Williams, M (1995) 'Role of the Multilateral Agencies After the Earth Summit', in M Haq, R Jolly, P Streeten and K Haq (eds) *The UN and the Bretton Woods Institutions: New Challenges for the Twenty-First Century*, MacMillan, London

World Bank (1991) *Urban Policy and Economic Development: An Agenda for the 1980s*, World Bank, Washington DC

— (1992) *World Development Report 1992: Development and the Environment*, World Bank, Washington DC

— (1994) *World Development Report 1994: Infrastructure for Development*, World Bank, Washington DC

World Commission on Environment and Development (1987) *Our Common Future* [The Brundtland Report], Oxford University Press, Oxford

Chapter One

Sustainable Development and Cities

Diana Mitlin and David Satterthwaite[1]

The term 'sustainable development' has become widely used to stress the need for the simultaneous achievement of development and environmental goals. As long as its meaning is kept this unspecific, few people disagree with it. But as governments or international agencies develop projects or programmes to implement it, so the disagreements surface as there are so many interpretations as to what is 'development' and how it should be achieved, what constitutes adequate attention to environmental aspects and what is to be 'sustained' by sustainable development. Among the proponents of sustainable development, there is a large gulf between those whose primary concern is conservation and those whose primary concern is meeting human needs (Adams, 1990). At present, the bias in most discussions on sustainable development is towards conservation. Even within 'environmentalists', there is the gulf between those whose primary concern is protecting the natural environment from destruction or degradation and those whose concerns include reducing environmental hazards for human populations and promoting environmental justice for those people lacking a healthy environment and adequate natural resource base for their livelihoods.

This primary concern of this chapter is how the unmet needs of city inhabitants, especially in the South, can be articulated and addressed,

---

1)   This chapter draws on a background paper entitled *Sustainable Development and Cities* that the authors wrote for Global Forum '94, the Forum in Manchester (UK) that brought together representatives of municipal authorities, trade unions, academics and NGOs and community organizations from 50 cities to discuss the issue of sustainable development and how it could be applied. This in turn developed themes that two of the authors first wrote about with Jorge Hardoy in Chapter 6 of Hardoy et al (1992).

23

without imposing environmental costs on other people (including those living in areas around cities) or depleting environmental capital (which in effect imposes environmental costs on future generations). This requires considerable change for most city and municipal authorities as the citizens within their jurisdiction acquire more power to define their needs and influence how they are addressed. It also means expanding the responsibilities of city and municipal authorities, for the use of resources and generation of wastes within city boundaries have to take account of the needs and rights of others living elsewhere and of future generations. This chapter seeks to provide a framework for considering the multiple goals that are embedded within the term 'sustainable development' for cities and to consider the potential that cities have for meeting the priorities of their citizens while also reducing the degradation or depletion of environmental capital. Before presenting this framework, we consider what sustainable development is seeking to sustain.

WHAT IS TO BE SUSTAINED?

One of the main sources of disagreement within the debate about sustainable development is what is to be 'sustained'. Some consider that it is natural or environmental capital that has to be sustained and that this commitment to sustaining environmental capital has to be combined with a commitment to ensuring that people's needs are met; this is how it is understood in the rest of this chapter and in our previous work on sustainable development and cities. But for many people writing on sustainable development, it is different aspects of development or of human activities that have to be sustained – for instance sustaining economic growth or 'human' development or achieving social or political sustainability. Thus, a discussion of sustainable development might be discussing how to sustain a person's livelihood, a development project, a policy, an institution, a business, a society or some subset of a society (for example a 'community'), culture or economic growth (in general or for some specific country). It may also be focusing on sustaining a nation, a city or a region. Box 1.1 gives more details of the different meanings given to the 'sustainable' part of sustainable development.

Box 1.1   THE MEANING OF SUSTAINABILITY

There is considerable confusion as to what is to be 'sustained'
by 'sustainable development'. For instance, is it natural systems or

human activities that are to be sustained and at what scale are they to be sustained (for example local projects, cities, nations, the sum of all activities globally).

The term 'sustainable' is most widely used in reference to eco-logical sustainability. But during preparations for the Earth Summit (held in 1992) and ever since, an increasing number of writers and international organizations began to include such con-cepts as 'social sustainability', 'economic sustainability', 'com-munity sustainability' and even 'cultural sustainability' as part of sustainable development. Meanwhile, many aid/development assis-tance agencies were giving another meaning to the term sustain-able development as this was the label given to ensuring that their development projects continued to operate and meet development objectives when these agencies' external support was cut off at the 'end of the project'. In this sense, 'sustainability' was far more about operation and maintenance (or 'institutional and managerial sustainability') than about any concept of ecological sustainability. A concern for project sustainability may give little or no consideration as to whether the sum of all the 'sustainable' projects would prove sustainable in an ecological sense.

Some of the literature about sustainable development discusses 'social sustainability' although there is no consensus as to what this means. For instance, some consider social sustainability as the social preconditions for sustainable development while others imply that it is the need to sustain specific social relations, customs or structures. But it is difficult to equate 'social sustainability' with the goals of Our Common Future. When judged by the length of time for which they were sustained, some of the most 'successful' societies were also among the most exploitative, where the abuse of human rights was greatest. These are not societies we would want to 'sustain'. Development includes strong and explicit social objectives and achieving the development goals within sustainable development demands social change, not 'sustainability' in the sense of 'keeping them going continuously'. Indeed, the achieve-ment of most of the social, economic and political goals which are part of 'sustainable development' requires fundamental changes to social structures including changes to government institutions and, in many instances, to the distribution of assets and income. This can hardly be equated with 'social sustainability'.

Discussions on 'social sustainability' when defined as the social conditions necessary to support environmental sustainability are valuable in so far as they stress that natural resources are used within a social context and it is the rules and values associated with this context that determine both the distribution of resources within the present generation and between the future generations and the present. Discussions of 'social sustainability' that stress the value of social capital or the social conditions that allow or support the meeting of human needs are also valuable. Our avoidance of the term is both because it can invite confusion with the other interpretations and because it can imply that there is only one way to achieve ecological sustainability whereas there is generally a range of possible options.

There has also been some discussion of 'cultural sustainability' because of the need within human society to develop shared values, perceptions and attitudes which help to contribute to the achievement of sustainable development. It is clear that development should include as a critical component a respect for cultural patrimony. Culture implies knowledge and a vast wealth of traditional knowledge of relevance to sustainable natural resource use (and to development) is ignored or given scant attention in development plans. But the term 'cultural sustainability' seems rather imprecise for the need to recognize the importance of culture and respect it within development. Culture is never static; to argue that it should be sustained is to deny an important aspect, changing and developing nature.

(Hardoy et al, 1993)

In contrast to this work that discusses how to sustain some aspect of 'development', there is also a large literature on sustainable development where there is no 'development' component at all in the sense of better meeting human needs (Mitlin, 1992). In such literature, it is common to find the terms 'sustainable development' and 'sustainability' used interchangeably with no recognition that the two mean or imply different things. A review of the literature on sustainable development (Mitlin, 1992:11) commented that:

Much of the writing, and many discussions, in the North concentrate primarily on 'sustainability' rather than sustainable development. These authors' main focus is how present environmental constraints might be overcome and the standard of living maintained. The need for development, of ensuring that all people in the world might obtain the resources they need for survival and development is ignored or given little attention.

This is also true for much of the literature on sustainable development published since then. The exclusive concentration of many authors on 'ecological sustainability' as the only goal of sustainable development is one reason why it has often proved difficult to engage the interest of development practitioners in environmental issues. There is much discussion under the heading of 'sustainable development' about the actions needed to sustain the global resource base (soils, biodiversity, mineral resources, forests) and about limiting the disruption to global cycles as a result of human activities – especially greenhouse gas emissions and the depletion of the stratospheric ozone layer. Such discussion tends to forget three other critical environmental issues or to downplay their importance. The first is the hundreds of millions of people in both rural and urban areas who lack access to safe and convenient supply of water for drinking and domestic use.[2] The second is the hundreds of millions of households who depend for part or all of their livelihood on raising crops or livestock. Their poverty (and the malnutrition and ill-health that generally accompanies it) are the result of inadequate access to water and fertile land. This lack of access to land and water for crop cultivation or livestock underlies the poverty of around a fifth of the world's population (see for instance, Jazairy et al, 1992). Yet many discussions about 'sustainability' with regard to soil erosion and deforestation give little or no consideration to the needs of these people and may indeed portray these people as 'the problem'.

The third environmental issue whose importance is often downplayed (or not even mentioned) is the ill-health and premature death caused by pathogens in the human environment – in water, food, air and soil. Each year, these contribute to the premature death of millions of people (mostly infants and children) and to the ill health or disability of hundreds of millions more. As the World Health Organization (WHO, 1992a) points out, this includes:

- the three million infants or children who die each year from diarrhoeal diseases and the hundreds of millions whose physical and mental development is impaired by repeated attacks of diarrhoea – largely as a result of contaminated food or water.
- the two million people who die from malaria each year, three quarters of whom are children under five; in Africa alone, an estimated 800,000 children died from malaria in 1991 (WHO,

---

2) Official statistics on water supply provision greatly overstate the proportion of the world's population with safe and convenient supplies; see Satterthwaite (1995).

1992b). Tens of millions of people suffer prolonged or repeated bouts of malaria each year.
- the hundreds of millions of people of all ages who suffer from debilitating intestinal parasitic infestations caused by pathogens in the soil, water or food, and from respiratory and other diseases caused or exacerbated by pathogens in the air, both indoors and outdoors.

The proportion of infants who die from infectious and parasitic diseases among households living in the poorest quality housing in Africa, Asia and Latin America is several hundred times higher than for households in west Europe or North America; all such diseases are transmitted by airborne, waterborne or foodborne pathogens or by disease vectors such as insects or snails. Of the 12.2 million children under the age of five who die each year in the South, 97 per cent of these deaths would not have occurred if these children had been born and lived in the countries with the best health and social conditions (WHO, 1995). One estimate suggested that in cities in the South, at least 600 million people live in homes and neighbourhoods in which the shelters are of such poor quality and so overcrowded and with such inadequacies in provision for piped water, sanitation, drainage and health care that their health and indeed their lives are constantly threatened (Cairncross et al, 1990:1–24).[3] This is more than the total urban population of the South just 30 years ago. Thus, much of the literature on sustainable development tends to 'marginalize the primary environmental concerns of the poor, even as they claim to incorporate them' (see Chapter 4 of this volume).

As soon as 'sustainable development' comes to include a concern for meeting human needs, so it must consider why so many people's needs are not currently met – and this means considering the underlying economic, social and political causes of poverty and deprivation. Most of the literature on sustainable development does not do so. It does not question the current distribution of power and the ownership of resources except where these are considered a factor in 'unsustainable practices'. It assumes that national conservation plans or national sustainable development plans can be implemented within existing social and political structures. Much of the literature assumes that the integration of conservation and development will meet people's needs which, as Adams (1990) points out, is disastrously naive.

---

3)   This estimate was subsequently endorsed by WHO (1992a) and by UNCHS (1996).

However, those whose primary concern within sustainable development is conservation or environmental protection can point to the fact that the most powerful government agencies or ministries concerned with 'development' and the largest and most powerful international development agencies also failed to consider the environmental implications of their projects or the sum of the environmental impacts of their projects on global problems. Development projects have often been a cause of environmental degradation rather than a solution to environmental problems (Adams, 1990). Although the debate about sustainable development has helped make such agencies more aware of environmental issues, this certainly does not mean that most international agencies and most governments in the South are taking these aspects seriously. For example, many development assistance agencies have never funded a public transport project and many may still not have considered the long-term implications for greenhouse gas emissions of the support they give to transport and energy.

While wanting to encourage greater attention in discussions about sustainable development to the needs, rights and priorities of low income groups, or of other groups whose needs and priorities are ignored, we do not think it appropriate to discuss this under 'sustainability'. We choose to use the concept of sustainability only with regard to natural capital, both because of the lack of consensus as to what sustainability might mean when applied to human activities and institutions and because we believe the term has been inappropriately applied. Ensuring that human rights are respected and that people have the right to express their own needs and to influence the ways in which they are fulfilled fall more clearly within the 'development' component of sustainable development.

This means that for governments and international 'development' agencies who wish to move from a concern with development to a concern with sustainable development, they have to add on to existing development goals the requirement that their achievement minimizes the depletion of natural capital – for instance the degradation of renewable resources such as soil and the depletion of scarce nonrenewable resources and/or the degradation of ecosystems. This allows one to avoid the confusions inherent in such concepts as social sustainability or cultural sustainability. Thus, desirable social, economic or political goals at community, city, regional or national level are best understood as being within the 'development' part of sustainable development, while the 'sustainable' component is with regard to ecological sustainability. It also required a consideration of the environmental implications of development initiatives that are not only concerned with their environmental impacts on their surrounds but also on their contribution to global environmental problems.

A FRAMEWORK FOR CONSIDERING SUSTAINABLE DEVELOPMENT AND CITIES

Most of the literature on sustainable development does not mention cities. As one paper commented (Houghton et al, 1994), this reluctance to discuss sustainable development and cities is probably because many of those who write on environmental issues have long regarded cities with disdain, even if they live in cities. Among those who write about sustainable development, many probably consider cities as a key part of 'the problem'. This has meant a rather poorly developed literature on sustainable development and cities, even though urban centres now include within their boundaries close to half the world's population and a higher proportion of the world's consumption of nonrenewable resources and generation of wastes (including much of the hazardous wastes and non-biodegradable wastes).

However, it is important to clarify that it is not cities that are responsible for most resource use, waste, pollution and greenhouse gas emissions, but particular industries and commercial and industrial enterprises (or corporations) and middle and upper income groups with high consumption lifestyles. A high proportion of such enterprises and consumers may be concentrated in cities but a considerable (and probably growing) proportion are not. In the North and in the wealthier cities or regions of the South, it is the middle or upper income household with two or three cars living in rural areas, small towns or low density outer suburbs of cities that has the highest consumption of resources – generally much more so than those with similar incomes living within cities.

In developing a framework for promoting sustainable development and cities, we will start with a key defining statement from *Our Common Future*, the Report of the World Commission on Environment and Development (also known as the Brundtland Commission), published in 1987.[4] Although a concern for combining environmental and development goals goes back several decades and was much discussed throughout the 1970s, this concern was made more explicit, and the use of the term 'sustainable development' promoted by this report.[5] It states

---

4) As noted in Barrow (1995) the importance of the Brundtland Commission was not so much in its innovative ideas but in rekindling environmental interests within development. The economic crises of the early 1980s and the political realignments in the North had hindered action on what might be termed 'Brundtland-like' demands made during the 1970s.

5) There is also an assumption that the concern for sustainable development is new when the key conceptual underpinnings of sustainable development were widely discussed and described in the early 1970s and possibly earlier. The term sustainable development arose primarily to acknowledge the development needs of low income groups

that we must meet 'the needs of the present generation without compromising the ability of future generations to meet their own needs' (WCED, 1987:8) and this has become the most widely quoted summary of the goals of sustainable development. Figure 1.1 elaborates on the different social, economic, political and ecological goals that fall under this that are relevant to sustainable development and cities.

Meeting the needs of the present can be interpreted as the 'development' component of sustainable development and so a discussion of this component brings in all the discussions and debates about whose needs are to be met, what needs, who defines needs and who obtains more power and resources to ensure they are met. These obviously include economic, social, cultural, health and political needs as outlined in Box 1.2.

Box 1.2   MULTIPLE GOALS OF SUSTAINABLE
DEVELOPMENT AS APPLIED TO CITIES

Meeting the needs of the present ...

- Economic needs – *include access to an adequate livelihood or productive assets; also economic security when unemployed, ill, disabled or otherwise unable to secure a livelihood.*
- Social, cultural and health needs – *include a shelter which is healthy, safe, affordable and secure, within a neighbourhood with provision for piped water, sanitation, drainage, transport, health care, education and child development. Also a home, workplace and living environment protected from environmental hazards, including chemical pollution. Also important are needs related to people's choice and control – including*

---

and low income countries within the growing interest in local, national and global environmental issues in the North and the understanding of the international dimensions of environmentalism. The need to reconcile these two aspects was widely discussed before, during and after the UN Conference on the Human Environment at Stockholm in 1972, even if this was not called 'sustainable development' at that time. The Brundtland Commission's stress on 'meeting the needs of the present without compromising the ability of future generations to meet their own needs' had been a central theme in the writings of Barbara Ward throughout the 1970s – although this was usually phrased as meeting the 'inner limits' of human needs and rights without exceeding the 'outer limits' of the planet's ability to sustain life, now and in the future. See for instance *The Cocoyoc Declaration* adopted by the participants of the UNEP/ UNCTAD symposium on 'Pattern of Resource Use, Environment and Development Strategies' in 1974 that was drafted by Barbara Ward and republished in Ward (1975). See also Ward and Dubos (1972); and Ward (1976 and 1979).

homes and neighbourhoods which they value and where their social and cultural priorities are met. Shelters and services must meet the specific needs of children and of adults responsible for most child-rearing (usually women). Achieving this implies a more equitable distribution of income between nations and, in most, within nations.

- Political needs – *include freedom to participate in national and local politics and in decisions regarding management and development of one's home and neighbourhood – within a broader framework which ensures respect for civil and political rights and the implementation of environmental legislation.*

... Without compromising the ability of future generations to meet their own needs

- Minimizing use or waste of non renewable resources – *includes minimizing the consumption of fossil fuels in housing, commerce, industry and transport plus substituting renewable sources where feasible. Also, minimizing waste of scarce mineral resources (reduce use, reuse, recycle, reclaim). There are also cultural, historical and natural assets within cities that are irreplaceable and thus non-renewable – for instance, historic districts and parks and natural landscapes which provide space for play, recreation and access to nature.*
- Sustainable use of renewable resources – *cities drawing on freshwater resources at levels which can be sustained; keeping to a sustainable ecological footprint in terms of land area on which producers and consumers in any city draw for agricultural crops, wood products and biomass fuels.*
- Wastes from cities keeping within absorptive capacity of local and global sinks – *including renewable sinks (eg capacity of a river to break down biodegradable wastes without ecological degradation) and non-renewable sinks (for persistent chemicals that cause ecological damage and that are not biodegradable or only degrade over long periods; these include most greenhouse gases and stratospheric ozone-depleting chemicals and many pesticides).*

Mitlin and Satterthwaite (1994)

Many city authorities have the fulfilment of many of these needs and rights as part of their official responsibilities. These are also contained in the United Nations Universal Declaration of Human Rights – i e meeting each person's right to a standard of living adequate for health and well-being including food, clothing, housing and medical care and necessary social services (See United Nations Universal Declaration of Human Rights, Article 25 (1)). This declaration, subsequent United Nations documents and *Our Common Future* all stress that development goals should include the right to vote within representative government structures. Perhaps the most relevant debate within this is the long-established discussion as to whether existing structures and institutions will ever improve their performance in ensuring human needs are met. For instance, there is much more discussion about 'governance' at city and municipal level and this is not only among community organizations, NGOs and other parts of 'civil society' but also among governments and international agencies (see, for instance, UNCHS, 1966). This is also not only about city and municipal authorities having more power and resources to enable them better to meet their responsibilities, but also about the need for them to be more accountable, transparent and democratic – and to give more responsibility and resources to community-based or neighbourhood based organizations, NGOs and other voluntary sector groups (UNCHS, 1966). The discussions about the changes in social structure that are needed to achieve sustainable development goals are also becoming more explicit. As an official United Nations report (UNCHS, 1966) states, 'strategies for achieving social equity, social integration and social stability are essential underpinnings of sustainable development.'

The 'sustainable' component of sustainable development can be taken as ensuring that the meeting of human needs today is achieved without a level of resource use and waste generation which threatens local, regional and global ecological sustainability. The 'sustainable' component requires no depletion or degradation of four kinds of 'natural capital' (or 'environmental capital') listed in the lower box in Figure 1.1. The first is *the finite stock of nonrenewable resources* – for instance fossil fuels, metals and other mineral resources. Most of these resources (especially the fossil fuels burnt for heat and power) are consumed when used, so finite stocks are depleted with use. Others are not 'consumed' since the resource remains in the waste – for instance metals used in capital and consumer goods. But for most nonrenewable resources, there are energy and cost constraints to recovering a high proportion of the total amount used from waste streams. These may be considered as partially 'renewable', with the extent defined by the proportion of materials in discarded goods which can be reclaimed and recycled. Biological diversity, one key part of environmental capital, might also be considered a nonrenewable resource.

The second component of environmental capital is what might be termed the *nonrenewable natural sink capacity*, which is the finite capacity of local and global ecosystems to absorb or dilute non-bio-degradable wastes without adverse effects. One area of concern is the increasing concentration of persistent biocides. There are also large volumes of non-biodegradable wastes arising from human activities that have to be stored and kept entirely isolated from ecosystems because of the damage to ecosystems and to human health they would pose, if not kept isolated – for instance there are large volumes of hazardous wastes that are generated by many industrial processes. The wastes from nuclear power stations are also a particular concern; these include wastes which will remain with dangerously high levels of radioactivity for tens of thousands of years. Globally, one of the most pressing problems is the finite capacity of global systems to absorb greenhouse gases without changes in climate that can pose very serious direct and indirect impacts on health and on ecosystems.

The third is the finite capacity of ecosystems to provide sustainable levels of *renewable resources*. Human use of some renewable resources (for example the direct use of solar power or its indirect use through wind or wave power) does not deplete the resource. But many renewable resources (especially pasture, crops and trees) are renewable only within finite limits set by the ecosystem within which they grow. Fresh water resources are also finite; in the case of aquifers, human use often exceeds their natural rate of recharge and such levels of use are unsustainable.

The fourth component of environmental capital is the *renewable sink capacity*, the finite capacity of ecosystems to break down biodegradable wastes. Although most wastes arising from production and consumption are biodegradable, each ecozone or water body has a finite capacity to break down such wastes without itself being degraded.

When considering whether some development initiative fits within a commitment to sustainable development, there is a further distinction needed between particular projects/activities and in reference to larger systems (sometimes city-wide, or nationwide or worldwide). It is useful to differentiate between the two applications of the term since both are important in considering sustainable development. Simple interrelation-ships between specific development activities (for instance, expanding a piped water supply or developing an irrigation system) and environ-mental capital can be assessed and judged according to whether there is a decrease in any of the four kinds of environmental capital outlined above. Alternatively, the focus can be much broader, concerned with large aggregates and systems of activities. The first approach is concerned with making a single part of the system compatible with ecological sustainability. The second approach recognizes that it is difficult to make all activities contribute towards ecological sustainability and that what is important is that the sum (or net effect) of the activities within a specific area are ecologically sustainable. The successful achievement of sustainable development requires society to establish institutions capable of ensuring that individual projects have an acceptable aggregate outcome without demanding such stringent conditions on individual projects that they inhibit the achievement of development goals.

Sustainable development and cities, not sustainable cities

This discussion about the territorial boundaries for sustainable development has particular importance for the debate about cities. This chapter is also about sustainable development and cities rather than sustainable cities. A concentration on 'sustainable cities' focuses too much on achieving ecological sustainability within increasingly isolated 'eco-regions' or 'bio-regions'. Seeking 'sustainable cities' implies that each city has to meet the resource needs of the population and enterprises located there from its immediate surrounds. But the goals of sustainable development are the meeting of human needs within all cities (and rural areas) with a level of resource use and waste generation within each region and within the nation and the planet that is compatible with ecological sustainability. It is unrealistic to demand that major cities should be supported by the resources produced in their immediate surrounds but entirely appropriate to require that consumers and producers in high-consumption, high waste cities reduce their level of resource use and waste and reduce or halt the damaging ecological impacts of their demands for fresh water and other resources on their surrounds.

Although the discussions and recommendations about 'sustainable cities' have much of relevance to reducing the depletion of environmental capital caused by production and consumption in cities in the North, they concentrate too much on individual city performance. What is more important for sustainable development is the local, national and international frameworks needed to ensure the achievement of sustainable development goals worldwide, including the appropriate frameworks for cities.

What sustainable development implies for city authorities

A commitment to sustainable development by city authorities means adding additional goals to those that are the traditional concerns of local authorities. Meeting development goals have long been a central responsibility of city and municipal authorities. Their objectives generally include a desire for greater prosperity, better social conditions (and fewer social problems), basic services, adequate housing and (more recently) better environmental standards within their jurisdiction. This does not imply that city and municipal authorities need be major providers of basic services – and they can act as supervisors and/or supporters of private or community provision.

A concern for 'sustainable development' retains these conventional concerns but with two more added. The first is a concern for the environmental impact of city-based production and consumption on the needs of all people, not just those within their jurisdiction. The second is an understanding of the finite nature of many natural resources (or the ecosystems from which they are drawn) and of the capacities of ecosystems in the wider regional, national and international context to absorb or break down wastes.

Historically, these have not been considered within the remit of city authorities. Indeed, many cities in the North have only made considerable progress in achieving sustainable development goals within their own boundaries (ie reducing poverty, ensuring high quality living environments, protecting local ecosystems and developing more representative and accountable government) by drawing heavily on the environmental capital of other regions or nations and on the waste absorption capacity of 'the global commons' (Rees, 1992). But in the long term, no city can remain prosperous if the aggregate impact of all cities' production and their inhabitants' consumption draws on global resources at unsustainable rates and deposits wastes in global sinks at levels that undermine health and disrupt the functioning of ecosystems.

Adding a concern for 'ecological sustainability' onto existing development concerns means setting limits on the rights of city enterprises or consumers to use scarce resources and to generate non-biodegradable wastes. This has many implications for citizens, businesses and city authorities. Perhaps the most important for cities in the North and the wealthier countries in the South is the role of city and municipal authorities in promoting the needed delinking of high standards of living/quality of life from high levels of resource use and waste generation.

WHAT IS CURRENTLY UNSUSTAINABLE?

There is growing evidence that many current global trends in the use of resources or sinks for wastes are not sustainable – and this is something that is unique to the late twentieth century (Houghton and Hunter, 1994). Although there are many examples of human activities destroying or seriously damaging natural resources and systems throughout history, only relatively recently has the sum of all human resource consumption and waste generation reached the point where it can adversely affect the present and future state of the global environment, seriously diminish biodiversity and reduce the availability of certain natural resources. This obviously alters the parameters of the environmental debate as the scale and scope of global environmental problems are recognized (Houghton and Hunter, 1994).

Although much uncertainty remains about the current level of risk and how much the risk will increase in the future (and its ecological consequences), the costs are already apparent (as in the health effects of stratospheric ozone depletion) or likely to become apparent soon. In the South, the problems are largely the worrying trends in terms of unsustainable levels of use for some renewable resources (for instance through deforestation and soil degradation and the use of groundwater resources much faster than their natural rate of recharge). In the North, the problem centres on the scale of renewable and nonrenewable resource use, waste, pollution and greenhouse gas emissions.

The link between what is unsustainable in terms of environmental capital and the resources needed to achieve 'development' goals through ensuring those with unmet needs have the resources to ensure these needs are met does not appear to be problematic in the short term. However, while the resources needed for meeting the needs of poorer women and men of all ages and ethnic groups in both the North and the South need not imply an unsustainable level of resource use, it is clear that extending the levels of resource consumption and waste generation currently enjoyed by the rich minority to an increasing proportion of the world's population almost certainly does (WHO, 1992). Thus, it is the ways in which 'development' is to meet human needs which determines the extent to which this is compatible with or contrary to ecological sustainability. If 'development' is 'high economic growth with very limited or no redistribution of assets and passes on the environmental costs to other regions or the future,' ie the pattern of development that was followed by the world's wealthiest countries today, this is not ecologically sustainable. The following subsections consider particular problems in relation to the four components of environmental capital defined earlier.

Cities and the use of renewable resources and sinks

Consideration of the sustainability of any city must take into account the ecological impacts of the city's concentrated demand for renewable resources drawn from forests, rangelands, farmlands, watersheds or aquatic ecosystems from outside its boundaries. The concept developed by William Rees (1992) of cities' 'ecological footprints' illustrates this phenomenon – see Box 1.2.

Box 1.2   THE ECOLOGICAL FOOTPRINT OF CITIES

*All cities draw on natural resources produced on land outside
their built-up areas (for example agricultural crops, wood products, fuel) and the total area of land required to sustain a city
(which can be termed its ecological footprint) is typically at least
ten times greater than that contained within the city boundaries or
the associated built-up area. In effect, through trade and natural
flows of ecological goods and services, all cities appropriate the
carrying-capacity of other areas. All cities draw on the material
resources and productivity of a vast and scattered hinterland.*

*Ecologists define 'carrying-capacity' as the population of a
given species that can be supported indefinitely in a given habitat
without permanently damaging the ecosystem upon which it is
dependent. For human beings, carrying-capacity can be interpreted
as the maximum rate of resource consumption and waste dis-
charge that can be sustained indefinitely in a given region without
progressively impairing the functional integrity and productivity of
relevant ecosystems.*

*Preliminary data for industrial cities suggest that per capita
primary consumption of food, wood, fuel and waste-processing
capacity, co-opts on a continuous basis several hectares of productive ecosystem, the exact amount depending on individual material
standards of living. This average per capita index can be used to
estimate the land area functionally required to support any given
population. The resultant aggregate area can be called the relevant
community's total 'ecological footprint' on the Earth.*

*Regional ecological deficits do not necessarily pose a problem if
import-dependent regions are drawing on true ecological surpluses
in the exporting regions. A group of trading regions remains
within net carrying-capacity as long as total consumption does not
exceed aggregate sustainable production. The problem is that
prevailing economic logic and trade agreements ignore carrying-
capacity and sustainability considerations. In these circumstances,
the terms of trade may actually accelerate the depletion of essential natural capital thereby undermining global carrying capacity.*

*Because the products of nature can so readily be imported, the
population of any given region can exceed its local carrying
capacity unknowingly and with apparent impunity. In the absence
of negative feedback from the land on their economy or lifestyles,
there is no direct incentive for such populations to maintain adequate local stocks of productive natural capital. For example, the*

> *ability to import food makes people less averse to the risks associated with urban growth spreading over locally limited agricultural land. Even without accelerated capital depletion, trade enables a region's population and material consumption to rise beyond levels to which they might otherwise be restricted by some locally limiting factor. Ironically then, the free exchange of ecological goods and services without constraints on population or consumption, ensures the absorption of global surpluses (the safety net) and encourages all regions to exceed local carrying capacity. The net effect is increased long-range risk to all.*
>
> *This situation applies not only to commercial trade but also to the unmonitored flows of goods and services provided by nature. For example, Northern urbanites, wherever they are, are now dependent on the carbon sink, global heat transfer, and climate stabilization functions of tropical forests. There are many variations on this theme, touching on everything from drift-net fishing to ozone depletion, each involving open access to, or shared dependency on, some form of threatened natural capital.*
>
> Rees (1992)

Certain natural resources are essential to the existence of any city – fresh water, food and fuel supplies. Many of the economic activities on which a city's prosperity depends require regular supplies of renewable resources; without a continuing supply of fresh water, agricultural goods and forest products, the economy of many cities would rapidly diminish. Many other formal and informal economic activities, although not directly linked to resource exploitation, depend on such exploitation to generate the income to support their own activities.

In the past, the size and economic base of any city was constrained by the size and quality of the resource endowments of its surrounding region. The relatively high cost of transporting food, raw materials and fresh water always limited the extent to which a city could survive by drawing resources from outside its region. The high costs of transporting city-generated wastes away from the surrounding region promoted local solutions, and there was a need to ensure that such wastes did not damage the soils and water on which local agricultural production (and often fishing) depended. If local ecosystems were degraded, the prosperity of the city suffered – or in extreme cases, its viability as a city was threatened. A city's ecological footprint remained relatively local.[6]

Motorized transport systems enormously cheapened the possibility of disassociating the scale of renewable resource use in cities from the productivity of its region. The more developed the transport system, the larger this disassociation. This has now reached the scale where the progress achieved in and around wealthy cities in terms of much improved protection of the region's forests, soils and areas of ecological importance is achieved by appropriating the soils and water resources of distant ecosystems (Rees, 1992). Wealthy nations now import many of the land-intensive and water-intensive goods their consumers or producers need so the depletion of soil and the over-exploitation of fresh water resources these cause are not environmental costs borne within their boundaries. The 'ecological footprint' is largely outside the national boundaries. Wealthy nations can also import goods whose production also has high environmental and health costs – for instance, the high use of pesticides which are applied without adequate protection for the workforce involved in the production – but with none of these health or environmental costs affecting their own inhabitants or ecosystems. Thus, the wealthiest nations can maintain the highest environmental standards within their own countries, even though the ecological and health costs of producing the goods they import are very high. Prosperous cities in the North now draw from the entire planet as their 'ecological hinterland' for food and raw materials. If consumers in (say) London or New York are drawing their fruit, vegetables, cereals, meat and fish from an enormous variety of countries, how can a link be established between this consumption and its ecological consequences in the areas where this food is produced?

Fresh water can also be drawn from distant watersheds and even pumped hundreds of metres up hills, as long as little consideration is given to the high energy costs that this entails (usually coming from thermal power stations, which also means not only high levels of fossil fuel use but also high levels of greenhouse gas emissions). Such technology and its high energy requirements obscure the link between a city's renewable resource use and the impact of this use on the ecosystem where the resource is produced. Prosperous cities can also transport their wastes and dispose of them beyond their own region – in extreme cases, even shipping them abroad. Or they can 'export' their air pollution to surrounding regions through acid precipitation and urban pollution plumes which can damage vegetation in large areas downwind of the city

---

6) There are many historic examples of wealthy and powerful cities that drew resources from a much wider region, but these were exceptions. See Giradet (1992).

(Conway and Pretty, 1991). Perhaps only when the cost of oil-based transport comes to reflect its true ecological cost in terms both of a depleting nonrenewable resource and its contribution to greenhouse gas emissions will a stronger connection be re-established between resource use within cities and the productive capacity of the regions in which they are located.

One example of a scarce 'renewable resource' is fresh water. Many cities around the world are facing serious shortages of fresh water, and this is even the case in cities where half the population is not adequately served with safe, sufficient supplies. Many cities have outgrown the capacity of their locality to provide adequate, sustainable water supplies. For instance, in Dakar (Senegal), local groundwater supplies are fully used (and polluted) and local aquifers over-pumped, resulting in saltwater intrusion; a substantial proportion of the city's water now has to be brought in from the Lac de Guiers, 200 kilometres away (White, 1992). Mexico City also has to supplement its very large groundwater supplies by bringing water from ever more distant river systems and pumping this water up several hundred metres to reach the Valley of Mexico where the city is located. Over-exploitation of its own underground water has also made the city sink – in some areas by up to nine metres – with serious subsidence damage for many buildings and sewage and drainage pipes (Damián, 1992; Postel, 1992).

Hundreds of urban centres in relatively arid areas have also grown beyond the point where adequate water supplies can be drawn from local sources. Examples include many of the coastal cities in Peru (including Lima), La Rioja and Catamarca in Argentina and various cities in northern Mexico. Many urban centres in Africa's dryland areas face particularly serious problems because of a combination of rapid growth in demand for water and unusually low rainfall in recent years, with the consequent dwindling of local fresh water resources.

For most urban centres worldwide, an examination of the use of renewable resources by consumers and enterprises within their boundaries reveals a scale and complexity of linkages with rural producers and ecosystems within their own region or nation which implies that 'sustainable urban development' and 'sustainable rural development' cannot be separated. The rural–urban linkages can be positive in both developmental and environmental terms. For instance, demand for rural produce from city-based enterprises and households can support prosperous farmers and prosperous rural settlements, where environmental capital is not being depleted. Few governments in the South appreciate the extent to which productive, intensive agriculture can support development goals in both rural and urban areas (see, for instance, Manzanal and Vapnarsky, 1986; Tiffen and Mortimore, 1992). Increasing agricultural production can support rising prosperity for rural populations and rapid urban development within or close to the main farming areas – the two supporting each other. There are also many examples of organic solid and liquid wastes, that originate from city-based consumers or industries, being returned to soils. These rural–urban links can also have negative aspects. For instance, agricultural land can be lost as cities' built-up areas expand without control and land speculation on urban fringes drives out cultivators; this appears more common in most nations.

With regard to the use of local sinks for city wastes, some progress has been achieved. In most countries, environmental legislation has limited the right of industries and utilities to use local sinks for wastes – for instance disposing of untreated wastes in rivers, lakes or other local water bodies or generating high levels of air pollution. However, the extent to which the environmental legislation is enforced varies widely and in many countries in the South there is little enforcement. Rivers, lakes and estuaries in or close to major cities or industrial complexes in the South are usually heavily polluted and this has often led to a drastic reduction in fish production and the loss of livelihoods for those who formerly made their living from fishing (Hardoy et al, 1992). In addition, most countries have been less successful in controlling air pollution arising from motor vehicles, except for the reduction in lead emissions that has been achieved in many countries by the increasing proportion of vehicles that use lead-free petrol.

But cities also have some important potential advantages with regard to the use of renewable resources. For instance, the close proximity of so many water consumers gives greater scope for recycling or directly reusing waste waters – and the techniques for greatly reducing the use of freshwater in city homes and enterprises are well-known, where freshwater resources are scarce (see Water Program, 1991) – although it is agriculture, not cities, that dominates the use of freshwater in most nations (see World Resources Institute, 1990:330–1). Cities also concentrate populations in ways which usually reduce the demand for land relative to population. In most countries, the area taken up by cities and towns is less than 1 per cent of the total surface area of the nation. The world's current urban population of around 2.6 billion people would fit into an area of 200,000 square kilometres – roughly the size of Senegal or Oman – at densities similar to those of high class, much valued inner city residential areas in European cities (for instance Chelsea in London). This is a reminder of how some of the most expensive and desired residential areas in the world also have densities that suburban developers and municipal authorities regard as 'too high' even though these are often areas that also have good provision for parks, a diverse employment structure and good cultural facilities.[7] There are also examples of increasing populations in the central districts of certain cities, as governments controlled private automobiles, improved public transport and encouraged a rich and diverse street life (UNCHS, 1996). The fact that cities also concentrate demand for fresh fruit, vegetables, fish and dairy products also means considerable potential for their production in the area around a city – especially if their promotion is integrated with a city-wide and region-wide plan to protect watersheds, control urban sprawl, encourage urban or peri-urban agriculture and ensure adequate provision for open space (see for instance, Smit et al, 1996). In many cities in Africa and Asia, this would support existing practices as a significant proportion of the food consumed by city inhabitants is grown within city boundaries or in areas immediately adjacent to the built up areas – often with city wastes also used to fertilize or condition the soil (Smit et al, 1996).

Cities and nonrenewable resources and sinks

It was a concern about possible global shortages of key nonrenewable resources (oil, natural gas and certain minerals) which provided a strong stimulus to the environmental movement in the early 1970s – as in, for instance, the Club of Rome report, *The Limits to Growth* (Meadows et al, 1974). If the concerns about environment and development in the early 1990s are compared to those in the mid-1970s, this concern now receives less prominence. Two other concerns have grown in prominence. The first is the much increased concern about damage arising from human activities to global natural systems; the depletion of the stratospheric ozone layer and atmospheric warming are now perceived as far more serious threats to sustainability than was the case in the early 1970s. The second is the much increased concern about the finite nature of many renewable resources (especially fertile soil and freshwater). As noted above, they are only renewable within particular limits.

Levels of resource use per person for nonrenewable resources vary by a factor of between 10 and 100 or more, when comparing per capita averages between wealthy and poor nations. The same is also true for

---

7) The example of Chelsea was chosen because it combines very high quality housing, very little of which is in high rises (and most of which is pre-twentieth century) with a diverse economic base, large amounts of open space and among the best educational and cultural facilities in London. With a population density of around 120 persons per hectare, it is an example of how relatively high density need not imply overcrowding or poor quality living environments. The world's urban population of around 2.6 billion in 1995 would fit into an area of land similar to that of Senegal (197,000 square kilometres) or Oman (212,000 square kilometres) at a density comparable to that of Chelsea.

levels of waste generation (UNCHS, 1996). The disparities become even larger, when considering the total consumption to date of nonrenewable resource use and the total contribution over time to existing concentrations of persistent chemicals or of greenhouse gases in the atmosphere. Even if prices for most nonrenewable resources have not risen to reflect their overall scarcity, many would be likely to do so if all countries in the South came to have consumption levels similar to those in the North.

But in one sense, comparisons of averages for resource use or waste (including greenhouse gas emissions) per person between nations is misleading in that it is essentially the middle and upper income groups who account for most resource use and most waste generation; this only becomes a North–South issue because most of the world's middle and upper income people with high consumption lifestyles live in Europe, North America, Japan and Australasia. High income households in Africa, Asia and Latin America may have levels of nonrenewable resource use comparable to high income households in the richest nations; it is the fact that there are so many fewer of them that keeps national averages much lower.

Levels of household wealth alone are insufficient to explain the disparities in terms of averages for resource use per person and other factors must be considered. For instance, figures for the use of gasoline per person in different cities are particularly interesting, since this represents both a draw on a finite nonrenewable resource (oil) and a major contributor to greenhouse gases. In 1980, gasoline use per capita in cities such as Houston, Detroit and Los Angeles was five to seven times that of three of Europe's most prosperous and attractive cities: Amsterdam, Vienna and Copenhagen (Newman and Kenworthy, 1989). Averages for resource use per person are not only linked to incomes and prices but also to the incentive and regulatory framework provided by governments to encourage resource conservation or penalize high levels of resource use and waste.

Although cities are generally considered as locations which concentrate high levels of nonrenewable resource use, they can also be viewed as places with tremendous potential to cut down the use of nonrenewable resources. By concentrating production and consumption, cities also make possible a greater range and possibility for the efficient use of nonrenewable resources – through the reclamation of materials from waste streams and its reuse or recycling – and for the specialist enterprises that ensure this can happen safely. Cities make possible material or waste exchanges between industries. The collection of recyclable or reusable wastes from homes and businesses is generally cheaper, per person served. Cities have cheaper unit costs for many measures to promote the use of reusable containers (and cut down on disposable containers). In many cities in the South, there are also long-established traditions which ensure high levels of recycling or reuse of wastes on which government's solid waste management can build (see Furedy, 1990; Furedy, 1992).

The fact that cities concentrate production and residential areas also means a considerable potential for reducing fossil fuel use in heating and/ or cooling and in transport. For heating, this can be achieved through the use of waste process heat from industry or thermal power stations to provide space heating for homes and commercial buildings. Certain forms of high density housing such as terraces and apartment blocks also considerably reduce heat loss from each housing unit, when compared to detached housing. There are also many measures that can be taken to reduce heat gain in buildings to eliminate or greatly reduce the demand for electricity for air conditioning. In regard to transport, cities represent a much greater potential for limiting the use of motor vehicles – including greatly reducing the fossil fuels they need and the air pollution and high levels of resource consumption that their use implies. This might sound contradictory, since most of the world's largest cities have serious problems with congestion and motor-vehicle generated air pollution. But cities ensure that many more trips can be made through walking or bicycling. They also make possible a much greater use of public transport and make economically feasible a high quality service. Thus, although cities tend to be associated with a high level of private automobile use, cities and urban systems also represent the greatest potential for allowing their inhabitants quick and cheap access to a great range of locations, without the need to use private automobiles.

Two points with regard to nonrenewable sources need to be emphasized. The first is that the finite nature of the resource base is not in doubt, even if the predictions as to when resource shortages (or price rises associated with shortages) will begin to have receded. The second is that high consumption levels for nonrenewable resources are also associated with high levels of waste generation and greenhouse gas emissions. Reducing greenhouse gas emissions certainly implies lower levels of use and waste in nonrenewable resources. There may be sufficient nonrenewable resources to ensure that 9–10 billion people on earth, late in the next century, have their needs met. But it is unlikely that the world's resources and ecosystems could sustain a world population of 9 or 10 billion with a per capita consumption of nonrenewable resources similar to those enjoyed by the richest households today or even the average figure for the world's high-consumption cities such as Houston and Los Angeles.

While there has been some progress in many countries in protecting renewable resources (especially soils and forests) and in limiting the ecological damage from city-generated wastes on their surrounding regions, there is much less progress on achieving more sustainable patterns of resource use and waste generation in the use of nonrenewable resources and sinks for non-biodegradable wastes. This includes the 'global sink' as the reduction in the stratospheric ozone layer brings new environmental and health costs and as global warming appears likely to continue and to bring increasingly serious health and environmental costs. Progress on addressing environmental problems is easier where those creating or exacerbating the problem (for instance the polluters) and those affected by the problem are within the same locality or nation. Even if those whose livelihoods and health have been adversely affected by the environmental consequences of other people's or businesses' activities have often found it difficult to get these activities halted or their environmental impacts reduced, at least within most societies there are laws and institutions which allow such problems to be addressed.

Where environmental problems are caused or exacerbated by activities in other countries, it is much more difficult to those affected to stop this. For instance, how can those people who are adversely affected by floods or extreme weather conditions that are probably linked to global warming get redress from the past and current middle and upper income households with high consumption levels who have been a major cause of global warming?

The problem becomes even more complex when considered across generations – how can those who are likely to lose their livelihoods (and possibly their lives) from storms and floods and changes in rainfall patterns that are linked to global warming in the future get redress from the people whose high consumption and waste levels were the main underlying cause of their losses? It has proved possible to halt or modify investment decisions which imply serious social and environmental costs either in the immediate locality or at least within that nation's boundaries (although much more needs to be done), but it is very difficult to halt or modify investment decisions that imply serious social and environmental costs in distant (foreign) ecosystems or for future generations.

In addition, if governments and international agencies give such inadequate attention to the needs and priorities of people who lack the income or assets adequately to meet their own needs, are they likely to act to safeguard the needs and priorities of future generations? The lack of a commitment to intra-generational equity i e to lessening unequal access to natural resources and to safe and healthy living environments within the contemporary world does not augur well for obtaining a real commitment to intergenerational equity. Achieving the intergenerational equity aspect of sustainable development is, in effect, a commitment by middle and upper income groups all round the world to change lifestyles and consumption patterns to safeguard the needs of future generations. Although the extent of the needed changes is strongly debated, the need for changes has become evident.

GLOBAL WARMING AND CITIES

Although there is still much uncertainty about the possible scale of global warming in the future, the scale of possible disruption to cities (and other settlements and ecosystems) and of increases in extreme weather events if there is a sustained trend towards atmospheric warming make curbs on greenhouse gas emissions particularly important. The most direct effects of global warming are higher global mean temperatures, sea level rises, changes in weather patterns (including those of rainfall and other forms of precipitation) and in the frequency and severity of extreme weather conditions (storms, sea surges). These can lead to major changes in the function and structure of ecosystems. They will also pose direct threats to human health and life, especially through increased incidence and severity of floods and storms and through decreased potential for crop production in particular areas.

Sea level rises will obviously be most disruptive to settlements on coastal and estuarine areas and this is where a considerable proportion of the world's population lives. Sea level rises will flood low-lying areas unless flood protection is built (and such protection may be prohibitively expensive for many settlements and societies). They will also bring rising ground-water levels in coastal areas that will threaten existing sewerage and drainage systems and may undermine buildings. Most coastal cities will need extensive and expensive modifications to their water supply and sanitation and drainage systems. Many of the world's most densely populated areas are river deltas and low-lying coastal areas. Many of the world's largest cities are ports that also developed as major industrial, commercial and financial centres and these will be particularly vulnerable to sea level rises. So too will the many industries and thermal power stations that are concentrated on coasts because of their need for cooling water or as the sea becomes a convenient dumping ground for their waste (Parry, 1992).

Global warming will also mean increased human exposure to exceptional heat waves. This is likely to cause discomfort for many and premature death for some. The elderly, the very young and those with incapacitating diseases are likely to suffer most (WHO, 1992). Those living in cities that are already heat islands where temperatures remain significantly above those of the surrounding regions will also be particularly at risk. High relative humidity will considerably amplify heat stress (WHO, 1992). Increased temperatures in cities can also increase the concentrations of ground-level ozone, as it increases the reaction rates among the pollutants that form ozone.

Global warming will also bring changes in the distribution of infectious diseases. Warmer average temperatures permit an expansion in the area in which 'tropical diseases' can occur. This is likely to be the case for many diseases spread by insect vectors – for instance global warming is likely to permit an expansion of the area in which mosquitoes that are the vectors for malaria, dengue fever and filariasis can survive and breed (WHO, 1992). The areas in which the aquatic snail that is the vector for schistosomiasis may expand considerably. Increasing temperatures and changes in weather patterns will lead to changes in ecosystems that in turn impact on the livelihoods of those who exploit or rely on natural resources for their livelihoods. Both traditional and modern agricultural practices may be vulnerable to the relatively rapid changes in temperature, rainfall, flooding and storms that global warming can bring. In many regions, the additional stress placed on farmers and pastoralists by changing temperatures and weather patterns will be added to what are already serious stresses on ecosystems' carrying capacities.

However, a long-term programme initiated now can, over time, greatly reduce the emission of 'greenhouse gases' that underlie global warming without high social and economic costs. Many of the actions needed to reduce the emissions of these gases have other social, economic or environmental benefits. The main difficulty in the more wealthy, urbanized societies where most greenhouse gas emissions currently take place is initiating a process that steadily reduces these emissions. The main difficulty in less wealthy societies is ensuring that the prioritization of economic growth and improved standards of living take place within resource efficient, waste-minimizing settlements. Both require ways to ensure that individuals and enterprises revise the basis on which investment and consumption decisions are made so these take sufficient account of dangers that are most acute several decades into the future.

Poverty and the loss of environmental capital

Much of the writing about sustainable development has not only ignored the needs and priorities of low-income groups but also cast low-income groups as major causes of environmental degradation.[8] But low-

---

8) See for instance UNDP (1991:28), which claims that 'significant environmental degradation is usually caused by poverty in the South'. Poverty is also considered as a major factor in environmental degradation in Holmberg (1992); Leonard (1989) and many publications by the Worldwatch Institute.

income groups contribute very little to the depletion of at least three of the four kinds of environmental capital discussed above. Their consumption per person of nonrenewable resources is very low – which is not surprising given the fact that they lack the income to own private automobiles and to own or use other resource-intensive capital goods. They generally use the least resource-intensive forms of transport – walking, bicycling and public transport. The levels of waste they generate per person are much lower than those of richer groups – and low income households in rural and urban areas often reuse or recycle much of what wealthier households would throw away.[9] Their contribution per person to greenhouse gases and to stratospheric ozone depleting chemicals both directly through their actions and indirectly through the goods they own or use is very low in comparison with wealthier groups. The same is true for other non-biodegradable wastes.

The only components of natural capital to whose depletion low income groups may contribute is in certain renewable resources – for instance to soil degradation or the degradation of forests or the overuse of freshwater. But a large proportion of low-income households contribute little or nothing to this – for instance those living in urban areas or those who are landless in rural areas and who make a living through wage labour. The only basis for accusing 'the poor' of contributing to unsustainable resource use is for that portion of 'the poor' that make their living as farmers (usually on smallholdings), pastoralists and forest users. But even for these, they cannot be a major force for the degradation of soils or forests worldwide since their poverty is a result of them having so little land and such inadequate access to forests. Most deforestation and soil erosion takes place on land which the poor do not own and to which they do not have access. Wealthy farmers, landowners, commercial companies and governments own most of the world's farmland and forests, so it is difficult to see how the poor can be blamed for their overuse. Thus, the discussion of the contribution of poverty to unsustainable resource use is only with regard to the very small proportion of the world's soils, forests, pastures and fisheries to which poor farmers, pastoralists, hunter gatherers and those who fish have access.

The fact that these people are poor will also mean that they generally have the most marginal or fragile renewable resources on which to draw their livelihoods. The more intense the competition for access to resources, the more the lowest income groups or indigenous peoples are

---

9) Some enterprises owned by low income groups do create or contribute to serious problems of air pollution and liquid and solid wastes within their locality – but this does not change the fact that low income groups in general generate far less wastes than middle and upper income groups.

pushed to the least valuable margins. As such, they have most difficulties in sustaining production levels and are most likely to forsake long-term sustainability because of short-term survival. It is common for many low-income households to be involved in deforestation on the agricultural frontier and to be expanding cultivation on land ill-suited to agriculture. But this does not mean that they are major contributors to unsustainable resource use on a global scale. And even if low income households have to sustain themselves on inadequate land-holdings and poor quality soil, there is not necessarily evidence of environmental degradation and many examples of low income groups involved in environmental protection and careful resource management (see for example Pretty and Guijt, 1992; and Chapter 6 of Satterthwaite et al, 1996). There are also many examples of 'low-income' communities whose indigenous knowledge and practices are far more oriented to long-term ecological sustainability than most modern farming and forestry practices (Ecologist, 1992).

There is certainly a link between poverty and serious problems of environmental health as low income groups lack access to safe and sufficient water supplies, provision for sanitation, safe and adequate housing and access to health care. But this should not be confused with the depletion of environmental capital. The environment-related diseases and injuries that low income households suffer are not depleting soils or forests or using nonrenewable resources or seriously disrupting ecosystems.

Development advantages of cities

The sections above have pointed to the current or potential advantages of cities in reducing a society's call on natural capital and thus contributing to a more 'ecologically sustainable' pattern of development. But it should also be recalled that cities present advantages in development terms. For instance, the higher densities in cities also mean much lower costs per household and per enterprise for the provision of piped, treated water supplies, the collection and disposal of household and human wastes, advanced telecommunications and most forms of health care and education. Higher densities also make much cheaper the provision of emergency services – for instance fire-fighting and the emergency response to acute illness or injury that can greatly reduce the health burden for the people affected.

However, in the absence of effective governance in cities, including the institutional means to ensure the provision of infrastructure and services, the control of pollution, and the encouragement of efficient resource use, environmental problems are greatly exacerbated. The concentration of human, household, commercial and industrial wastes causes major environmental health problems for city inhabitants and overwhelm local sinks' capacity to break them down or dilute them. In the absence of an adequate drainage system, flooding and waterlogging usually cause serious problems. And cities' potential advantages for high quality infrastructure and service provision and efficient use of resources is not utilized. Meanwhile, in the absence of a planning framework, city expansion takes place haphazardly and often with urban sprawl over the best quality farmland. Meanwhile, poorer groups usually live in illegal or informal settlements which develop on land ill-suited to housing – for instance on floodplains or steep slopes with a high risk of landslides or mudslides – because these are the only land sites which they can afford. It is much more this failure of effective governance within cities that explains the poor environmental performance of so many cities rather than an inherent characteristic of cities in general.

The achievement of sustainable development goals in cities should also be viewed more positively in terms of employment creation. There is a considerable employment potential in moving towards more resource conserving, waste-minimizing patterns of production and consumption in the North and in the wealthier cities in the South. The main reason is that levels of resource use, waste generation and pollution are so high that there are many possibilities for substituting labour and knowledge for resource use and waste. There is great potential for combining employment generation with the transition to a more resource-efficient, minimum waste production and consumption pattern in:

- improving insulation levels in residential, commercial and industrial buildings and in adopting other innovations which limit electricity or fossil fuel consumption;
- the manufacture, installation and maintenance of machinery and equipment that are more resource efficient and less polluting; and
- the industrial and service enterprises associated with waste minimization, recycling, reuse and resource reclamation.

Extending the life of capital goods to reduce levels of resource use also generally means more employment in maintenance and repair, although for many old capital goods and polluting equipment, the focus should be on replacement (including inefficient, high pollution level motor vehicles, poorly insulated CFC-coolant fridges, and inefficient space and water heaters and electric lights).

One of the factors constraining action by governments towards resource conservation and waste reduction is the worry about the loss of jobs that this might create. There are employment losses arising from the greater cost of certain goods or services, especially those whose production or use requires major changes to reduce unacceptable levels of resource use or waste generation. But there are many examples of industrial processes where resource use and pollution levels have been cut with no overall increase in costs and, in some cases, with significant cost savings (Schmidheiny et al, 1992). In addition, even if costs do rise, they only do so to compensate for environmental costs that previously had been ignored.

A move to patterns of production within cities that are more compatible with sustainable development (because they are more resource conserving with minimal wastes) implies a series of shifts in the relative importance of employment in different sectors.[10] For instance, declining employment in the manufacture of automobiles and the material inputs into this process is compensated through expanding employment in public transport equipment and systems, traffic management, air pollution control equipment for motor vehicles, and reclamation and recycling of materials used in road vehicles. Similarly, declining employment in the coal, oil, natural gas and electricity industries is balanced by increasing employment in energy conservation in all sectors and in the manufacture and installation of energy-efficient appliances. Employment also grows within the renewable energy sector as higher prices for nonrenewable fuels, technological advances and public support for renewable resource use expand the potential to tap renewable energy sources. It is quite feasible in the North for living standards and the number of households to continue growing but with a steady decline in the level of fossil fuel use.[11] Investments in energy conservation are generally more labour intensive than investments in increasing the energy supply – especially when comparing the cost of increasing the electricity supply with the cost of reducing demand through conservation or the use of more efficient appliances, so that supplies no longer need to increase.

Another employment shift within this move to more sustainable production patterns is declining employment in mining and primary metals industries and paper and glass industries (and other industries associated with packaging production) and expanding employment in urban management systems that maximize recycling, reuse and reclamation, and promote waste minimization. There is also an employment shift is declining employment in producing and selling the fertilizers and biocides now widely used in industrial agriculture and horticulture but with increased employment in lower input farming, ecologically-based farming and land management, and resource efficient, high intensity crop

---

10) This point is developed in more detail in UNCHS (1996).
11) Several studies in the late 1970s and early 1980s demonstrated this – for instance see Leach (1979) for details of how increasing prosperity need not imply increased fossil fuel use in the UK.

production systems such as those based on hydroponics and permaculture. This includes much increased scope for urban agriculture and horticulture which can also bring considerable ecological advantages, as well as employment and incomes (see Smit et al, 1996).

There are also likely to be increased employment opportunities in the water supply and sewage treatment industries as higher standards are met and water conservation programmes implemented, and in the managerial and technical staff within municipalities and companies or corporations whose task is environmental management.

Although there are employment benefits in moving towards more ecologically sustainable patterns of production and consumption, the employment losses fall heavily on certain employees and on urban centres or regions that have the traditional logging, 'smokestack' and mining industries. Most of the job losses in these industries in Europe and North America over the last two decades have little to do with environmental regulation and much more to do with the gradual shift in production to cheaper areas or to new technologies that greatly reduce the need for labour. But it is little comfort to the miners and steelworkers and their families when jobs disappear, to know that policies promoting resource conservation and waste minimization are creating more employment elsewhere. Thus, one of the most important roles for government in promoting this transition is addressing the needs of the workforce in the resource and waste intensive industries that lose their employment. There are some interesting cases of this – for instance the case of Hamilton-Wentworth in Canada which lost a large part of its employment base as the steel mills closed down, moved away or cut down their workforce and whose response was to try to promote the city as a good location for industries concerned with environmental protection and resource conservation and to develop its environmental quality as a key part of attracting new investment (Wilkins, 1993; Regional Municipality of Hamilton-Wentworth, 1993a and 1993b; Staff Working Group on Sustainable Development, 1993).

LINKING GLOBAL AND LOCAL SUSTAINABILITY

The possible contradictions between ecological sustainability at global and at local level have been noted already. So too has the fact that most of the world's wealthiest nations have been relatively successful at meeting some sustainable development goals within their own nation or region by drawing heavily on the environmental capital of other regions or nations and on the global sink. In effect, they have imported environmental capital and depleted the world's stock of such capital; it is often their production and consumption patterns which underlie (or contribute significantly to) unsustainable forest, soil or freshwater exploitation in poorer nations.

This implies the need for international agreements which set limits for each national society's consumption of resources and use of the global sink for their wastes. But it is also clear that most action to achieve sustainable development has to be formulated and implemented locally. The fact that each village, province or city and its insertion within local and regional ecosystems is unique implies the need for optimal use of local resources, knowledge and skills for the achievement of development goals within a detailed knowledge of the local and regional ecological carrying capacity. This demands a considerable degree of local self-determination, since centralized decision making structures have great difficulty in implementing decisions which respond appropriately to such diversity. Nevertheless, some new international institutions are required to ensure that individual cities or countries do not take advantage of others' restraint.

National governments inevitably have the key role in linking local and global sustainability. Internationally, they have the responsibility for reaching agreements to limit the call that consumers and businesses within their country make on the world's environmental capital. Nationally, they are responsible for providing the framework to ensure local actions can meet development goals without compromising local and global sustainability. But there is little evidence of national governments setting up the regulatory and incentive structure to ensure that the aggregate impact of their economic activities and citizens' consumption is in accordance with global sustainability – although a few in Europe have taken some tentative steps towards some aspects (see for instance UNCHS, 1996). Such an incentive and regulatory structure is relatively easy to conceive, as an abstract exercise. Certainly, poverty can be greatly reduced without an expansion in resource use and waste generation which threatens ecological sustainability. It is also possible to envisage a considerable reduction in resource use and waste generation by middle- and upper-income households, without diminishing their quality of life (and in some aspects actually enhancing it). The prosperity and economic stability that the poorer nations need to underpin secure livelihoods for their populations and the needed enhancement in the competence and accountability of their government can be achieved without a much increased call on environmental capital. However, the prospects for actually translating what is possible into reality both within nations and globally remains much less certain. Powerful vested interests oppose most if not all the needed policies and priorities. Richer groups are unlikely willingly to forsake the comfort and mobility that they currently enjoy. Technological change can help to a limited extent – for instance, moderating the impact of rising gasoline prices through the relatively rapid introduction of increasingly fuel-efficient automobiles and the introduction of alternative fuels derived from renewable energy sources. But if combatting atmospheric warming does demand a rapid reduction in greenhouse gas emissions, this will imply changes in people's right to use private automobiles, which cannot be met by new technologies and alternative ('renewable') fuels – at least at costs that will prove politically acceptable. So many existing commercial, industrial and residential buildings and urban forms (for instance low density suburban developments and out-of-town shopping malls) have high levels of energy use built into them and these are not easily or rapidly changed (Gore, 1991).

At the same time, in the South, the achievement of development goals that minimize the call on local and global environmental capital demands a competence and capacity by local governments that is currently very rarely present. The achievement of key development goals is also unlikely without strong democratic pressures and processes influencing decisions about the use of public resources.

Governance

Achieving three of the main principles that underlie sustainable development (Houghton and Hunter, 1994) – more intergenerational equity, more intragenerational equity and greater transfrontier responsibility by resource users and waste generators – implies substantial political changes. It implies major changes in ownership rights for land and natural resources (von Amsberg, 1993). It also implies changes in the configuration of the political systems at local and global levels that had previously allowed or even encouraged undesirable environmental impacts (Houghton and Hunter, 1994).

This helps explain why the discussion of urban problems has been moving away from discussing 'what should be done' to discussing what kind of 'governance' structure is needed to allow effective decisions to be made about what has to be done. The discussion of governance is much broader than the roles and responsibilities of governments as 'governance' includes the contribution of community and voluntary organizations and other social groups and their relations with 'government' (UNCHS, 1996). One of the most important aspects of this change is the move from discussing 'what poor people need' to 'what decision-making powers, access to resources and political influence should low-income people have to allow them to ensure that their needs are met, their rights respected and their priorities addressed. One example of this comes from the discussion of 'Future Cities'. The April 1996 issue of the journal we edit, *Environment and Urbanization*, is a special issue for Habitat II and is on this theme of 'Future Cities'. Most of the papers submitted for this issue are not about a future city as a physical structure (and the usual discussion of the benefits that advanced technology will apparently bring) but a future society where power is reclaimed by citizens and community organizations from governments, corporations and international agencies. Cities and community organizations not only have more influence on their 'future city' but they also require governments, corporations and international agencies to be more accountable for the actions and investments they make (see for instance Ortiz, 1966; Korten, 1966; and Balvin Diaz et al, 1966).

The debate about city and municipal authorities in the South has also moved in this direction. The concern in the late 1970s and early 1980s was largely that they lacked the power, authority and resources to meet their responsibilities. More recently, the concern has come to include how democratic, accountable and transparent they are and their capacity to work with, encourage and support a great range of community organizations, voluntary associations and social groups.

An important part of this move from 'government' to 'governance' has been the greater appreciation of the role of individuals and households and of community and voluntary organizations in building and managing each city. All cities are the result of an enormous range of investments of capital, expertise and time by individuals, households, communities, voluntary organizations and NGOs, as well as by private enterprises, investors and government agencies. Over the last 20 years, many of the most effective initiatives to improve housing conditions among low income groups have come from local NGOs or community organizations. These include new models for housing finance which provide loans to households whose incomes are too low or uncertain to get finance from the private sector, but which nonetheless achieve lower levels of loan default than banks obtain from loans to higher income groups (Mitlin, 1995). They include new ways for governments to work with low income groups and their community organizations in improving housing conditions and health (UNCHS, 1996). They include municipal authorities that make their whole budgeting process more open and more subject to the demands of citizens (Bretas, 1996). Many more governments and a few donor agencies are learning how to support these processes that build and develop cities. What can be achieved by supporting the efforts of several hundred community organizations in a single city can vastly outweigh what any single government agency can do by itself.

Another important change is the innovation showed in many local Agenda 21 plans developed by cities in both the North and the South

(UNCHS, 1996; Mega, 1996). These seek to address environment and development issues that are of direct relevance to the citizens. Many have pioneered new ways of fully involving the inhabitants in their formulation and implementation. But many have also sought to address environment and development problems of relevance to people outside their boundaries and to the depletion of environmental capital elsewhere (Mega, 1996). These are showing a new commitment to intergenerational equity and transfrontier responsibility. While these provide encouraging examples, what is so lacking in most countries and within international negotiations is any sign of the national and international framework that is needed to support such initiatives and to ensure they become the norm rather than the exceptions.[12]

National governments in both North and South are unlikely to set the incentives and regulations needed to promote sustainable development outside their national boundaries without international agreements. One of the key international issues for the next few decades will be how to resolve the pursuit of increased wealth by national societies (most of whose members have strong preferences for minimal constraints on their consumption levels) within a global recognition of the ecological and material limits of the biosphere. There is little doubt that the world's natural resource endowments and natural systems can sustain the world's population both now and in the near future with absolute poverty eliminated, human needs met and all nations having life expectancies comparable to those in the richer nations. In the richest nations, it is also possible to envisage much more resource-conserving societies without a fall in living standards; indeed, as outlined earlier, in many aspects, far more resource conserving societies will have higher living standards and broader and more fulfilling employment structures. What is far more in question is whether the political processes within nations and internationally can put in place both the agreements and the regulatory and incentive structures to ensure that this is achieved. The power and profitability of many major corporations and the authority of national governments will be reduced by such a move. Many jobs may also be threatened although, as noted earlier, more attention to resource conservation is likely to create more jobs than it removes. Some necessary measures are likely to prove politically unpopular. Even when international agreement is reached, the world has little experience of the institutions needed to ensure compliance.

---

12) For instance, initial steps have been taken at national level of Sweden and The Netherlands to encourage a move towards sustainable development goals among urban authorities – see Expert Group on the Urban Environment (1994).

Achieving this is made all the more difficult by incomplete knowledge about the scale and nature of the environmental costs that current production and consumption patterns are passing on to current and future generations (Serageldin, 1993). The precautionary principle may be well understood and widely quoted but it is not being integrated into economic decisions. One of the most difficult issues to resolve is on what basis to value the different kinds of environmental assets widely used in production and consumption (Serageldin, 1993; Winpenny, 1991) and how to ensure that this valuation contributes to greater intergenerational and intra-generational equity. Another is the extent to which other forms of capital are substitutable for natural capital (see, for instance, Serageldin, 1995).

Another is how to ensure that social capital (including social institutions that have great importance to ensuring human needs are met) and human capital (including people's knowledge and level of education and their health) are also not also depleted (Serageldin, 1995). There is an increasing recognition of the importance of what is often termed the 'social economy', not only for the benefits it brings to each street or neighbourhood but also for the economic and social costs it saves the wider society. (This material on the social economy is drawn largely from Korten, 1995; and Boyd, 1995.) The social economy is a term given to a great variety of initiatives and actions that are organized and controlled locally and that are not profit-oriented. It includes many activities that are unwaged and unmonetized – including the work of citizen groups, residents' associations, street or neighbourhood (*barrio*) clubs, youth clubs and volunteers who help support local schools and prevention-oriented health care and provide services for the elderly, the physically disabled or other individuals in need of special support. It includes many initiatives that make cities safer and more fun – helping provide supervised play space, sport and recreational opportunities for children and youth (Korten, 1995; Boyd, 1994; UNCHS, 1996).

There are also international factors far beyond the competence and capacity of national and municipal governments that influence the quality of city environments. The very poor environmental conditions evident in most Southern cities are an expression of the very difficult circumstances in which most Southern countries find themselves. *Stagnant economies and heavy debt burdens do not provide a suitable base from which to develop good governance.* Governments from the North and international agencies may promote environmental policies but there is little progress on changing the international economic system to permit more economic stability and prosperity among the poorest nations. Many Southern economies have no alternative but to increase the exploitation of their natural resources to earn the foreign exchange to meet debt repayments. In the end, despite the possibility of pointing to innovative programmes and practices in both the North and the South that move cities towards a more successful combining of environmental and development goals, the present economic and political structures within which they operate and the great lack of progress in introducing even modest changes to these do not augur well for their spread and further development.

References

Adams, W M (1990) *Green Development: Environment and Sustainability in the Third World*, Routledge, London and New York

Balvin Diaz, Doris, Jose Luiz Lopez Follegatti and Micky Hordijk (1996) 'Innovative Environmental Management in Ilo, Peru', *Environment and Urbanization*, 8 (1), April, special issue of on 'Future Cities'

Barrow, C J (1995) 'Sustainable Development: Concept, Value and Practice', *Third World Planning Review*, 17 (4), November, pp 369–86

Boyd, Graham (1995) 'The Urban Social Economy', *Urban Examples*, UNICEF, New York

Bretas, Paulo Roberto Paixão (1996) 'Participative Budgeting in Belo Horizonte: Democratization And Citizenship', *Environment and Urbanization*, 8 (1), April

Cairncross, Sandy, Jorge E Hardoy and David Satterthwaite (1990) 'The Urban Context', in Jorge E Hardoy, Sandy Cairncross and David Satterthwaite (eds) *The Poor Die Young: Housing and Health in Third World Cities*, Earthscan Publications, London, pp 1-24

Conway, Gordon R and Jules N Pretty (1991) *Unwelcome Harvest*, Earthscan Publications, London

Damián, Araceli (1992) 'Ciudad de México: Servicios urbanos en los Noventas', *Vivienda*, 3 (1), January–April, pp 29–40

Ecologist, The (1992) *Whose Common Future: Reclaiming the Commons*, Earthscan Publications, London

Expert Group on the Urban Environment (1994), *European Sustainable Cities Part 1*, European Commission, X1/95/502-en, Brussels

Furedy, Christine (1990) 'Social Aspects of Solid Waste Recovery in Asian Cities', *Environmental Sanitation Reviews*, 30, ENSIC, Asian Institute of Technology, Bangkok, pp 2–52

— (1992) 'Garbage: Exploring Non-Conventional Options in Asian Cities', *Environment and Urbanization*, 4 (2), October, pp 42–61

Giradet, Herbert (1992) *The Gaia Atlas of Cities*, Gaia Books, London

Gore, Charles (1991) 'Policies and Mechanisms for Sustainable Development: The Transport Sector', mimeo

Hardoy, Jorge E, Diana Mitlin and David Satterthwaite (1992), *Environmental Problems in Third World Cities*, Earthscan Publications, London

Holmberg, Johan (1992) *Poverty, Environment and Development: Proposals for Action*, Swedish International Development Authority, Stockholm

Houghton, Graham and Colin Hunter (1994) *Sustainable Cities*, Regional Policy and Development series, Jessica Kingsley, London

Jazairy, Idriss, Mohiuddin Alamgir and Theresa Panuccio (1992) *The State of World Rural Poverty: An Inquiry into its Causes and Consequences*, IT Publications, London

Korten, David C (1966) 'Civic Engagement in Creating Future Cities', *Environment and Urbanization*, 8 (1), April, special issue of on 'Future Cities'

— (1995) 'Civic Engagement to Create Just and Sustainable Societies for the 21st Century', Conference Issues Paper prepared for Habitat II

Leach, Gerald et al (1979) *A Low Energy Strategy for the United Kingdom*, London, Science Reviews Ltd

Leonard, H Jeffrey (1989) 'Environment and the Poor: Development Strategies for a Common Agenda', in H Jeffrey Leonard et al, *Environment and the Poor: Development Strategies for a Common Agenda*, Overseas Development Council, Transaction Books, New Brunswick and Oxford, pp 3–45

Manzanal, Mabel and Cesar Vapnarsky (1986) 'The Development of the Upper Valley of Rio Negro and its Periphery within the Comahue Region, Argentina', in Jorge E Hardoy and David Satterthwaite (eds), *Small and Intermediate Urban Centres: Their Role in Regional and National Development in the Third World*, Hodder and Stoughton, London and Westview, USA

Meadows, Donella H, Dennis L Meadows, Jorgen Randers and William W Behrens III (1974) *The Limits to Growth*, Pan Books Ltd, London

Mega, Voula (1996) 'Our City, Our Future: Towards Sustainable Development in European Cities', *Environment and Urbanization*, 8 (1), April

Mitlin, Diana (1992) 'Sustainable Development: A Guide to the Literature', *Environment and Urbanization*, 4 (1), April, pp 111–24

— (1995), 'Building with Credit: Housing Finance for Low-Income Households', IIED, London

Mitlin, Diana and David Satterthwaite (1994) 'Cities and Sustainable Development', the background paper to Global Forum '94, Manchester City Council and IIED, June

Newman, Peter W G and Jeffrey R Kenworthy (1989) *Cities and Automobile Dependence: An International Sourcebook*, Gower Technical, Aldershot

Ortiz, Enrique (1966) 'Towards a City of Solidarity and Citizenship', *Environment and Urbanization*, 8 (1), April, special issue on 'Future Cities'

Parry, Martin (1992) 'The Urban Economy', presentation at Cities and Climate Change, a conference at the Royal Geographical Society, 31 March

Postel, Sandra (1992) *The Last Oasis: Facing Water Scarcity*, Worldwatch Environmental Alert Series, Earthscan Publications, London

Pretty, J N and Irene Guijt (1992) 'Primary Environmental Care: An Alternative Paradigm for Development Assistance', *Environment and Urbanization*, 4 (1), April, pp 22–36

Rees, William E (1992) 'Ecological Footprints and Appropriated Carrying Capacity', *Environment and Urbanization*, 4 (2), October, pp 121-30

Regional Municipality of Hamilton-Wentworth (1993) *Implementing Vision 2020: Directions for Creating a Sustainable Region*, The Regional Chairman's Taskforce on Sustainable Development

— (1993b) *Towards a Sustainable Region: Hamilton-Wentworth Region, Official Plan (Draft)*, September, Regional Planning and Development Department, September, Hamilton-Wentworth

Satterthwaite, David (1995) 'The Underestimation of Poverty and its Health Consequences', *Third World Planning Review*, 17 (4), November, pp iii-xii

Satterthwaite, David, Roger Hart, Caren Levy, Diana Mitlin, David Ross, Jac Smit and Carolyn Stephens (1996) *The Environment for Children*, Earthscan Publications, London and UNICEF, New York

Schmidheiny, Stephan, with the Business Council for Sustainable Development (1992) *Changing Course: A Global Business Perspective on Development and the Environment*, The MIT Press, Cambridge, Massachusetts

Serageldin, Ismail (1993) 'Making Development Sustainable', *Finance and Development*, 30 (4), December, pp 6-10

— (1995) 'Sustainability and the Wealth of Nations: First Steps in an Ongoing Journey', Paper presented at the Third Annual World Bank Conference on Environmentally Sustainable Development

Smit, Jac et al (1996) *Urban Agriculture: Food, Jobs and Sustainable Cities*, UNDP, February

Staff Working Group on Sustainable Development (1993) *Hamilton-Wentworth's Sustainable Community Decision-Making Guide*, Regional Municipality of Hamilton-Wentworth, August

Tiffen, Mary and Michael Mortimore (1992) 'Environment, Population Growth and Productivity in Kenya: A Case Study of Machakos District', *Development Policy Review*, 10, pp 359–87

UNCHS (Habitat) (1996), *An Urbanizing World: Global Report on Human Settlements, 1996*, Oxford University Press, Oxford and New York

UNDP (1991) *Human Development Report 1991*, United Nations Development Programme, Oxford University Press, Oxford and New York

von Amsberg, Joachim (1993) *Project Evaluation and the Depletion of Natural Capital: An Application of the Sustainability Principle*, Environment Working Paper No 56, Environment Department, World Bank, Washington DC

Ward, Barbara (1975) *World Development*, 3 (2/3), February–March

— (1976) 'The Inner and the Outer Limits', The Clifford Clark Memorial Lectures 1976, *Canadian Public Administration*, 19 (3), Autumn, pp 385-416

— (1979) *Progress for a Small Planet*, Penguin and subsequently republished by Earthscan Publications, London

Ward, Barbara and René Dubos (1972) *Only One Earth: The Care and Maintenance of a Small Planet*, Andre Deutsch, London

Water Program (1991) *Water Efficiency: A Resource for Utility Managers, Community Planners and other Decision Makers*, Rocky Mountain Institute, Snowmass

WCED (1987) *Our Common Future*, Oxford University Press, Oxford

White, Rodney R (1992) 'The International Transfer of Urban Technology: Does the North have Anything to Offer for the Global Environmental Crisis?', *Environment and Urbanization*, 4 (2), October, pp 109–20

WHO (1992a) *Our Planet, Our Health*, Report of the Commission on Health and Environment, Geneva

— (1992b) 'World Malaria Situation 1990', Division of Control of Tropical Diseases, World Health Organization, *World Health Statistics Quarterly*, 45 (2/3), pp 257–66

— (1995) *The World Health Report 1995: Bridging the Gaps*, World Health Organization, Geneva

Wilkins, Charles (1993) 'Steeltown Charts a New Course', *Canadian Geographic*, 113 (4), July/August, pp 42–55

Winpenny, J T (1991) *Values for the Environment: A Guide to Economic Appraisal*, HMSO, London

World Resources Institute (1990) *World Resources 1990-91: A Guide to the Global Environment*, Oxford University Press, Oxford

Chapter Two

The Idea of Healthy
Cities and its Application

Trudy Harpham and Edmundo Werna

The issue of health in the cities of developing countries has recently emerged on agendas of national and international agencies. Harpham and Tanner (1995) discuss the reasons for this. The last decade has witnessed health issues being addressed in urban development projects and programmes which would previously have focused only on physical infrastructure, for example slum improvement projects (Harpham and Stephens, 1992). One action or intervention which emerged as a result of growing discussions on urban health is the Healthy Cities Project (HCP) of the World Health Organization (WHO). The Healthy Cities Movement, which generated the project, was launched in Lisbon in 1986. Eleven European cities were first selected. The initial idea was to apply to urban life, the theory and principles of WHO's strategy of 'health for all by the year 2000'. The HCP is a long-term development project which seeks to put health on the agendas of decision makers in cities and to build a strong lobby for public health at the local level. Ultimately, the project seeks to enhance the physical, mental, social and environmental wellbeing of the people who live and work in urban areas. The aim is to bring the public, the business and voluntary sectors and communities together in a partnership to focus on urban health and health related issues (Werna and Harpham, 1995). Since Tsouros (1990) reviewed the achievements of the HCP in Europe, there has been a growing interest in HCP in developing countries. WHO Geneva, with Dutch government funding, launched in 1995 a major new initiative in HCP in developing countries. This initiative is one of the most significant in the health sector, which emphasizes sustainability in terms of urban development and it is therefore timely to introduce the concept and its application in this volume. The current chapter aims to consider sustainable urban development against discussions of sustainability in the health sector; to describe the concept of healthy cities, and to provide two case studies of the application of healthy cities (CCC/WHO, 1993; BMA, 1994). The chapter should be read alongside that by McGranahan et al in order to understand both health problems and health actions currently emphasized in the cities of developing countries.

HEALTH IN URBAN AREAS

The general concept of sustainable development has been used in the study of specialized fields, such as urbanization. This section[1] presents the current trends in the growing literature on sustainable urban development and analyses their relation to urban health. This will pave the ground for understanding the relationship between the HCP and sustainability in urban health.

The contemporary discussion about sustainable development in general started in the 1970s, focusing on the environmental impact of development policies (for example Meadows et al, 1974; Sachs, 1979; Schumacher, 1973; Ward and Dubos, 1972 – see also Mitlin, 1992, for a review). There were loose or no references to urban issues within this general discussion (for example Atkinson, 1994; Hardoy et al, 1992). However, the concept of sustainability eventually found its way into the specific literature on urban development.

The discussion about sustainable urban development also started with a strong environmental bias – for example examining how cities and towns have affected the physical milieu through hazardous activities such as pollution, and exhaustion of nonrenewable resources. Issues regarding both the construction of urban areas (for example building materials, construction techniques, patterns of land occupation) and their maintenance (for example supply of urban services, consumption habits) were explored in this way.

However, the concept of sustainable urban development eventually went beyond the environmental domain, thus encompassing social, political and/or cultural aspects (for example Atkinson, 1994; Bhatti, 1988; Brugman, 1994; Hardoy et al, 1992). Also, a multi-actor view has evolved, ie the belief that different actors such as local authorities, non-

---

1)   This section is a version of the section 'Sustainable Urban Development and Health' published in Harpham and Werna (1996).

governmental organizations (NGOs) and community-based organizations (CBOs) play specific roles and have to be involved for the achievement of sustainable urban development.

Another important advancement in the sustainable urban development literature was the disaggregation of the two components of 'sustainable development', and the identification of an intrinsic conflict between the idea of 'sustaining' something (which entails conservation) and the idea of 'developing' it (which entails change). Hardoy et al (1992) provide a good clarification of this conflict. The term 'sustainable' should be used mainly in reference to ecological sustainability, because 'sustaining societies or cultures is more ambiguous. Indeed, the achievement of many social, economic and political development goals requires fundamental changes to social structures including government institutions and, in many instances, to the distribution of assets and income' (Hardoy et al, 1992:177–8). Therefore, instead of applying the concept of sustainability to every single activity, one should note that 'what is important is that the sum (or net effect) of the activities within a specific area is sustainable' (Hardoy et al, 1992:182). Consequently, the sustainability of urban areas relates to their impact on environmental capital, and the developmental component relates to their performance and that of their institutions in catering for the needs of the population.[2]

The literature has not reached a consensus regarding which specific issues should be sustainable and which issues should develop. However, the point to emphasize now is that the concept of sustainable urban development has been elaborated far beyond the environmental domain, including other fundamental aspects (political and cultural) on their own and/or associated with environmental/ecological aspects, and also encompassing a multi-actor approach. As will be shown later, such a broad approach is important for the discussion about sustainable urban health in general and about the HCP in particular.

However, despite the aforementioned elaborations regarding sustainable urban development, a number of authors and policy-making agencies still have a strong environmental bias (for example Choguill, forthcoming; Leitmann, 1994; Serageldin and Cohen, 1994; Stren et al, 1992; UNCHS, 1990; White, 1994). This part of the sustainable urban development literature does refer to economy, politics, culture and society. However, it discusses such issues *within* an environmental/ecological perspective – for example the economic, political, cultural and/or social aspects of environmental sustainability. Of course this is

---

2) The needs of the population also include, but are not limited to, environmental issues such as protection from different types of pollution.

not the same as discussing the sustainability and developmental aspects of these issues *on their own* and/or *associated with* environmental/ecological issues. In short, the literature on sustainable urban development has varied from a focused concern with environmental issues to a broad multisectoral concern. These different approaches have diverse consequences for sustainable urban health. In order to understand this fully, the relation between urban development and health will be clarified.

The current concept of health is distinct from (and much broader than) the traditional view which emerged in industrialized societies from the mid-twentieth century. The traditional view narrowly treats health care (which is an activity) as a synonym of health itself (which is a state of being), and places emphasis on the cure of diseases (for example CCC/WHO, 1993). The WHO epitomizes the current concept by defining health as a state of complete physical, social and mental wellbeing – which is much more than the mere absence of disease or infirmity; and whose attainment therefore requires far more than the supply of health services. Thus, 'That health is a state of wellbeing indicates that health is not an activity . . ., rather it is the outcome of all activities which make up the lives of individuals, households, communities and cities' (CCC/WHO, 1993:3). Such a statement, when applied to the specific realm of urban settlements, shows the importance of the different aspects of urban development to health. For instance:

> Physical, economic, social, and cultural aspects of city life all have an important influence on health. They exert their effect through such processes as population movement, industrialization, and changes in the architectural and physical environment and in social organization. Health is also affected in particular cities by climate, terrain, population density, housing stock, the nature of the economic activity, income distribution, transport systems, and opportunities for leisure and recreation.
>
> (WHO, 1993:10–11)

In sum, it is necessary to act upon the several issues which enable a city/town to improve the health of its citizens. Consequently, an approach to sustainable urban development that is able to connect such a wide range of issues may constitute a solid basis for achieving sustainable urban health. However, by comparison, a unisectoral approach to sustainable urban development is bound to have notable constraints.

As shown before, there have been different approaches to sustainable urban development, from a specific focus on environmental issues to a much wider focus. Paying attention to the environment is fundamental.

However, a specific concern with this aspect of sustainable urban development will exclude other issues which are also pivotal for addressing sustainable urban health, such as education, employment, domestic and street violence and recreation habits, to name a few. In short, actions to achieve sustainable urban health need a wide approach. An important initiative in this respect is the HCP, whose main concept is explained in the next section.

THE CONCEPT OF HEALTHY CITIES

WHO (1995:1) has declared that 'the designation of a Healthy City signifies that new initiatives are being undertaken or planned, which through a new coalition of government and community organizations address priority urban health and environment problems.' In the same document WHO suggests that there may be 100 such cities in the American region, 30 in the African region, 30 in the eastern Mediterranean region, 30 in the western Pacific region and 10 in the Southeast Asian region. It acknowledges that, at present, an adequate reporting system is lacking in all regions with the exception of the European region.

Unusually for a UN programme, the HCP is characterized by good links with other organizations. For example, many activities designed to improve the capacity of municipal government to manage the urban environment and improve living conditions in cities have taken place in the wake of the United Nations Conference on Environment and Development (UNCED). HCP is linked to the UNDP's LIFE Programme, the UNDP/World Bank/UNCHS's Urban Management Programme, the ILO's Labour Intensive Public Works Programme, the World Bank/UNDP's Metropolitan Environment Improvement Programme and Metropolitan Development Programme, the UNCHS's Sustainable Cities Programme, the ESCAP/UNDP's CITYNET/Asia–Pacific 2000 Programme, the Megacities Programme and the Metropolis Programme (WHO, 1995:6). However, recent criticisms of WHO and the loss of its AIDS programme to UNDP puts into question the ability of WHO to play a key coordinating role among UN agencies.

The WHO emphasizes that HCP may be a stand alone project in a given city, or it may be a health component of a larger urban development effort that involves urban infrastructure, land management, municipal finance and industrial development, with the city *health* plan being an integral part of the wider development plan for the city. The programme's mission statement is:

Healthy Cities strive to improve the health and the living conditions in urban areas with local governments as the key partners in this process. This is achieved through a process of political commitment, institutional strengthening, innovative action that involves all sectors, community participation and networking. The focus is on inter-programme cooperation, with special emphasis on health and environment and health promotion, and close cooperation with all other related programmes.

(WHO, 1995:7)

WHO (1995:13) has identified two key concepts that help define the programme – intersectoral collaboration for health and supportive environments. In terms of intersectoral collaboration all agencies concerned with energy, food, agriculture, macroeconomic planning, housing, land use, transportation and other areas are required to examine the health implications of their policies and programmes, and adjust them to better promote health and a healthy environment. WHO acknowledges that such collaboration has often failed because it was unclear how the health sector was to be involved and there was little political support for intersectoral collaboration. It is suggested (WHO, 1995:13) that such collaboration requires (a) a measurement of the health impacts of various development activities, (b) policies on health for particular sectors (for example health in housing, health in the workplace, health in schools) and (c) advocacy by the health sector in relation to each implementing ministry or agency. The more successful HCPs have obtained political support by involving mayors, universities, NGOs, private companies and community organizations. This partnership then contributes to the formation of a municipal health plan (see Box 2.1).

The idea of a supportive environment and the 'settings' approach is based on the premise that health status is determined more by conditions in certain settings such as work, school, home than by the health care services or facilities that are provided. For example, a 'Healthy Marketplaces' Programme has established partnerships between all concerned in order to address issues such as:

- infrastructure (water, toilets, physical layout);
- practices for the storage and handling of raw and semi-processed foodstuffs (meat, vegetables);
- safety of street vendor food;
- solid and liquid waste management;
- role of government authorities, for example food inspectors; and
- consumer education.

The above description of the healthy cities' concept emphasizes several characteristics that can contribute to sustainable urban health, namely a broad definition of health, an intersectoral approach and the involvement of a wide range of actors. An additional important characteristic is that WHO provides limited funding and instead places emphasis on mobilizing local resources. This factor makes redundant any idea of sustainability merely meaning the ability of a national government to continue activities after the withdrawal of funding from bilateral or multilateral agencies. Instead, it places emphasis on the process of the HCPs ensuring sustainability. This is illustrated in the next section where two case studies of HCPs are presented in relation to the 'sustainability' characteristics identified above.

Box 2.1   OUTLINE OF A MUNICIPAL HEALTH PLAN

This is based on the development of municipal health plans (MHPs) in the cities of Rio de Janeiro, Accra and Lahore during 1991/2.

Who formulates the plan? *A multisectoral team of community representatives and organizations including Ministry of Health (MOH) staff, NGOs, the university, a representative from the mayor's office, and representatives of hospitals and the media. The plan is consistent with national urban health/planning guidelines of the MOH and of ministries of urban development, and is endorsed by the mayor.*

Goals of the plan

- *To get health education and the other health-related activities incorporated into the community-level activities of municipal staff working in water, sanitation, solid waste, housing, education, social support and other areas; and*
- *to improve the performance of the municipality both in provision of services and in supporting local community initiatives and greater community participation in activities that promote health.*

Prerequisites
- *Community organization and representation in formulation of the plan;*
- *health leadership, which may be found in the MOH, NGO or municipal office; and*
- *a public hearing to allow broad public discussion.*

Content

- *Identify and review all studies and reports that are available that describe and quantify the social, economic and environmental health problems, and environmental conditions in the city;*
- *attempt to rank the contribution that problems make to the burden of ill-health;*
- *identify the existing municipal agencies and organizations, including UN bilateral agencies and NGOs, that can potentially contribute to solutions to health problems;*
- *identify potential mechanisms for partners to work in a more coordinated manner in addressing problems; and*
- *identify and rank the priority actions and programmes, including setting of targets, and evaluation plans.*

Ensure action

- *Commitment of community leaders;*
- *training of municipal staff and community participants;*
- *publish stories and reports in local media;*
- *monitor, evaluate and publish annual health status and activity data.*

The MHP may have programmes or projects for specific settings, such as schools, workplaces, the marketplace, and health care settings.

In preparing the plan, the project staff must keep in mind that there may be some government functions (policy-making, services) that are outside the responsibility of the city government and are controlled by national ministries. Identification of these functions will be critical, as will information about which city and national politicians and officials are sympathetic to health issues, or to the involvement of citizen groups in local government, and therefore may be prepared to support the project.

The MHP is collated and analysed by the project, and distributed to government agencies, NGOs and the public in one or more HCP meetings. The plan is not so much a blueprint but a tool to promote discussion and raise awareness that there are possibilities of changing living conditions in the city for the better, through cooperative efforts and partnerships.

(WHO, 1995:15, 16)

CASE STUDIES

Chittagong

Chittagong is an old city, which in 1960, had a population of approximately 300,000 and an area of 10.24 square kilometres (CCC/UNICEF, 1993). However, from the 1960s the city grew rapidly. Its population in 1993 was between 1.5 and 2.5 million, and its area was 183.4 square kilometres (CCC/UNICEF, 1993; CCC/WHO, 1993). At present Chittagong is the main industrial and commercial centre and main sea port of Bangladesh, and the country's second largest city. However, this accelerated process of urban growth has been accompanied by a multitude of health problems. The conditions in the 110 slums of Chittagong, which house around 40–67 per cent of the city's population, have been particularly critical (CCC/WHO, 1993). Aiming to ameliorate this situation, the Chittagong HCP was launched.

The Chittagong project[3] started with a series of meetings and workshops in 1993, coordinated by WHO. During this period a local coordinator for the project was chosen, and a number of working groups to be responsible for actions in different fields of urban development were chosen. The attributes of the Chittagong project in respect of sustainable urban health are explained below.

A broad definition of health   A broad definition of health, as already noted, is a basic tenet of the healthy city concept itself. The very fact that the Chittagong project includes a wide range of actors (most of whom are not linked to health services) and intersectoral activities (explained below) confirms the adoption of such a broad approach.

However, experiences in developing countries have shown that such a broad approach is not easily understood by the social actors responsible for the several aspects of urban development, and by the population in general. Equating healthy cities solely with improvements in health services is the most common (although not the only) problem. Thus, the broad concept of health was widely explained in the Chittagong project, through: (a) seminars and workshops with the participation of professionals with expertise in the HCP, (b) approaching the media, (c) the activities of a local consultant in Chittagong, and (d) a wide distribution of key texts such as the plan of action of the Chittagong project (CCC/ WHO, 1993) and of newsletters (prepared by the local consultant). The importance of each specific aspect of the development of the city (housing, education, transport, culture) to the health of the population

---

3)   In this chapter the terms 'project' and 'HCP' are used interchangeably.

has been emphasized through the methods mentioned above, so that the social actors responsible for each one of them clearly understand their role (and those of the others) in the process.

The adoption of a broad definition of health also means that the local coordinator of an HCP does not necessarily have to be a medical doctor, or any other professional linked to health services. A primary requisite for a coordinator, in addition to leadership skills, is the understanding of the process of urban development and of its impact on the wellbeing of citizens – rather than expertise in health services. In Chittagong, the initial coordinator was a magistrate of the city corporation, who was succeeded by a civil engineer belonging to the same local authority. Such a choice of coordinators substantiates the adoption of a broad definition of health in the Chittagong project. At the same time, it helps to clarify to the lay public that an HCP is not specifically related to health services.

Intersectoral activities   This element is illustrated by the type and range of, and integration between, topics and actions which constitute the Chittagong HCP. First, this project is formed by seven sectoral task forces, which encompass the major fields of urban development in Chittagong: (a) town planning, infrastructure and economic development; (b) slum improvement; (c) literacy and unemployment; (d) water and sanitation; (e) environmental protection; (f) drainage and sewerage; and (g) primary health care and maternal and child health (despite its restricted title, the seventh task force is responsible for health services in general).

Also, improvements in the aforementioned areas are to be achieved by the implementation of a multisectoral plan of action comprising 73 specific activities as diverse as a transport development strategy, a mechanism to attract inward investment to Chittagong, community business investment support mechanisms, extension of technical and vocational training, legislation to prevent hill cutting, and support for rag pickers to sell and distribute low cost latrines (CCC/WHO, 1993). The comprehensiveness of these activities as well as their inter-relationship are explicit in the plan of action, which states that if any parts of this package are missing, the overall effectiveness of the HCP will be compromised (CCC/WHO, 1993).

Wide range of actors   The institutional organization of the Chittagong project reflects the involvement of a wide range of actors. In addition to an office (headed by the coordinator), the project includes: (a) a coordination council (or steering committee), (b) the sectoral task forces and (c) zonal task forces.

The coordination council has the supreme authority within the HCP, and has the final say on any policy or action. It is formed by the main organizations from all sectors (the public, community, voluntary and private sectors as well as international agencies) involved in the different aspects of the development of Chittagong. Bottom-up participation is particularly encouraged (CCC/WHO, 1993).

Table 2.1 *Actors involved in the Chittagong HCP*

Public sector	Private sector	NGOs	Community organizations	International orgs[4]
Bakrabad Gas Co	Chamber of Commerce	ADAB Concern	community associations	UNCHS
Bangladesh Inst of Technology	leading banks	Ghashful	slum leaders	UNDP
Bangladesh Railway	Lions Club	NGO Forum		UNICEF
Bangladesh Road Transport Corporation		World Vision		WHO
Chittagong City Corporation	Rotary Club	other NGOs to be incorporated later on		
Chittagong Development Authority				
Chittagong University				
Civil Surgeon				
Defence Service				
Department of Environment				
Dept of Forests				
Export Processing Zone				
Facilities Dept				
Housing and Settlement Directorate				
Liquidified Petroleum Gas Plant				
MOH				
Port Authority				
Power Development Board				
Primary/Secondary/ Higher Education Depts				
Public Works Dept				
Roads and Highways Dept				

Source: CCC/WHO (1993) and UNDP/UNCHS office in Chittagong.

Each sectoral task force, whose role has already been explained, is

---

4) All these international organizations have had projects in Chittagong.

constituted by all the actors involved in the specific field. For instance, the water and sanitation task force is formed by the Chittagong Water Development Authority, the department of engineering of the city corporation, all the NGOs and CBOs with activities in this field, among others. Each zonal task force is responsible for the plans and actions in a specific geographical area of Chittagong. Thus, it is constituted by all the social actors with a strong concern with this area – for example local councillors, all NGOs and CBOs with projects in the area, and informal or traditional community leaders. There is indeed overlap between actors in sectoral and zonal task forces. However, this does not constitute a problem. By integrating the plans of the sectoral task forces with those of the zonal task forces, the overall plan of action of the HCP is formulated.

The actors involved in the Chittagong project are outlined in Table 2.1. The plan of action (CCC/WHO, 1993) includes details of the roles of each one of these actors.

Limited funding   Funding given by WHO to the Chittagong HCP has been restricted to setting up the project's office (for example furniture and equipment), technical advice (for example a part-time local consultant) and field studies commissioned to local academics. The fact that HCP is not about bringing 'a basket full of money' to Chittagong has been emphasized since the inception of the project. This has led local actors to take more sustainable routes. In 1994 the city corporation initiated a number of activities in a pilot area (which it termed 'Healthy Ward') with its own resources. Also, a number of development projects (for example eight maternal and childcare centres) to be considered for external funding have been under discussion by the task forces and coordination council. It has been a sine qua non condition of the Chittagong HCP that the identification of such development projects and the initiative to seek external funding should be taken by the local actors, and not spoon-fed 'top-down' by WHO.

Bangkok

The Bangkok Metropolitan Administration (BMA, 1994) has identified the priority urban health problems as environmental pollution, solid waste management and malnutrition. In 1994 the BMA identified three districts within Bangkok to start a HCP. Two key objectives were to mobilize participation and networks between government and private sectors and to improve health through improved living conditions in key settings (namely housing, workplace, schools and food outlets). A key outcome identified by the BMA is the formulation of a sustainable process of urban development that enhances cultural heritage (BMA, 1994:24).

A broad definition of health   In its background to the HCP, the BMA has explicitly stated the recognition of the interaction between physical, mental, social and spiritual dimensions of health. One of the desired outcomes is that community members can cooperatively identify existing resources to enable them to support each other mutually in improving their quality of life in relation to infrastructure, socioeconomic status, physical health status, mental health and environmental wellbeing.

Intersectoral activities   The nature of the intersectoral action being taken under the Bangkok HCP can be illustrated by one of the activities within the project: that of the 'healthy and safe workplace' programme. This operates at two levels – one, the traditional occupational health service that emphasizes factory-level work by health inspectors and two, the newer challenge of the small-scale and cottage industries that are not amenable to traditional approaches and that demand community based and participatory approaches that may be best implemented by local government with national government support (BMA, 1994:35). Goldstein (in BMA, 1994) identifies issues that such a programme will address, including (a) education of workers (for example about risk assessment in plain language and safe procedures for various occupations), (b) support and training of NGOs that can undertake worker education in small-scale industries, (c) worker participation and representation in industry trade associations, (d) mass media role in education, (e) health services for workers, (f) attention to the needs of women workers and a support role for women's associations, (g) establishing channels of communication between industry decision makers, workers and authorities responsible for environmental protection, (h) proper management of solid and liquid wastes and (i) attention in urban planning for siting of industries with a view to reducing pollution and environmental damage. Thus, it can be seen that, to meet this objective alone, a variety of sectors have been involved and this takes the project outside the MOH or the Bangkok Metropolitan Administration's health department. It should be noted at this point that metropolitan authorities are often in a stronger position to undertake multisectoral action given the variety of departments under their mandate. Activities or projects within the MOH often suffer from the problem that MOHs are often isolated and weak in relation to other ministries at the central government level.

Wide range of actors   Figure 2.1 demonstrates the actors in the Bangkok HCP (source BMA, 1994). The inner circle represents the project's committee, while the middle ring represents the various departments of the BMA which are brought together for the project. The outer ring represents other organizations and actors contributing to the project within Bangkok. This demonstrates the wide range of actors involved in the project.

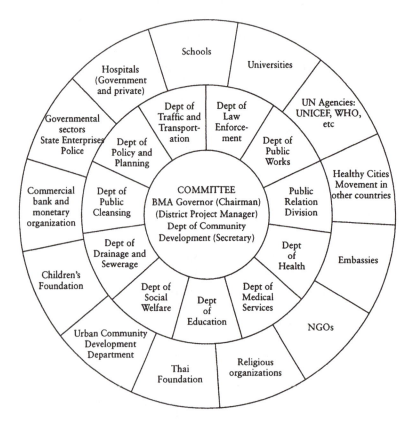

Figure 2.1 *The actors in Healthy City Bangkok project*

Limited funding The budget for 1994 was nearly four million baht, which covered the 20 steps for developing an HCP given in Figure 2.2. Additional international funding was obtained by a university in Bangkok to undertake a costing exercise of the HCP. One of the criticisms that has been levelled at the healthy cities initiative is that there is no evidence of what the initiative costs in real terms (for example participation of various actors involved). This costing exercise is currently underway and is due to be completed in 1996.

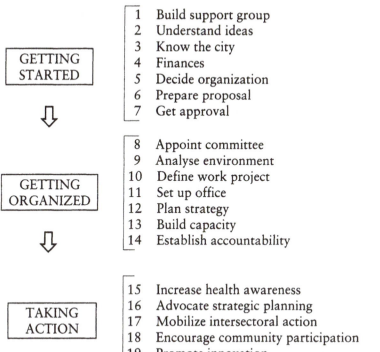

GETTING STARTED	1 Build support group 2 Understand ideas 3 Know the city 4 Finances 5 Decide organization 6 Prepare proposal 7 Get approval

⇩

GETTING ORGANIZED	8 Appoint committee 9 Analyse environment 10 Define work project 11 Set up office 12 Plan strategy 13 Build capacity 14 Establish accountability

⇩

TAKING ACTION	15 Increase health awareness 16 Advocate strategic planning 17 Mobilize intersectoral action 18 Encourage community participation 19 Promote innovation 20 Secure healthy public policy

Figure 2.2 *Twenty steps for developing a Healthy Cities Project of Bangkok Metropolitan Administration*

CONCLUSION

This chapter has shown the importance of having a wide and integrated approach for achieving sustainability in urban development and health. The HCP has been presented as a significant initiative in this respect.

As HCPs are relatively new in developing countries, a special note is made here about the need for monitoring and evaluation. Any HCP should be monitored from its inception. Thus, it is important to have appropriate indicators to use in monitoring. One could argue that long-term outcomes are what really matter, i e the project may only be deemed successful if it has a positive impact on indicators such as overall morbidity and mortality rates, child and infant mortality and life expectancy. However, such impact indicators are likely to show significant changes only after a number of years and it is difficult to attribute change to the project itself. It is important to monitor the earliest years of each HCP in order to keep the morale of the participating actors high (by demonstrating progress) and/or to correct potential problems. Donor agencies may also be willing to monitor the development of HCPs from the early stages. Sound monitoring should include an evaluation based on process indicators, which assess issues such as level of community organization, awareness and participation of different actors in the project, and cooperation between institutions. These indicators are able to spot changes more quickly than impact indicators. In addition to these points, process evaluations – especially those focusing on institutional strengthening – are important for assessing the capacities of local actors to support the project (which is a *sine qua non* condition for its sustainability). A proposal for such an early stage evaluation has been developed elsewhere (Werna and Harpham, 1995).

This type of evaluation has been already applied in the Chittagong project (Werna, 1995). Between 1993 and 1995 Chittagong received two visits from WHO–Geneva. The WHO office in Bangladesh has also paid a number of visits. Finally, the hiring of a local consultant was an important step, not only to monitor progress but also to address the problems detected. The Bangkok project, which started after Chittagong, has also been visited. However, it also needs an evaluation exercise in the near future.

Although HCP is now an international WHO programme, its sustainability should not be understood through the narrow approach usually adopted by international agencies – ie that a programme or project should continue to survive after the departure of the implementing agency. HCP's sustainability is ultimately due to its long-term contribution to health and wellbeing.

In this chapter we have analysed four attributes of the HCP. However, the emphasis on a broad definition of health, intersectoral activities, a wide range of actors and limited funding does not represent a claim that all possible factors required for sustainability in urban development and health have been identified here. As a suggestion for the improvement of HCP, we will end this chapter with an analysis of the supra-local dimension of urban sustainability.

The literature on sustainable urban development shows that it is important to have a broad approach not only in an intra-urban sense. It is also vital to have this approach in a multilayer/supra-urban sense, because cities and towns are dependent upon and influenced by regional, national and international factors such as macroeconomic policies, recession, capital flows, trade, and technology transfer (for example

Atkinson, 1994; Hardoy et al 1992; White, 1994). The importance of the impact of supra-urban issues on the specific realm of urban health has also been noted (for example Werna et al, forthcoming).

Thus, only part of the actions to achieve sustainable urban development and health lies within cities and towns themselves (and the HCP has been comprehensive regarding this set of actions). However, another important part lies outside the local realm – changes in the supra-urban issues that affect urban areas, and also the particular roles for supra-urban actors to enable changes within cities or towns.

In this chapter we suggest that HCP will be further strengthened by giving more attention to supra-urban issues. Of course one should not expect HCP to curb global recession and the like. However, there are more feasible actions that could be taken. For instance, actions in the realm of supra-urban national authorities that affect the places where the project is being implemented. To give one example, in Chittagong there are many public agencies connected to eight different ministries, which are involved in several aspects of the administration of the city and in the provision of its public services. These agencies are not accountable to the city corporation, which coordinates the Chittagong HCP. Intersectoral action within Chittagong does ameliorate this problem. However, there is still a need for actions to be taken in Dhaka, the capital city of Bangladesh (see Werna, 1995).

In another paper on the subject of sustainability (Harpham and Werna, 1996) we have highlighted that supra-urban actions can be carried out through two complementary approaches – the involvement of the supra-urban actors (for example federal and regional governments); and the activities of local actors outside the urban/local domain. The first approach has received more attention in the literature. However, despite its relative neglect, the second approach is also important. In the other paper we have shown the need for local actors to 'think locally and act globally', to take the local issues that they know only too well to broader forums and domains where consequential decisions are made. Now, we suggest that healthy cities themselves, through their burgeoning networks, may be a strong lever for local actors to implement wider actions.

References

Atkinson, A (1994) 'Introduction: The Contribution of Cities to Sustainability', *Third World Planning Review*, 16 (2), pp 97–101

Bhatti, M (1988) 'From Consumers to Prosumers: Housing for a Sustainable Future', *Housing Studies*, 8 (2), pp 98–108

BMA (1994) *Pilot Project: Healthy Cities*, unpublished monograph, Bangkok Metropolitan Administration

Brugman, J (1994) 'Who Can Deliver Sustainability? Municipal Reform and the Sustainable Development Mandate', *Third World Planning Review*, 16 (2), pp 129–45

CCC/UNICEF (1993) *City Plan of Action on Some Basic Services for Women and Children*, Chittagong City Corporation, Chittagong

CCC/WHO (1993) *Chittagong Healthy City Project: Health for All – All for Health*, Chittagong City Corporation/World Health Organization, November

Choguill, C (ed) (forthcoming) 'Special Issue on Sustainable Development', *Habitat International*

Hardoy, J E, D Mitlin and D Satterthwaite (1992) *Environmental Problems in Third World Cities*, Earthscan, London

Harpham, T and C Stephens (1992) 'Policy Directions in Urban Health in Developing Countries: The Slum Improvement Approach', *Social Science and Medicine*, 35 (2), pp 111–20

Harpham, T and M Tanner (1995) *Urban Health in Developing Countries: Progress and Prospects*, Earthscan, London

Harpham, T and E Werna (1997) 'Sustainable Urban Health', *Habitat International* (forthcoming)

Leitmann, J (1994) 'The World Bank and the Brown Agenda: Evolution of a Concept', *Third World Planning Review*, 16 (2), pp 116–28

Meadows, D H, D L Meadows, J Rangers and W W Behrens (1974) *The Limits to Growth*, Pan Books, London

Mitlin, D (1992) 'Sustainable Development: A Guide to the Literature', *Environment and Urbanization*, 4 (1), pp 111–24

Sachs, I (1979) 'Ecodevelopment: A Definition', *Ambio*, 8 (2/3)

Schumacher, E F (1973) *Small is Beautiful: A Study of Economics as if People Mattered*, Abacus, London

Serageldin, I and M A Cohen (eds) (1994) *The Human Face of the Urban Environment*, A Report to the Development Community on the Second Annual Conference on Environmentally Sustainable Development, Washington DC, 19–23 September, Environmentally Sustainable Development Proceedings Series No 5

Stren, R, R White and J Whitney (1992) *Sustainable Cities: Urbanization and the Environment in International Perspective*, Westview Press, Boulder

Tsouros, A (ed) (1990) *World Health Organization Healthy Cities Project: A project becomes a Movement, Review of Progress 1987–1990*, World Health Organization, Copenhagen

UNCHS (1990) *El Pueblo, Los Asentamientos, El Medio Ambiente y El Desarrollo: Mejorar el Entorno de Vida para un Futuro Sostenible*, United Nations Centre for Human Settlements, Nairobi

Ward, B and R Dubos (1972) *Only One Earth: Care and Maintenance of a Small Planet*, Penguin, London

Werna, E (1995) *The Chittagong Healthy City Project: Follow-Up Analysis One Year After its Initiation*, Research Report, Urban Health Programme, London School of Hygiene and Tropical Medicine, January

Werna, E and T Harpham (1995) 'The Evaluation of Healthy City Projects in Developing Countries', *Habitat International*, 19 (4), pp 629–41

Werna, E, I Blue and T Harpham (forthcoming) 'The Changing Agenda for Urban Health', in M Cohen, B A Ruble and J Tulchin (eds) *How Cities Survive: Coping with Global Pressures and Local Forces* (provisional title), Woodrow Wilson Center, Washington DC

White, R R (1994) 'Strategic Decisions for Sustainable Urban Development in the Third World', *Third World Planning Review*, 16 (2), pp 103–16

WHO (1993) *The Urban Health Crisis: Strategies for Health for All in the Face of Rapid Urbanization*, World Health Organization, Geneva

WHO (1995) *A Review of the Operation and Future Development of the WHO Healthy Cities programme*, World Health Organization, Geneva

Chapter Three

Towards Sustainable Infrastructure for Low-Income Communities

Charles L Choguill
and Marisa B G Choguill

ABSTRACT

Until the low-income populations of the rapidly growing cities of the Third World obtain acceptable forms of physical infrastructure, the urban environment will continue to deteriorate. In this chapter we suggest, based on a review of selected case studies of the experience of such communities, that the concept of progressive improvement is as relevant to infrastructure as it is to housing development.[1] Evidence exists that the poor are willing to contribute to their community infrastructure if they have stability and security of tenure. Partnerships between the community and outside organizations are necessary, particularly as a means of obtaining access to technology. The payoffs of such alliances are significant, particularly in terms of obtaining infrastructure at costs well below those which result when such facilities are provided by government. However, as the local community has planned, built and financed their facilities, there is no reason why they should not retain ownership of them and that they should not be viewed as a community asset. Thus, as the urban environment improves because of the existence of local infrastructure, community wealth will increase as well.

---

1) This chapter is based on a study sponsored by the UK Overseas Development Administration and draws heavily upon a report from that study entitled 'Developing Self-Sustaining Infrastructure in Third World Urban Areas'. The views expressed here are those of the authors and should not be construed as policy of the Overseas Development Administration.

83

INTRODUCTION

Although much has been written about 'sustainable development' in recent years, based upon the definition suggested by the World Commission on Environment and Development (WCED, 1987:8) as meeting 'the needs of the present without compromising the ability of future generations to meet their own needs', remarkably little attention has been given to cities in the sustainability debate (Choguill, 1993). This is somewhat surprising when it is realized that it is in cities where a disproportionate amount of resource use and pollutant generation takes place.

Since about 1950, for many complex and interrelated reasons, cities in the developing world have experienced unprecedented growth. This growth is self-perpetuating in that it continues to attract people, jobs, services, interests and opportunities. Urban populations have increased at rates which have had profound implications for the demand for housing and the provision of urban services. As a result, in almost all developing countries there has been an inability of authorities to respond adequately to rapid urbanization and, in particular, to provide adequate basic urban services, a situation which is proving detrimental to the maintenance of a congenial and healthy living environment. The plight of the urban poor is particularly acute.

Environmental health conditions in many cities are severely threatened. An increasing proportion of urban housing is hurriedly built and cities that have experienced this rapid growth are largely unplanned. Informal settlements now make up as much as 32 per cent of São Paulo, 33 per cent of Lima, 34 per cent of Caracas and 59 per cent of Bogotá, and these are the lucky ones, for in Addis Ababa the proportion of people who live in informal settlements is 85 per cent, as are 70 per cent in Luanda and 60 per cent in Dar es Salaam (UNCHS, 1987:77). Even in cities that are growing by as much as 10 per cent a year, in many instances the percentage of slum dwellers and squatters is growing at twice that rate.

These growing populations have stretched the available urban services as well. As a result, urban environmental quality has degenerated. Air and water pollution may be the most noticeable manifestations of this malaise, yet growing populations have denuded nearby forests for firewood, while construction projects have stripped peripheral land and hillsides of topsoil, resulting in serious erosion problems. Such construction has a detrimental effect upon local hydrology. Overuse of water can be responsible for the saline invasion of underground water, as in Jakarta. Massive cities have even had an effect upon microclimates. Municipal and government agencies frequently lack personnel and other resources to halt and counteract the deterioration of environmental conditions in cities.

It is apparent that much that has been done in cities in the past can scarcely be described as sustainable.

The purpose of this chapter is to explore alternative methods of providing urban infrastructure. In it we concentrate on provision in low-income neighbourhoods, recognizing that these areas are generally provided with the fewest urban services and as a result, through no fault of their inhabitants, are most out of balance with the surrounding natural environment. Although infrastructure alone does not guarantee urban sustainability, its provision does go some way toward insuring the compatibility of urban areas with their surrounding natural environments. Not only does infrastructure help to reduce the impact of urban pollution but it also facilitates the meeting of basic needs of urban residents (Hardoy, et al, 1992, Chapter 6; Choguill, 1993), which is equally important in making urban sustainability possible.

THE STATE OF URBAN INFRASTRUCTURE

The development of an adequate infrastructural base in urban areas is a prerequisite to the achievement of urban sustainability. Simplistically, infrastructure can be divided into two components. The first of these is social infrastructure, including educational and health care facilities. The second category, which forms the focus of the present analysis, is physical infrastructure, including water supply, sanitation facilities, drainage, urban roads and solid waste disposal facilities. The terminology used by different analysts to describe infrastructure varies. The World Bank (1994:13), for example in its 1994 *World Development Report*, refers to this latter category of investments as economic infrastructure, including 'the long lived engineered structures, equipment and facilities, and the services they provide which are used in economic production and by households'. Within this category, the World Bank places public utilities (power, piped gas, telecommunications, water supply, sanitation and sewerage, solid waste collection and disposal), public works (major dam and canal works for irrigation and roads), and other transport sectors (railways, urban transport, ports, waterways and airports).

Although the importance of the World Bank's broader definition is recognized, the focus here is placed upon that part of physical infrastructure that is of primary relevance to low-income communities. At the higher level, the objectives of investing in physical infrastructure are multifaceted. Such facilities contribute to economic production and therefore, not surprisingly, are closely correlated with levels of development (Kessides, 1993; Anas and Lee, 1988; Lee, 1988). Infrastructure can be seen as one way of reducing adverse environmental impacts within the city and within the vicinity surrounding the city. Infrastructure can also be seen as a way of improving the health of urban residents. Infrastructure is an instrument in the creation of a well-run and managed urban area. Finally, physical infrastructure can contribute to the standard of living of residents of such urban areas (Menendez, 1991).

As such, the provision of physical infrastructure must be seen as a prerequisite for the achievement of the sustainability of human settlements in that it is directly related to environmental conditions. It is also an integral part of the meeting of basic human needs. If a city fails to provide an adequate level of infrastructure for any group of its inhabitants, including the poor, it is unlikely either that the city can maintain a balance with its environment nor will standards of living for the residents of the community be acceptable. Unfortunately, much urban development that has taken place in the past has ignored, or short-changed, investment in urban infrastructure with dire results.

THE DEVELOPMENT OF INFRASTRUCTURE SYSTEMS

The traditional model for the development of urban infrastructure systems, a model that until recently has been widely accepted and rarely questioned, involves the provision for the public of infrastructure elements by a central or local government authority. This model is based on the premise that the benefits of infrastructure, such as clean water, sanitation and roads, are shared by the entire population, but are beyond the capability of any single part of that population to provide. Furthermore, it is assumed that only government is in a position to collect the revenues required to support this infrastructure from all parties who receive the benefits. Given the hierarchical nature of most infrastructure, namely a central source of supply with branches increasingly subdivided to serve each consumer, a model that seems relevant to many different types of infrastructure networks, only government has the capability of maintaining the central elements of this system and, for this reason, the responsibility is its.

In fact, this was never a universal model of infrastructural provision, for different countries at various points in time employed different approaches. In the USA, for example, such utilities as gas and electricity have traditionally been supplied by private enterprise under governmental regulations. Monopoly franchises were granted to firms in specific geographical areas and the prices charged by these firms were controlled either by state or federal government directly, or by independent commissioners appointed by the state to avoid the possible abuse of monopoly pricing power.

This traditional model has, however, led to situations that have had unfortunate effects in countries with lower incomes. Cost recovery has long been an underlying assumption of such a model (UNCHS, 1984:6). Within countries where average per capita incomes are relatively high, the recovery of such costs was possible over the long run. When applied to developing countries, where the variation in income can be extreme between the very rich and the very poor, the effect of adopting this centrally-driven model was to exclude those customers who were unable to pay from the provision of such a service. As a result, from the time when this model was first applied in the developing world, unserved customers were in some way expected to provide the services of such infrastructure themselves.

Despite the rather callous sounding result of this model, it should be recognized that even in areas for which the model was originally designed not all people within an urban area were served. In the nineteenth century, a large proportion of the urban population solved their own sanitation problems, for example in the United Kingdom, in the USA and elsewhere, by on-site facilities. Even today, many suburban and peri-urban families in urban USA are dependent upon septic tanks for the provision of sanitation facilities.

In a sense then, adoption of the model in the rapidly growing urban areas of the developing world has resulted in the evolution of two parallel systems of infrastructural provision. This is particularly noticeable when examining the cases of water and sanitation. A 'town system' has developed within the central areas of cities and in areas where high income residences are located, served by the municipal system and financed by something resembling, but rarely quite achieving, a full cost recovery basis. Those who are unable to afford the service, provide their own system, such as pit latrines, septic tanks and drinking water wells. This latter alternative might be called the 'on-site system'.

Unfortunately, in many urban areas of the developing world, a significant proportion of residents participate in neither system. Numerous residents of cities in the poorer countries of the world solve their sanitation problems by a trip to the bush to meet personal needs and to rivers or ponds to obtain water supplies. Although one might think this is strictly the result of low incomes, in fact it is probably due to the fact that such residents have no legal right to the land they occupy and, realizing the uncertainty of their future at any given location, are unwilling to allocate their own scarce resources to solve their water and sanitation problems in an on-site manner. The environmental and health impacts of such a situation are obviously negative.

Within the terms of the definition suggested above, it is unlikely that any of these approaches are strictly sustainable in the accepted sense of the term. All too often town systems of infrastructural provision fail to recover the costs of providing that system because accounting systems are inefficient, payment collection systems do not work, the richer more powerful members of society refuse to pay their due through one means or another or the system itself is based on elaborate systems of subsidies from the central treasury or elsewhere and therefore in the strictly economic sense run at a loss. On-site systems may well fail to meet environmental standards inherent in that definition in that they pollute ground water resources or have other unhealthy aspects. The use of the bush may be one way of meeting basic human needs, but is hardly acceptable in environmental or health terms.

The solution to this problem would seem to be one that is based on progressive improvement of on-site facilities to meet the standards in effect within the town system. Given the low income nature of the people who use facilities of this type, it is obvious that a full cost recovery is impossible at the moment. However, progressive improvement must be viewed as a long-term proposition. If complementary urban and employment development policies are in force, seemingly essential if urban sustainability is taken as a serious objective, it would be expected that the incomes of this target group would rise over time allowing the eventual payment for the services which would be provided. The objective of infrastructure, if it is to provide the kinds of universal benefits for which it is designed, whether it be a solid waste collection programme, sanitation or roads, must become a city-wide system with service provision for all, whether they be rich or poor.

Twenty-five years ago, development policy for housing the poor was in a similar situation. The public provision of housing had failed to deliver more than a proportion of the housing units which were needed and, as a result, new approaches were obviously required. Two housing analysts, Turner and Mangin, after lengthy periods of fieldwork in Peru, concluded that in attempting to house themselves, the poor were just as rational as middle and upper income classes in terms of a response to their situation but that middle-class observers too frequently misinterpreted their motivation because of a cultural gap (Turner, 1967; Mangin, 1963 and 1967). Although the centralized government housing provision model viewed the tumbledown shanty in a slum area as evidence of social malaise, the poor themselves viewed the shack in quite a different light, as a rational step on the way to self-improvement. Turner noted that such families who earned erratic incomes in an unstable economy viewed property as a primary means of security in much the same way as middle and upper classes viewed insurance, banking services and access to credit. He argued that if the poor could achieve geographical stability then, as they became fully urbanized, they could be expected over time, as their circumstances (in terms of income, employment and derived living standards) improved, to add to and improve their existing houses by adding another room, a better roof, or merely wooden window frames. As Turner (1967:168) noted, ordinary families in urbanizing countries preferred to live in large unfinished houses than in small finished ones of the type delivered by government agencies. Yet, Turner noted, certain prerequisites had to be met if this self improvement was to take place:

> Secure possession of land where they can live now is far more important to them than the promise of a modern house that may never materialize. But given the land and the right circumstances – that is, adequately located, properly planned and with a secure title – experience has shown that development to contemporary standards would surely take place, even if slowly.

It would seem that there could be a direct parallel between the progressive improvement of housing as seen by Turner and Mangin and the progressive improvement of infrastructure to conventional standards. Where the analysis by Turner and Mangin fails, however, is in taking the view that all poor people within an urban area can, through their own efforts, improve their situation. The image of a ladder of progressive improvement is popular among urban analysts. The progressive improvement model, as proposed by Turner and Mangin, sees the poor as progressing from one rung to the next in the course of self improvement. Unfortunately, a significant proportion of urban residents in most cities of the developing world are unable to get onto the first rung of that ladder (Choguill, 1994:1). As a result, progressive improvement may be no more than a distant dream to them. What is required then, if the housing problem is to be met, is to design policies to get the poor onto the first rung of the ladder.

A similar situation exists in infrastructure. The progressive improvement of infrastructure, implying the almost total rejection of the traditional model of infrastructural development, has emerged as a salient discussion point. Glennie (1982) has proposed a model of infrastructure development which has four stages: initial, consolidation, expansion and maintenance. In this model, the main objectives of the initial phase are to lay the framework of the progressive improvement of infrastructure using measures that would be expected to favour success, such as small project size, a suitable community, technical simplicity, good quality field staff and accessibility of the project area. In the consolidation phase, more sophistication is added to the process including the development of standardized procedures and techniques and the definition of technical standards of construction. Glennie's expansion phase involves the spread of these techniques and procedures to other promising areas. Finally, completed projects would enter the maintenance phase in which long-term project benefits would be realized and the assets created during the previous phases would be preserved by sound maintenance.

Choguill et al (1991) and Cotton and Franceys (1991) proposed a similar model which incorporated three sets of objectives in terms of health, social necessity and convenience. Although specific levels of service were seen, including a primary level, an intermediate level and an expansion phase, this work went beyond that of Glennie in detailing how specific elements could be incorporated into such a system in a manner to insure progressive improvement from a technical perspective.

Building on this foundation, the most efficient way to improve the capability of infrastructure is through a system of progressive improvement. However, past models of progressive improvement in low income neighbourhoods have involved a strong, top-down input from governmental authorities. In both of the models referred to above, the government was seen as playing a key role, although in the latter this role could be taken over by non-governmental organizations (NGOs). The problem with NGOs is, of course, that whereas they work very well on a one-off project basis, difficulties frequently arise in trying to sustain this work over a series of projects. If such a deficiency were to arise in the progressive improvement of infrastructure, much potential in terms of the achievement of a town based system would be lost.

As a result, it seems important that two elements be recognized in the attempt to meet the conventional system of infrastructural provision. In terms of the town system, there is no reason why government cannot be central to the driving of this system, although in recent years it has become increasingly accepted that private enterprise can probably do this job at least as well as government. The lower circuit of this chain is more problematic. It is within this area that progressive improvement is absolutely critical. It has been argued (Choguill et al, 1995) that the improvements that can be made to on-site facilities, or where no facilities exist, can be made by the community itself with minimal external inputs. Initial assistance might be concerned with training related to the system as well as technical assistance at key points in the implementation process, but little else.

It is crucial to include one additional element to this progressive improvement process: once the system has been completed, it should belong to the community itself. After all, they built and financed it and must maintain and operate it as well. As incomes rise and the technology of the on-site system approaches that of the town system, then the option arises for the community to transfer, or sell, the system to the municipal operating authority.

Some outside observers, as well as supporters of the strong role of government may question whether a community is capable of undertaking this role. In the following section, a number of cases are presented in which the community, with, although frequently without, the assistance of outside authorities, have worked together to obtain improvements in infrastructure. The objective of this discussion is to demonstrate that progressive improvement to town standard is possible through community effort and that, in so doing, low income people are in a position to participate because of the savings in money that result from such an approach.

THE BOTTOM RUNG OF THE IMPROVEMENT LADDER

In this section, a selected number of case studies that focus on the establishment of infrastructure elements by self-help are reviewed as a means of demonstrating that the theoretical assertions made earlier can in fact be substantiated in reality, i e that infrastructure, with little more than outside technical assistance, can be planned, constructed, maintained and operated by the community. Particularly in cases where infrastructure is not provided by the state for whatever reason – whether it be considered too expensive or impossible to meet full cost recovery conditions, or whether there is a lack of political will on the part of decision-makers to provide it – the members of the community may have no option if they want it but to provide such facilities themselves and to strive to improve it, over time, to town standards.

The case studies included here are but a small sample of a larger number collected and analysed in two recent research studies into the potential of self-help (Choguill and Silva-Roberts, 1993; Choguill et al, 1995). In the course of these studies, various hypotheses have been tested to demonstrate how far self-help principles and progressive improvement can be used to meet public facility needs. In total, nearly 700 such studies were reviewed.

Despite this enormous literature that was uncovered in these efforts, it should be noted that remarkably few of the studies are concerned with low income communities attempting to reach the bottom rung of the ladder by self-help methods for infrastructural improvement. The reasons for this limited number of case studies are several. It is probable that this approach to infrastructural improvement has been followed far less frequently than in the case of housing. This is hardly surprising given that individual house construction is far less complex than the construction of, say, water or sanitation systems.

It is also suspected that the literature itself is incomplete. In many instances it is thought that the community may well have improved its infrastructure, but that this accomplishment has not been recorded in the literature. This may well be because it has not attracted the attention of consultants, international civil servants or academics who are more likely than other people to have recorded these accomplishments. Rather, such improvement efforts have been undertaken quietly and have avoided the glare of academic investigation and evaluation. There are probably also instances where self-help has been attempted and failed. If the reasons for this failure had been made public, they could have formed a significant contribution to the literature, as failure and the study of failure are probably as important as the study of success. However, understandably, low income communities, and even academics, may not wish to spend time studying failure, but prefer to look at successes.

In all likelihood, a bias exists in the kinds of case studies that have been recorded in the literature. It is probably likely that successes initiated by government or NGOs have a higher probability of appearing in this literature than those that are strictly done by the community. Involvement of academics, whether in the guise of consultants to multilateral organizations, to governments or working with NGOs, is also more likely to lead to publication as this is, after all, one of the prime responsibilities of academics. Efforts that are strictly initiated by the community (implemented, managed and paid for by it) are unlikely to appear in the literature, except in the most unusual of circumstances.

Despite these reservations, much can be learned from published case studies of community efforts within this field. The three studies summarized here are from geographically diverse areas. They do, however, reflect what can be accomplished through community effort, particularly in cases where there is a supportive government or, in particular, a dedicated NGO. As will become apparent, certain common elements occur in the case study material presented (and in that not presented here as well) which provide guidance on how the probability of community successes can be maximized.

Self-help in the Philippines

The first study presented is from Bagumbayan in the Philippines. It represents the case of a low income community that became involved in upgrading its facilities and in putting pressure on government agencies to provide assistance (National Housing Authority, 1990; Sadain and Toledano, 1985a and 1985b; Abanil and Toledano, 1986; Alonzo, 1994). Activities undertaken included housing, drainage, sewer lines and water supply. The study illustrates what can be achieved by a local community when it obtains the enabling cooperation of a central governmental authority. Bagumbayan is located in Quezon City in Metro Manila. Greater Manila, with a population of around 8 million, is eight times larger than the next largest urban centre. The primacy of Metro Manila, brought about by natural forces, natural endowments, as well as economic policies, has made this city the political, administrative, commercial and industrial centre of the country. This has, however, led to very high rates of migration to the city and the establishment of squatter communities throughout the area. About 30 per cent of the total urban population are squatters, and past attempts at resettlement and high rise solutions have proven impractical and beyond the economic capacity both of governments and the squatters themselves.

In 1984, Bagumbayan's *barangay* had a population of about 4110, distributed among 734 households. The residents of the community organized the Bagumbayan Home Owners' Association in 1983. The objective of this community organization was to supervise, manage, direct and implement the upgrading of the community's physical, social and economic conditions. Organizationally, the association divided the community into 12 blocks, each block having two leaders, and the resulting 24 leaders formed the members of the organization's executive committee.

Other organizations with similar aims existed in the area at the time of its creation, and linkages were made to these community organizations to increase effectiveness. Approaches were made to government organizations to achieve funding for specific projects, such as for the establishment of a daycare programme from the Ministry of Social Services and Development, and for primary health care from the Ministry of Health. In addition, the community was fortunate to be adopted by one of Manila's many Rotary Clubs under the club's 'Adopt a *Barangay*' programme. This eventually led to the Rotary Club playing a significant role in the community's self-help programme.

At about the same time, the Philippine government was attempting to respond to the ever growing need for urban housing, particularly from those low-income residents who lacked sufficient funds to build what was considered to be adequate standard housing. As the government switched away from the provision of housing for the poor, programmes were developed which recognized their needs, the necessity of including appropriate technology in such programmes, and in helping communities in determining their own needs and realizing their own aspirations

mainly through their own efforts. One approach used by the national
housing authority was the Community Self-Help Programme. This
approach departed from the conventional and institutionalized upgrading approaches previously used by the Philippines' National Housing
Association in which the federal agency assumed a lead role in all aspects
of the community development process. Under the Community Self-Help
Programme, the authority limited its role to mere provision of technical
assistance. Technical assistance did, however, take a number of different
forms, including the facilitation of the development of the community to
implement and manage entire projects in the development process by
itself. Furthermore, the Community Self-Help Programme did not
preclude the community from seeking external resources and assistance
as necessary.

In 1984, Bagumbayan became a pilot project of the National Housing
Association's Self-Help Community Programmes. In this project, the
Bagumbayan Homeowners' Association defined its own project objectives as the completion of drainage and sewer lines, the provision of
water lines and the construction of community facilities. Within a year,
the drainage lines had been completed with the financial support of the
Quezon City local government, and a plan for the community facility to
house medical, library, daytime and village functions was approved and
work begun on it.

In the case of Bagumbayan, the community successfully met its own
objectives. A study by the National Housing Association suggested that
this was largely due to the community's own efforts and that the major
reasons for the self-help being effective were because the community
leaders themselves were responsive to the needs of the community, the
community was properly disposed towards the project, the technical
assistance provided by the professional project team members was effective, and the project requirements were simple enough for such a project
to be successfully carried out by the local community.

The analysis of the project concludes that successful self-help in a
community depends on a combination of external assistance and internal
initiative. External assistance may be necessary to provide the resources
the community cannot generate by itself and, in the case of Bagumbayan,
adequate but benign support originated from the central government. In
addition, the funds necessary for the construction of the community hall
were provided by the Rotary Club. A further example of the initiative
shown by the community association was that it solicited the assistance
of neighbouring factories to allow the installation of connections from
the factory's own water pipes, while another enterprise donated lot
boundary markers for subdividing the area to the community.

The Bagumbayan case study illustrates the need for cooperation between local community organizations and central authorities. This co-operation could not have been promoted had tenure problems with respect to the land occupied by the low income settlement not been resolved at the outset. It is essential that community leaders represent the desires of the local community and that they do not pursue their own agendas. If these points can be achieved, then self-help stands a chance of succeeding in meeting project objectives, if resources and technical assistance of the correct sort are provided to support it.

Obtaining urban water in Honduras

The second study is based in Tegucigalpa, Honduras, and is a case of devising means of extending water services to peripheral low income communities of that city (Friedlander, 1990; Choguill, 1991; UNICEF, nd a; UNICEF, nd b). The approach, in a funded project, involved training and community contributions for construction, administration, maintenance and financial responsibility.

Although most major cities in the developing world have some kind of utility system designed to distribute water and collect sewage, these systems provide only partial coverage. Tegucigalpa, the capital of Honduras, has served as a magnet attracting rural residents. With an urban growth of 5.2 per cent a year, it is almost inevitable that the city will double in size over the next 15 years. It is estimated that 60 per cent of the population of Tegucigalpa live in peripheral areas, known locally as *barrios marginales*.

As in many Latin American cities, virtually no urban services are provided to peripheral areas. The water shortage in the city is particularly acute as there is not even enough water in the system to supply customers who are already connected to the municipal system, much less those who are outside the distribution network. Not surprisingly, diseases associated with unclean water and water shortages are prevalent, particularly in peripheral areas. Between one-quarter and one-third of all infant and child deaths in Tegucigalpa are caused by dysentery and diarrhoea-related diseases, diseases which are caused or aggravated by using contaminated water or having too little water.

Many inhabitants of the *barrios marginales* receive their water from private vending operations. Unregulated water vendors truck 55-gallon barrels of water up to the *barrios* and sell each drum of water for the equivalent of $1.75. Depending on family size, water use and income, a household may go through one barrel a day, one a week or somewhere in between. Here lies the irony of the situation: the price people pay to water vendors in the *barrios* is estimated to be 34 times higher than the official government rate to better-off families who are connected to the town system. It is apparent that if even a fraction of the total annual cost of water paid by people in the peripheral areas could be allocated to an urban system, the same level of service could be provided at a fraction of the cost.

In order to meet the growing water needs of the community, the Honduras National Water and Sanitation Agency has explored alternative methods of water supply and come up with what appears to be a revolutionary set of solutions in a project funded by the governments of Canada and Sweden and by the UNICEF Committee of Canada. One of these solutions is the wholesale vending of water. In this case, the community itself builds a water cistern in the peripheral areas and the central water authority regularly fills it with water from the municipal system which has been pumped to smaller storage tanks in the hills above the community and fed by gravity to public standpipes. The water is then sold by the community to public taps at various locations throughout the neighbourhood at a rate far below that charged by unregulated water vendors.

In all of the approaches considered by the central water authority, a crucial element in the water supply process is community participation. A community must request help for the construction and building of a system. Once the request is received, a study is done by the water authority to determine which approach best serves the community and whether or not the community is sufficiently organized and enthusiastic enough to construct and administer such a system. Thus, the city acts as a wholesaler of water to the community, which in turn acts as a retailer. The water source belongs to the municipal authority, but the community is responsible for operating and maintaining the system and must provide all necessary repairs. The central authority designs the system, covers many of the initial costs and provides technical assistance. The community forms a water association, supplies the manpower to construct the facilities, purchases some of the materials, is responsible for the administration and maintenance of the system upon completion and collects the fees from users who pay for the water supplied.

One of the most interesting aspects of the project is that the communities are realizing that they can make changes in their lives. Water supply is viewed as only the first step. Some already have plans to add sanitation systems to what they have accomplished as a means of further improving health and hygiene. Thus, the water schemes appear to be serving as a catalyst for further community development.

The Tegucigalpa project clearly illustrates what potentials can be realized through community participation and self-help in urban development projects. Too often, the incorporation of the community is seen just as a source of cheap labour. In Tegucigalpa, the community is involved in planning to meet its own needs and then takes on a management function that assures the neighbourhoods safe water at a price they can afford. It should be apparent that such an approach could, with training and organization, be successfully applied to a range of such activities.

Building a sanitation system in Pakistan

The final case study is from Orangi District, Karachi, Pakistan and represents a case in which a low income community, with the assistance of an NGO, has installed a sanitation system (Hardoy et al, 1992:147; Hassan, 1990; Turner, 1980).

Orangi is an unauthorized settlement within Karachi of about 800,000 inhabitants. Initially, there was no public provision for sanitation and most residents used bucket latrines which were emptied periodically into the unpaved lanes between houses. The cost of having local government put in a sewage system would have been too high for the low income residents.

A local NGO, Orangi Pilot Project (OPP), initiated a self-help sanitation system that has been very successful. Meetings were held between staff of the NGO and residents to explain the benefits of such a system and to offer technical assistance. Lane leaders were elected who formally applied for technical help and organized the local project. Technicians from the OPP drew up plans for the local scheme and the sewers were then installed with maintenance organized by local groups. As the project was seen to work, others in Orangi wished to undertake it as well. To date, nearly 70,000 sanitary pour-flush latrines have been constructed.

The important aspect of the project has been its low cost. Simplified designs and the use of standardized steel moulds reduced the cost of sanitary latrines in manholes to less than one quarter of contractors' rates. The cost of the sewerage line was also greatly reduced by eliminating the profits of the contractor. The average cost of a small bore sewer system is no more than $US 66 per house. It has been noted that conventional urban sewerage systems have investment costs of five times the cost of labour and materials, increasing by over 200 per cent if international tenders are involved. Today, almost 75 per cent of Orangi houses have sanitary latrines with an underground sanitation system.

An interesting sidelight on the Orangi project concerns the solid waste management system that is evolving in the community (UNCHS, 1986 and 1990). The community has found that a project for producing composting from organic waste is economically and commercially feasible. Such compost is used to fertilize Pakistan's own fields, but some is exported to the Gulf States for cash.

The Orangi experiment is one of the best known sanitation examples that exists within low-income communities of the developing world. Cost savings have been significant and have resulted in a system that works. The importance of outside technical assistance from OPP should not be underestimated. The efforts by the NGO are commendable, working in difficult situations where the municipality did not even attempt to operate. (For an overview of other activities run by OPP, see OPP, 1995.)

LEARNING FROM EXPERIENCE

A number of interesting lessons emerge from the case studies. Such studies, and many others like them, confirm the ability of local communities to plan and construct their own infrastructure. The necessary ingredient to achieve this state appears to be a willingness and desire of the community to work together within an environment of support. The support can come either from government agencies or from an NGO. In the case of Tegucigalpa, government was instrumental in facilitating water development. In Orangi, the OPP (an NGO) played this essential role. In the Philippine example, interestingly, steps taken by an agency of central government led to NGO involvement with the community.

This cooperative arrangement between the community and the outside body seems to be crucial to long-term success in such endeavours. Yet much literature on community participation seems to underestimate its importance. In part, this is probably the result of context. The most widely quoted analysis of participation is probably that of Arnstein (1969), which provides a basis for evaluating and measuring community involvement in projects. The Arnstein system is, however, designed for assessing the degree of citizen participation in federal programmes within the USA. The interactive roles played by the community and government (or NGOs) in just these three studies reveals the great gap that exists between analysing citizen participation in the developed world, such as Arnstein's USA, and analysis in the developing world.

The basis of the Arnstein scheme is an eight-level classification, which moves from nonparticipation to various degrees of citizen power. The analogy of rungs on a ladder are used. Hence, the bottom two rungs, 'manipulation' and 'therapy', are seen as representing nonparticipation. The next three rungs on the ladder, 'informing', 'consultation' and 'placation', represent decreasing degrees of tokenism in the participation process. The final three steps to the top of the ladder, 'partnership', 'delegated power' and ultimately 'citizen control', indicate increasing degrees of citizen power.

Yet in the most successful cases of participation in the developing world in terms of actually accomplishing specific project goals, in this case building infrastructure, various forms of community/government/

NGO partnerships are apparently more productive than pure control by local residents. This was certainly evident in each of the three case studies examined.

On the other hand, empowerment, as seen by different analysts, takes different forms. In a recent study, M B G Choguill (1996), after reviewing the Arnstein ladder, constructs a new series of steps based on developing world experience. In this case, empowerment still edges out partnership for the highest position, but only if empowerment is defined as government action on behalf of the community that results from social pressure of that community.

A further conclusion to emerge from the case studies is the financial feasibility of constructing community infrastructure. Although the groups that were central to the case study description may be the poorest in any given society, through their own efforts, with little more than outside technical assistance, they were able to afford infrastructure improvements. Moreover, through such a process, it is apparent that large savings were made compared to the costs of top-down, conventional approaches.

THE WAY AHEAD IN INFRASTRUCTURE DEVELOPMENT

This chapter has been concerned with devising ways for low-income communities to obtain infrastructure. If this can be achieved, the cities in which they reside will take a large step toward sustainability. If not, the quality of urban environments will continue to decline, the health of urban inhabitants will deteriorate and basic human needs will remain unfulfilled.

The approach suggested, based on a review of actual case studies of the experiences of low-income communities from around the world, parallels in many respects conventional wisdom concerning shelter construction by low-income urban residents. With stability and security of tenure, it is expected, as demonstrated by numerous published examples from urban development literature, that inhabitants of such low-income communities would be willing to contribute to their own urban equipment. Such an approach reduces costs and brings infrastructure within their financial grasp. It has been argued that what is needed to bring this theoretical process to reality is a partnership with an outside organization, whether it be from government or from beyond government, to provide, in an appropriate manner, a measure of technical assistance.

However, once such infrastructure is constructed, it is suggested that since it was planned, built and financed by the low-income communities themselves, like their houses, it should be owned by them as well. Presumably, in time, as urban incomes rise and municipal financial capability improves, the ownership of such facilities will be transferred to municipal government, providing not only a windfall gain to local residents, but the transformation of a locally-oriented infrastructure system into a city-wide one. In this way, progressive improvement will, it is hoped, be assured.

These arguments are seen as one means of contributing to urban sustainability. Infrastructure is seen as a necessary, but not sufficient condition for urban sustainability. Such equipment will itself facilitate economic production within the community, as well as ensure better health and lives for its residents. If infrastructure can be provided in this manner, the possibility of making cities sustainable, even cities in poor countries, will be greatly enhanced.

References

Abanil, C and A Toledano (1986) *Report on Bagong Barrio Workshops on Self-Help Conceptualization and Functional Delineations*, National Housing Authority, Manila

Alonzo, A (1994) 'The Development of Housing Finance for the Urban Poor in the Philippines', *Cities*, 11 (3–6) pp 398–401

Anas, A and K S Lee (1988) 'Infrastructure Investment and Productivity: The Case of Nigerian Manufacturing', *World Bank Urban Development Division Discussion Paper INU14*, Washington DC, May

Arnstein, S (1969) 'A Ladder of Community Participation', *Journal of the American Institute of Planners*, vol 35, pp 216–24

Choguill, C L (1991) 'Infrastructure for Low-Income Communities: A Study from Honduras', in S Meikle and B Mumtaz (eds) *Successful Shelter Strategies*, Development Planning Unit for the Overseas Development Administration, London, pp 63–67

— (1993) 'Sustainable Cities: Urban Policies for the Future', *Habitat International*, vol 17 (3), pp 1–12

— (1994) 'Sustainable Housing Programmes in a World of Readjustment', *Habitat International*, vol 18 (2), pp 1–11

Choguill, C L and A M Silva-Roberts (1993) *Factors and Conditions in the Developing World Which Result in Successful Self Help in Housing, Infrastructure and Other Community Developments*, A Research Report to the ODA from the University of Sheffield Centre for Development Planning Studies

Choguill, C L, M B G Choguill and A M Silva-Roberts (1995) *Developing Self-Sustaining Infrastructure in Third World Urban Areas*, A research report to the UK Overseas Development Administration by the University of Sheffield Centre for Development Planning Studies, vol 1

Choguill, C L, A Cotton and R Franceys (1991) *The Preparation of a Planning Manual for the Infrastructural Provision of Water Supply, Drainage and Sewage Disposal Based on a Literature Review*, A research report to the UK Overseas Development Administration by the University of Sheffield Centre for Development Planning Studies and the Loughborough University of Technology Water, Engineering and Development Centre

Choguill, M B G (1996) 'A Ladder of Community Participation for Under-developed Countries', *Habitat International*, 20 (2)

Cotton, A and R Franceys (1991) *Services for Shelter*, Liverpool University Press, Liverpool

Friedlander, P (1990) 'Water for the Urban Poor', *Waterlines*, 9 (1), pp 6–8

Glennie, C (1982) 'A Model for the Development of a Self-Help Water Supply Program', *World Bank Technical Paper Number 2*, Technology Advisory Group of the World Bank, Washington DC

Hardoy, J E, D Mitlin and D Satterthwaite (1992) *Environmental Problems in Third World Cities*, Earthscan, London

Hassan, A (1990) 'Development through Partnership: The Orangi Project in Karachi', in D Cadman and G Payne (eds) *The Living City: Towards a Sustainable Future*, Routledge, Andover, Hants, pp 221–6

Kessides, C (1993) 'The Contributions of Infrastructure to Economic Development: A Review of Experience and Policy Implications', *World Bank Discussion Paper Number 213*, Washington DC

Lee, K S, (1988) 'Infrastructure Constraints in Industrial Growth in Thailand', *World Bank Urban Development Division Working Paper 88-2*, Washington DC, September

Mangin, W (1963) 'Urbanization Case History in Peru', *Architectural Design*, 33 (August), pp 366–70

— (1967) 'Latin American Squatter Settlements: A Problem and a Solution', *Latin American Research Review*, 2, pp 65–98

Menendez, A (1991) 'Access to Basic Infrastructure by the Urban Poor', *World Bank EDI Policy Seminar Report Number 28*, Washington DC

National Housing Authority/Philippines (1990) 'Evaluative Study: The Community Mortgage Program in NHA', Manila

OPP (Orangi Pilot Project) (1995) *Environment and Urbanization*, 7 (2), pp 227–36

Sadain, M K and A M Toledano (1985a) *Project Documentation Report Bgy Bagumbayan, Libis, Quezon City, Philippines – Self-Help Project*, National Housing Authority/Philippines, Manila

— (1985b) 'A Study of NHA Technical Assistance in Barangay Bagumbayan Self-Help Area', National Housing Authority/Philippines, Manila

Turner, B (ed) (1980) *Building Community: A Third World Case Book*, Building Community Books, London

Turner, J F C (1967) 'Barriers and Channels for Housing Development in Modernizing Countries', *Journal of the American Institute of Planners*, 33 (3), pp 167–81

UNCHS (1984) *A Review of Technologies for the Provision of Basic Infrastructure in Low-Income Settlements*, United Nations Centre for Human Settlements, Nairobi

— (1986) 'Converting Garbage into Compost Proves Profitable in Pakistan', *Bulletin of the International Year of Shelter for the Homeless*, 5, July

— (1987) *Global Report on Human Settlements 1986*, Oxford University Press, Oxford

— (1990) 'Cash from Trash: Making Refuse Pay', World Habitat Day, 1 October 1990, *Shelter and Urbanization Information Kit*, New York

UNICEF (n d a) 'Urban Example – Prospective for the Future: Water Supply and Sanitation to Urban Marginal Areas of Tegucigalpa, Honduras', United Nations Children's Emergency Fund

— (n d b) 'Water Supply and Environmental Sanitation for *Barrios Marginal* Areas (Slums, Squatter Settlements in Urban Tegucigalpa)', UNICEF submission to the UNICEF executive board on behalf of the government of Honduras

World Bank (1994) *World Development Report*, Oxford University Press, Oxford

WCED (1987) *Our Common Future*, Oxford University Press, Oxford

Chapter Four

Sustainability, Poverty and Urban Environmental Transitions

Gordon McGranahan, Jacob Songsore and Marianne Kjellén

The relationship between sustainability, poverty and the environment is complex and at times confusing. The problem is not just that it can be hard to discern where the sustainability arrow is pointing. The very status of sustainability remains unclear. Is it 'a good thing' by definition or by implication? If, especially at certain times and in certain places, the single minded pursuit of sustainability seems to be 'a bad thing', does this indicate that the definition needs to be reworked, or that sustainability should be only one objective, or constraint, among many? Here it is argued that the primary environmental concerns of the more disadvantaged urban dwellers are not issues of sustainability, narrowly defined. Should a broader definition of sustainability be adopted, or should the pre-eminence of sustainability concerns be rejected?

Given the current popularity of sustainability, it is tempting to stretch the concept to fit one's preoccupations. Thus, for many, poverty alleviation and the elimination of severe environmental health hazards are clearly of critical importance and, hence, ought to be central to sustainability. Munasinghe (1993:3), whose discussion of sustainability provides the starting point for the use of the term in this book, associates poverty alleviation with the social side of sustainability: 'The socio-cultural concept of sustainability seeks to maintain the stability of social and cultural systems, including the reduction of destructive conflicts. Both intragenerational equity (especially elimination of poverty) and intergenerational equity (involving the rights of future generations) are important aspects of this approach.'

In common with many other attempts to incorporate poverty-related concerns under the rubric of sustainability, there are some serious problems with the manner in which a concern with poverty is being justified here. The underlying logic is that sustainability entails social stability, that poverty leads to conflict which undermines social stability, and hence that poverty is unsustainable. But the legitimate objection to poverty is surely the misery it entails, not the disruptions that occur when the immiserated protest. If this is the sort of means through which poverty alleviation can gain a place on the sustainability bandwagon, then it is probably better not to have a place there at all, but to plod along independently, or to latch on to alternative concepts wherein sustainability qualifies rather than incorporates alternative goals, such as sustainable development or sustainable poverty alleviation.

Somewhat surprisingly, there are many urban environmental problems whose relations to sustainability are also tenuous. Faecal matter is probably the most hazardous pollutant in many low-income cities. To say that the sanitation systems in these cities are unsustainable suggests quite a different set of issues, however. It could mean that the infrastructure or facilities cannot be maintained: a very real problem in many cities, but not of great relevance in areas with no facilities at all. Taking a more ecological perspective, it could mean that nutrient cycles are being disrupted – again not a priority problem in areas where, say, open defecation is practised. It could even mean that sanitation is so bad that the cities are under threat from devastating epidemics or pandemics. But in the late twentieth century, faecal pollution is causing primarily endemic health problems, which threaten the welfare and lives of many urban dwellers, but not to the point of undermining the sustainability of whole cities.

The most serious problem with broad definitions of sustainability is that they tend to marginalize the primary environmental concerns of the poor, even as they claim to incorporate them. As described below, increasing urban affluence changes the nature of the environmental challenge. The environmental priorities of the affluent clearly relate to sustainability: it is not so much the present as the future of the world's affluent minority that is at risk. Many of the environmental priorities of the urban poor, on the other hand, must be manipulated to be portrayed as sustainability issues: it is in the here and now that many of their most serious problems have their effects, and their burden on resources and global sinks is comparatively minor. Since the international environmental agenda in any case tends to be dominated by the concerns of the more vocal and powerful, adopting sustainability as an overarching principle reinforces existing tendencies to ignore the priorities of low-income groups.

On the other hand, it is important not to exaggerate the difference between those environmental problems that threaten sustainability, narrowly defined, and those that do not. There are many similarities, both physically and in terms of the collective action problems they pose, between the primarily local problems of the urban poor and the more extensive and long-term problems of more concern to the affluent. Moreover, if the poor majority can gain effective control over their local environments, and successfully reduce the hazards which are now such a burden, they are far more likely to become active participants in efforts to prevent the global scale environmental abuse which threatens the future of the poor and the affluent. Similarly, if the environmental nature of many water, sanitation and housing problems in Southern settlements is recognized, the poor are more likely to be able to take advantage of the global environmental movement to help address short-term problems. Thus the goal of creating a common platform for environmental improvement is laudable, even if concepts such as sustainability are not up to the task.

In the remainder of this chapter we attempt to situate the environmental problems of the urban poor in their international environmental context and to draw some action-oriented conclusions. In the section headed 'urban environmental transitions', we provide the rough outlines of such a transition and link affluence to the scale and timing of environmental burdens. It is argued that with increasing affluence, environmental burdens tend to become spatially more diffuse, temporally more delayed, and causally less directly threatening (ie environmental degradation is relatively more likely to undermine life support systems and relatively less likely to threaten health directly). The next section continues with a presentation of selected results from a study of Accra, Jakarta and São Paulo, illustrating elements of this transition. Accra, the poorest of these three cities, faces the worst household-level environmental problems, while São Paulo, the largest and most affluent, has some of the worst city-level problems and contributes the most (even per capita) to global problems. In the final section we focus on the local environmental problems of disadvantaged neighbourhoods and attempt to link their physical and institutional character with the qualities needed for improvement efforts to succeed.

URBAN ENVIRONMENTAL TRANSITIONS

In the urban context,[1] affluence is not unambiguously harmful or beneficial to the physical environment. Under existing patterns of economic development, however, affluence does change the locus of the urban environmental challenge. Where one perceives the worst problems to be will vary depending upon whether one is concerned with very localized problems such as bad household water and sanitation and indoor air pollution, city-level problems such as ambient air and water pollution, or global problems such as global warming and ozone depletion. Generally:

- The urban environmental hazards causing the most ill-health are those found in poor homes, neighbourhoods and workplaces, principally located in the South.
- The most extreme examples of city-level environmental distress are found in and around middle-income megacities and the industrial cities of the formerly planned economies.
- The largest urban contributors to global environmental problems are the affluent, living preponderantly in the urban areas of the North.

Whether one looks across cities, at the history of affluent cities, or even across different groups within a city, it is possible to discern the outlines of an environmental transition relating to affluence. There tends to be a spatial shifting of environmental problems, as affluence increases, from the local to the regional and global. There also tends to be a temporal shifting from immediate health problems to, in the case of global warming, intergenerational impacts. These tendencies only reflect dispositions: policies, as well as demography and geography, can make an enormous difference, and vastly different environmental conditions can be found in and between cities of comparable affluence. Generally, however, the poor create environmental problems for themselves and their neighbours, while the affluent create problems for an expanding public.[2]

Thus, in poor cities and particularly their poor neighbourhoods, the most threatening environmental problems are usually those close to

---

1) This section develops ideas presented in McGranahan and Songsore, 1994.
2) When epidemics and pandemics were a common cause of death, the environmental problems of the poor were a serious threat to the health of the affluent. Indeed, the sanitary reforms of the nineteenth century were predicated on an awareness of this interdependence. Responses to recent outbreaks of cholera and the plague indicate that current efforts to improve sanitary conditions in poor neighbourhoods would also proceed very differently if there was felt to be a serious threat to the well off.

home (McGranahan, 1993). The dangers of exposure are high, especially for women and children. Inadequate household water supplies and sanitation are typically more crucial to people's wellbeing than polluted waterways (Cairncross and Feachem, 1993). There is often more exposure to air pollution in smoky kitchens than outdoors (Smith, 1993). Waste accumulating, uncollected, in the neighbourhood often poses more serious problems than the waste at the city dumps. Flies breeding in the waste and mosquitoes breeding in water sites can add considerably to the local health risks (Chavasse et al, 1994; Schofield et al, 1990). In the most disadvantaged neighbourhoods, these problems combine to create a complex of environmental health problems, whose most evident burdens are high prevalences of diarrhoeal diseases (Bradley et al, 1991; Cairncross and Feachem, 1993; Huttly, 1990) and acute respiratory infections (Berman, 1991; Chen et al, 1990; Graham, 1990) among young children, but also extend to numerous other health problems (Hardoy et al, 1990; Satterthwaite, 1993).

A more affluent urban lifestyle employs more resources and creates more waste, but the rich devote part of their wealth to measures which protect themselves from environmental hazards. The problems close to home are the first to improve as affluence increases because they are the most clearly threatening and are institutionally the easiest to address. Moreover, the physical displacement of environmental problems is at once a means of avoiding personal exposure and a possible route to larger scale environmental problems. Waterborne sewerage systems, for example, reduce personal exposure to faecal material, but can lower the quality of the cities' waterways and strain the cities' water supplies. Electricity is a clean fuel where it is used, but electric power plants can be an important source of ambient air pollution. Industries may provide the incomes to allow people to take better care of their home and neighbourhood environments, but they can also bring pollution which degrades the ambient environment.

Thus, even as household and neighbourhood-level environmental problems recede from prominence for a growing segment of a city's population, there are pressures to increase ambient air pollution, hazardous waste problems, pollution of the waterways and, more generally, the regional environmental burden of the city. If the broader environmental problems are not on the political agenda (and in most industrializing countries they have not been) these pressures will tend to lead to a general worsening of the ambient urban environment. The fact that interest in environmental protection has no strong power base within a city probably contributes to delays in implementing even relatively uncontroversial environmental controls.

Affluent cities, like affluent households and neighbourhoods, can and often do take measures to protect themselves. Over the past few decades, many cities in the North, and a growing number in the South, have improved the quality of their ambient air (UNEP/WHO, 1988) and, to a lesser extent, water (World Bank, 1992). Remedial measures to cope with many of the worst excesses are well known (Douglas, 1983), if not always applied. An affluent city can more easily afford the public finance and administration needed to regulate the more perceptible forms of pollution; and in any case affluent cities are more likely to be economically dependent on the services and commercial sector than on highly polluting heavy industry. Moreover, with a rise in national income, pollution by a range of water and air pollutants is seen to increase and then fall (Grossman and Krueger, 1995; Shafik, 1995), but, according to economic analysis, such a pattern is to be expected from the introduction of economically efficient abatement strategies (Selden and Song, 1995).

Attempts to address city-wide environmental problems do not, however, prevent economic growth from increasing global environmental problems. The resources consumed and greenhouse gases emitted to support even the cleanest of Northern cities are, on a per capita basis, far larger than those associated with the poorer cities of the South. Recent research confirms a general tendency for carbon dioxide emissions to rise continuously with economic growth (Holtz-Eakin and Selden, 1995; Shafik, 1995). Relatively little progress has yet been made in introducing 'clean' production in the broadest sense of the term (Jackson, 1993), or in shifting from the linear material flows which characterize most modern technologies to the closed cycles which some environmentalists argue ought to characterize postmodern technology (Wallgren, 1994). The image of an 'ecological city' remains as utopian in the North as in the South, and it would require radical changes even to begin to approach what could be legitimately termed sustainable cities (White, 1994). Since the institutional basis for negotiated restrictions on global environmental burdens are still rudimentary, the economic incentive for affluent countries to take effective measures remains negligible.

Accompanying the shift in the scale of environmental problems from household and neighbourhood, to city and regional, to global, is a shift from issues of health to those of ecology and sustainability. Threats from intense environmental insults in and around people's homes usually affect the health of the inhabitants directly. Threats from broader environmental burdens are typically more indirect, affect life-support systems in often subtle ways and take more time to manifest themselves. The environmental health problems that are more critical in affluent cities are typically those that are very poorly or only recently understood, involve delayed effects or cumulative low-level exposures, or are particular aspects of large-scale environmental change (Chivian et al, 1993).

Whether the broader environmental burdens are sustainable, even in the narrow sense, can be a very pertinent question. The burdens themselves are often the long-term side effects of the creation of wealth. On the other hand, the sustainability of the more local burdens, such as inadequate household water and sanitation or indoor air pollution, is not really an issue. Such problems derive from practices people do not sustain by choice, and the burdens have already shown themselves all too able to persist.

In its broad outlines, the transition summarized above applies to cities. It suggests an association between a city's affluence, its environment and the health of its citizens. However, there are both poor and affluent people in almost every city. The average income of a city makes a difference, but environmental burdens are borne unevenly. People living in poor neighbourhoods are not only likely to face more household and neighbourhood-level environmental problems, but more than their share of the broader problems as well. For a variety of reasons, low income settlements are more likely to be located near polluting industrial establishments, waste dump sites and heavily polluted waterways. Indeed, there is a sense in which the poor in rapidly industrializing cities face the worst of two worlds (Harpham et al, 1988), and in some cases the environmental risks of poverty and industrialization can overlap and create destructive interactions (Smith and Lee, 1993).

While the local character of many of the environmental problems of poverty means that it is necessary to look closely at intra-urban differences in environmental health, there is an inherently public aspect to the environmental problems of almost every level. Acting independently and selfishly, cities and nations would not contribute significantly towards solving global environmental problems; industries, transporters and neighbourhoods would not contribute towards solving city-wide problems; and individuals and households would not contribute towards solving neighbourhood problems. At every level, institutional mechanisms are needed to ensure that people are acting in the collective interest. And at every level, social movements have played and will probably continue to play an important part in ensuring that institutional as well as technical innovations are forthcoming. This holds despite the enormous differences in both the physical nature of the problems and their institutional contexts.

Alternatively, rapid population growth can act as a compounding factor at every level. Local environmental problems are often most severe where the urban population is growing rapidly, and migrants are particularly exposed to environmental health hazards. City-wide problems are typically more severe in larger cities. And more people, particularly more affluent people, generally mean a greater global environmental burden.

Looking at environmental priorities in this manner, it seems reasonable to ascribe the disproportionate attention given to sustainability issues in the international environmental movement to the fact that the movement is dominated by the concerns of the affluent. It might seem fanciful, however, to suggest that when the now affluent cities were dominated by more localized environmental problems, the international agenda was too. But this would indeed seem to be the case.

A nineteenth-century precursor to the modern environmental movement was the sanitary movement and, at the time, sanitation was very much an environmental concern. Average urban mortality rates in European cities were far higher than in their rural surroundings (Bairoch, 1988). Bad sanitation, which then referred to a range of poorly understood environmental hazards rather than just excreta disposal, was increasingly seen as responsible for this urban disadvantage (Wohl, 1983). Prominent scientists studied water, sanitary conditions and health, and reformers in urban centres around the world discussed both the technical and moral aspects of urban sanitary reform (Hamlin, 1990; Ladd, 1990; Luckin, 1986). The topic was even of popular interest in many countries. The General German Exhibition of Hygiene and Lifesaving in 1883 attracted 900,000 visitors over a period of five months (Ladd, 1990). As in environmental discussions today, one of the most heated debates was about the appropriate role for government and whether attempts to impose sanitary improvements constituted an infringement on what we would now call the private sector. Eventually, the reformers won out. While the health problems were far worse in poor areas, the affluent were also at risk. Moreover, the ill health of the poor was itself felt to be a burden on the whole society. Politicians were even concerned that the military strength of their nations was being undermined (Shapiro, 1985). It was gradually accepted by the politically powerful that the threat was indeed public and required a public response.

The environmental concerns of the world's affluent have moved on, and international attention has followed suit. Now, comparisons of average urban and rural mortality rates do not display the same urban disadvantage, even in countries with poor urban sanitation (Mosley et al, 1993). However, averages hide gross disparities in the health status of urban dwellers (Harpham et al, 1988; Schell et al, 1993). Much the same applies to sanitary conditions and other localized environmental hazards. Many urban dwellers currently face environmental conditions roughly comparable to those that shocked the bourgeoisie in the nineteenth century. Even for the urban poor (now located primarily in the South), the environmental health burden may not be as high as it once was. Nevertheless, local environmental inadequacies in disadvantaged neighbourhoods probably remain the most important avoidable environmental causes of ill health. Indeed, the 1993 *World Development Report*, which focused on health, estimated that improving household environments could avert the annual loss of almost 80 million 'disability free' years of human life – more than the feasible improvement attributed to all other identified environmental measures combined (World Bank, 1993b).

While the health risks of bad water, poor sanitation and the like have not been forgotten, it is no longer conventional to treat them as complex environmental problems requiring better science, innovative responses and social mobilization. Rather, by and large they are viewed as problems whose solution is known, but for which the requisite finances are not always available, to which insufficient priority is given, or which require a somewhat different mix of private and public sector involvement. This view has been reinforced by efforts to promote price reform in environmental service delivery, which have led the World Bank and other development agencies to emphasize the extent to which water, and to a lesser extent sanitation and other household environmental services, are like normal commodities, whose supply ought to be determined through efficient market mechanisms, with full costs recovered from user fees whenever possible (Briscoe and Garn, 1995; World Bank, 1993a). In some cities, efficient provision on a commercial basis would indeed be an improvement over existing provisions through underfinanced public utilities.[3] But the complex of household and neighbourhood environmental problems, which burden so many of the world's more disadvantaged neighbourhoods, deserves far more in the way of response than yet another shift along the private–public axis, this time in the private direction.

FROM ENVIRONMENTAL HEALTH TO SUSTAINABILITY: EVIDENCE FROM A THREE-CITY STUDY

As indicated above, the most severe urban environmental health problems are concentrated in the South (Hardoy et al, 1992; McGranahan, 1993), where contributions to global environmental problems are comparatively small. There is, however, enormous variation within and between urban centres in the South. The cities that receive the most publicity are the mega-cities, where only a relatively small share of urban

---

3) It is important not to make too much of this comparison: there is little reason to assume that the more commercially oriented utilities will resemble the market ideal any more than public utilities resemble the ideal public service provider.

dwellers live. Often, these Southern mega-cities are portrayed as the epitome of environmental distress. The concentrated environmental burdens of these cities, as indicated by their ambient air pollution, water requirements, release of water pollutants, solid waste generation and local resource degradation, are often immense. However, in the light of the environmental transition described above, there is no reason to assume that city-level and household-level problems go hand in hand. Indeed, the results of a recent study of Accra (Benneh et al, 1993), Jakarta (Surjadi et al, 1994) and São Paulo (Jacobi, 1995) suggest that the opposite is more likely to be true. Many of the worst environmental health problems are probably most severe in smaller, poorer settlements.

Table 4.1 *Selected indicators of city affluence and size of Accra, Jakarta and São Paulo*

Selected indicators	Accra (Ghana)	Jakarta (Indonesia)	São Paulo (Brazil)
1. Total area	935 sq km[a]	660 sq km[b]	1577 sq km[c]
2. Population	1.6m[a]	8.2m[b]	9.5m[c]
3. Average annual population growth 1970–90	3.8%[a]	3.1%[b]	1%[d]
4. National GDP per capita (measured at PPP[e]) 1992	$2100	$3000	$5200

Notes:
a   Greater Accra Metropolitan Area, which includes Accra, Ga and Tema districts.
b   Jakarta DKI. The metropolitan area, often referred to as Jabotabek (including the districts of *Jakarta* DKI, *Bogor*, *Tanggerang* and *Bekasi*) had an estimated population of 16.8 million in 1990. Much of Greater Jakarta's recent growth is taking place in the periphery outside of Jakarta DKI and Jabotabek. Previously, low density areas such as Depok and Cibinong have population growth rates of 10 per cent a year (Douglass, 1989).
c   City of São Paulo. The São Paulo Metropolitan Region had a population of 15.2 million according to the 1991 census.
d   Refers only to the 1980s for the city of São Paulo. Excluding the capital and considering the 37 municipalities of the São Paulo region, the average annual growth rate jumps to 3.1 per cent.
e   Purchasing power parity

Sources: (1) Leitmann, 1993; (2) Benneh et al, 1993; Surjadi et al, 1994; (3) Benneh et al, 1993; Leitmann, 1993; Jacobi, 1995; (4) UNDP, 1995

The three cities, Accra in Ghana, Jakarta in Indonesia, and São Paulo in Brazil, span three continents, and have no obvious cultural similarities. Table 4.1 provides summary statistics on the three cities.

Jakarta and São Paulo are both mega-cities, while Accra is considerably smaller and poorer. However, even Accra is larger and more affluent than the settlements most Southern urban dwellers live in. More than half of urban dwellers in the South live in cities of less than half a million people (UN, 1995), and Ghana has one of the highest per capita incomes of the 47 countries ranked low on the human development index (UNDP, 1995).

In all three countries, the average income in the cities selected is higher than that of the country as a whole. At about the time of the survey, the estimated per capita expenditure in Accra was 50 per cent higher than the national average and that of Jakarta was 130 per cent higher. Alternatively, the São Paulo Metropolitan Region, with less than 12 per cent of Brazil's population in 1990, accounted for an estimated 18 per cent of the GDP of Brazil (Oliveira and Leitmann, 1994).

As described above, many of the most severe urban environmental hazards are found in and around poor people's homes and workplaces. Table 4.2 below summarizes some of the indicators of household-level environmental problems derived from representative surveys administered as part of the three-city study. While individually the comparability of such indicators is often doubtful, the overall picture is clear.

All these indicators involve health risks for either diarrhoeal diseases or respiratory infections, two of the most significant causes of childhood morbidity and mortality.[4] Not having a water source at home is not only burdensome for women, but restricts hygiene practices. High levels of toilet sharing often leads to poor sanitary conditions in the toilets themselves, creates more opportunities for faecal-oral diseases to be transmitted between households, and can lead to open defecation and faeces being mixed with solid waste. Without household garbage collection, waste often accumulates in the neighbourhood, providing ideal habitats for flies and rats. Where biofuels are used without proper ventilation, indoor air pollution may be severe and contribute to respiratory diseases. Flies observed in a kitchen, apart from providing a general indication of the sanitary state of the household, can facilitate the faecal-oral route of many diarrhoeal diseases.

---

4) For a statistical analysis of the relation between these or similar indicators and selected health problems in Accra, see the city report (Benneh et al, 1993).

Table 4.2 *Household environment indicators in Accra, Jakarta and São Paulo, 1991/2*

Environment indicator	Accra % of sample (N=1000)	Jakarta % of sample (N=1055)	São Paulo % of sample (N=1000)
Water			
No water source at residence	46	13	5
Sanitation			
Share toilets with > 10 households	48	14–20	<3
Solid Waste			
No home garbage collection	89	37	5
Indoor Air			
Main cooking fuel wood or charcoal	76	2	0
Pests			
Flies observed in kitchen	82	38	17

Source: McGranahan and Songsore, 1994.

In every case, the indicator improves between Accra and Jakarta and improves further between Jakarta and São Paulo. The more detailed household statistics confirm this trend. The most obvious explanation for the tendencies observed is the relative affluence of the three cities. Indeed, as indicated in Table 4.3, similar patterns are observed looking across different neighbourhoods of Accra.

The affluent neighbourhoods of Accra would seem to have roughly the same access to water and sanitation as the São Paulo averages, while the middle-class neighbourhoods are roughly comparable to the Jakarta averages. While affluent Accra dwellers are more likely to use a smoky cooking fuel than citizens of Jakarta and São Paulo – a fact that probably reflects Accra's smaller size – they use smoky fuels far less frequently than the poorer Accra dwellers, and among the most affluent households in Accra the cook exposed to the smoke may actually be a servant or poor relative.

Almost half of the urban population in Accra have incomes below the World Bank's absolute poverty threshold. The poor tend to be concentrated in high-density indigenous settlements and migrant residential areas with poor access to environmental services (Amuzu and Leitmann, 1994). The lack of infrastructure faced by the poor majority is reflected in Table 4.3 below.

Table 4.3 *Selected household environment indicators in poor, middle-class and affluent neighbourhoods of the Greater Accra Metropolitan Area, 1991/2*

Environment indicator	Poor % of sample (N= 790)	Middle Class % of sample (N=160)	Affluent % of sample (N=50)
Water			
No water source at residence	55	14	4
Sanitation			
Share toilets with > 10 households	60	17	2
Solid Waste			
No home garbage collection	94	77	55
Indoor Air			
Main cooking fuel wood or charcoal	85	44	30
Pests			
Flies observed in kitchen	91	56	18

Note: The three neighbourhoods classes are an aggregation by affluence of the eight socio-ecological strata presented in Benneh et al, 1993.

Source: Stockholm Environment Institute/University of Ghana household survey.

These indicators give a clue to the health risks and the level of inconveniences households, particularly women and children, face in order to secure the necessities of daily life. Still, these problems are suffered by individuals and their close neighbours, with the dominant environmental processes involving local interactions, and they are not intended to indicate the level of strain on the city's resource base.

It was argued in the previous section that the strain placed on a city's resources tends to be less where many people are poor and consumption levels low. A selection of indicators related to city-level environmental burdens are provided in Table 4.4. These indicators are taken from a variety of sources, and some are less comparable than the household-level indicators. Most reflect the extent of the burden rather than the damage done (partly because the damage depends heavily on local geography) and tend to be even less comparable.

While the differences are in some cases more ambiguous than with the household-level indicators, they do confirm the general tendency suggested and illustrate the extent and manner in which some of the local environmental problems are displaced to the city level. Both aggregate and per capita indicators are presented because, although the largest cities tend to be found in middle income countries, a relation between urban affluence and the scale of environmental burdens also exists independently of city size.

Table 4.4 *Selected indicators of city-level environmental burdens in Accra, Jakarta and São Paulo, 1990–92*

Environment indicator	Accra (metro)	Jakarta (city)	São Paulo (city)
Water			
1. Household water consumption (litres per capita per day)	82	138	215
2. Total water consumption ('000 cubic metres per day)	263	1469	5017[b]
Sanitation			
3. Sewage flow ('000 cubic metres per day)	46	35	2400[b]
4. Sewage treatment (% treated)	20	1	26
Solid Waste			
5. Household solid waste generation (kgs per capita per day)	0.5–0.6	0.6[a]	1–1.2
6. Municipal solid waste generation (tons per day)	1000	5000[a]	11,000
7. Percentage of waste collected	75	79	90
Outdoor Air			
8. Automobile ownership (% of households)	16	26	33
9. Suspended particulate matter mid-1980s ($\mu g/m^3$ air)	107–9	204–71	98

Notes: (a) Includes both household and industrial waste; (b) metro.

Sources: (1) Stockholm Environment Institute/University of Ghana/Atma Jaya Catholic University household surveys; Leitmann, 1993; (2, 3 and 4) Leitmann, 1993; (5, 6 and 7) Amuzu and Leitmann, 1994; Leitmann, 1993; Oliveira and Leitmann, 1994; (8) Stockholm Environment Institute/University of Ghana/ Atma Jaya Catholic University/Centro de Estudos de Cultura Contemporânea household surveys; (9) World Bank, 1992.

Regional water scarcities are an increasing problem globally, and can be particularly acute in the vicinity of large cities where they can lead to sharp increases in the cost of supplying water (Anton, 1993; World Bank, 1993a). As shown in Table 4.4, water consumption per capita is about 70 per cent higher in Jakarta than in Accra, and about 60 per cent higher again in São Paulo. Because of their relative sizes, these differences are magnified in the city-wide figures. Water consumption increases with affluence both because it becomes more convenient and affordable to use, and because new demands for water, such as for washing cars, develop. As noted above, the share of households with water sources in their homes increases from about half in Accra to 95 per cent in São Paulo and, as indicated in Table 4.4, the share of households with cars doubles. Many other measures of convenience and water using devices would show similar patterns.

The principal water sources for Accra are the Densu and Black Volta rivers, which have the capacity to provide far more water than the current demand. The city-wide impacts of Jakarta's water demands are somewhat difficult to determine. The majority of households in Jakarta use shallow wells, at least for washing (Surjadi et al, 1994). Groundwater salination affects some 40 per cent of Jakarta's residents (Surjadi et al, 1994), and this is often attributed to excess abstraction (Douglass, 1989). However, the salination of the shallow aquifer used by households may be a long-standing natural phenomenon (Rismianto and Mak, 1993), and it is possible that the more serious long-term supply problems lie in the piped water system. The high consumption levels in São Paulo are all met through the piped water system, which is severely straining the city's water supplies (Anton, 1993). Water scarcity is exacerbated during the dry winter and rationing is applied (Jacobi, 1995).

Pollution of the waterways is a serious problem in the vicinity of all three cities. Many of São Paulo's and Jakarta's water quality problems are related to industrial activity, which is particularly intensive in and around São Paulo. Even faecal water pollution is more of a city-level problem in São Paulo, where the sewerage system reaches some three quarters of the residents, but 75 per cent of the sewage is released untreated (Jacobi, 1995). Forty cubic metres per second of raw sewage and industrial effluent are discharged into the Tietê river which has become almost entirely devoid of oxygen (Leitmann, 1993). In Accra and Jakarta, where the sewerage systems are negligible, a larger share of the faecal material degrades in the neighbourhoods, where is poses its main risks. This does not, however, prevent the waterways of Accra and Jakarta from being very severely polluted with faecal material.

As shown in Table 4.4, solid waste generation is somewhat higher in São Paulo than in Accra or Jakarta. Most solid waste in the three cities is eventually collected by the city authorities, with a somewhat higher share in São Paulo. Overall, with its large size, high waste generation and high collection share, São Paulo's authorities cope with by far the largest solid waste burden. Alternatively, as depicted in Table 4.2, only 11 per cent of the households in Accra, and 63 per cent in Jakarta have their refuse collected from the house. Households without a home collection dump their wastes at collection points, official dump sites, or other, often illegal, sites. While the rubbish that is brought to the collection or dumping sites officially becomes the responsibility of the city authorities, when collection is intermittent, much of the environmental burden is carried by the nearby residents.

São Paulo is famed for its poor air quality. During 1989 health warnings due to air pollution from carbon monoxide were issued for a total of 250 days, ozone for 108 days and particulates for 54 days. However, lead and sulphur dioxide levels have declined[5] with the increased use of alcohol fuel (Hardoy et al, 1992). The lowering of sulphur dioxide and lead pollution is a trend São Paulo shares with most cities in the North. As depicted in Table 4.4, both Jakarta and Accra show measurements for suspended particulate matter well beyond the WHO guidelines (60–90 µg/cbm). According to these measurements, São Paulo's air pollution is considerably less, despite the large number of cars and the greater industrial activity. However, in Accra, air pollution problems are concentrated mainly in the industrial areas. Sites with traffic congestion also bring localized problems of airborne lead (ROG/UNDP/UNCHS, 1989). Overall, outdoor air pollution is not a significant problem for Accra (Amuzu and Leitmann, 1994). Actually, the high levels of indoor air pollution among wood and charcoal users (Benneh et al, 1993) are more alarming, indicating that the main concerns for Accra remain in the home sphere.

As with the household-level indicators, the attempt to find quantifiable indicators diverts attention from many of the more unique environmental problems characteristic of these cities. All these cities face problems with watershed management, urban-led deforestation and land degradation, and a wide range of other environmental resources. Moreover, just as the household environmental problems were shown to vary significantly in Accra, as well as between the cities, so not all residents within a city place the same strain on the city-level environment.

Table 4.5 provides two of the indicators for city-level burdens for the same types of neighbourhoods in Accra that were depicted in Table 4.3. Again, the figures for the middle-class and affluent neighbourhoods of Accra are closer to the averages for Jakarta and São Paulo than they are to the figures for the poor neighbourhoods of Accra.

---

5)   In the 1980s sulphur dioxide concentrations decreased by over 10 per cent a year and the annual lead average was below the WHO guideline range (UNEP/WHO, 1988).

In summary, the household environment appears far better in São Paulo than in the other two cities, reflecting higher levels of private affluence as well as organized efforts and ability by the city authorities towards providing infrastructural facilities for the bulk of the population. On the other hand, even on a per capita basis, the levels of activities creating city-level environmental problems are highest in São Paulo, though the effects have been mitigated by somewhat more vigorous pollution control efforts in some areas, such as air pollution.

Table 4.5 *Selected indicators of city-level environmental burdens in poor, middle-class and affluent neighbourhoods of the Greater Accra Metropolitan Area, 1991/2*

Environment indicator	Poor % of sample (N= 790)	Middle-class % of sample (N=160)	Affluent % of sample (N=50)
Water Consumption (daily litres per capita)	61	153	173
Outdoor Air Automobile ownership (% of households)	9	34	58

Note: The three neighbourhoods classes are an aggregation by affluence of the eight socio-ecological strata presented in Benneh et al, 1993.

Source: Stockholm Environment Institute/University of Ghana household survey.

Jakarta appears, at least superficially, to have the worst of two worlds environmentally; it faces severe city-level problems affecting fishing, agriculture and its watersheds (Douglass, 1989; Hardoy et al, 1992), but, due to poorly developed environmental infrastructure, has made little headway towards solving the unhealthy environment in many neighbourhoods. Still, most households are far more affluent than those in Accra, which is reflected in the many private solutions towards improving the household environment (Surjadi et al, 1994).

Accra's residents face the most pervasive environmental health problems, related mainly to the low development of infrastructure to displace the environmental burdens away from the household sphere. Except for localized air and water pollution problems in areas of traffic congestion, industrial sites and lagoons, fishing and agriculture have not (yet) been adversely affected by city activities (Amuzu and Leitmann, 1994).

THE ENVIRONMENTAL PROBLEMS OF UNSERVICED HOUSEHOLDS AND THEIR NEIGHBOURHOODS

The foregoing empirical generalizations do not imply fixed relationships between affluence and environmental distress. It would be a mistake to think that low income neighbourhoods are all insanitary, smoky, waste strewn and pest infested (Bapat and Crook, 1984), that the open air and waterways of middle income cities are always heavily polluted, or that affluence has to create a global environmental crisis. Similarly, there are circumstances when the homes of the affluent become environmentally hazardous, and other circumstances when the poor contribute significantly to environmental problems of a global scale. Indeed, part of what makes environmental management such a challenge is that the connections between human activity and the environment cannot be reduced to a few simple relationships, and environmental problems of different scales interrelate.[6] The generalizations described in the previous sections do, however, locate what appear to be the weakest links – the levels at which the most serious problems are likely to surface in the absence of good environmental management.

The remainder of this chapter focuses on local environmental problems in low-income settlements, again using examples from Accra, Jakarta and São Paulo. The level of poverty is taken to be such that most households in the settlements are not offered environmental amenities such as in-house piped water, sewers, and door-to-door waste collection, and would not be willing to pay for such services if they were offered.[7] It is argued that in the absence of such services, local environmental management is both physically and socially extremely complex, and must be tailored to local conditions. Partly as a result, the most effective strategies are likely to be in large part locally driven, not in the sense of individualistic private initiatives, but of concerted efforts to achieve

6) For example, local environmental changes that alter the manner in which infections spread and develop can lead to very different health risks in broader populations, including, for example, the emergence of more or less virulent disease strains (Ewald, 1993; Ewald, 1994).
7) It is sometimes argued that, since the urban poor already pay a high prices for vendor water, a large share would be willing to pay for water piped into their homes if they were offered it at cost. However, the fact that low-income households are, if it is absolutely necessary, willing to pay high prices for water does not mean that, given all the options available at cost, they would choose in-house connections.

locally defined goals. Simultaneously, effective local environmental management must be multifaceted, not only taking local environmental interconnections into account, but combining government programmes with contributions from non-governmental organizations (NGOs) and community-based organizations (CBOs), combining scientific research with public participation, and combining education with public debate and mechanisms for applying popular pressures to governments. In short, attempting simply to emulate the engineering solutions applied in affluent areas, but using less expensive technologies, is likely to fail.

In Accra, Jakarta or São Paulo, and indeed in virtually any city, the local environmental problems of disadvantaged neighbourhoods would undoubtedly be transformed if residents became appreciably more affluent, or if large sums of public funds were devoted to improving local infrastructure and providing environmental services. It is important, however, not to make the mistake of assuming that little can be done until it is possible to afford the standard 'modern' solutions. Indeed, the notion that everyone knows what needs to be done, and the only problem is to find the resources to do it, can be very pernicious.

Poverty elimination is a more comprehensive and ultimately far more important goal, intimately linked to international as well as national economic relations, but it could be greatly assisted by local environmental improvement. Much recent work emphasizes that a lack of economic opportunity is only one aspect of urban poverty (Amis, 1995a; Amis, 1995b; Moser, 1995; Rakodi, 1995; Wratten, 1995). For a variety of reasons, local environmental conditions, especially in unserved neighbourhoods, can easily become worse than income poverty alone would dictate (McGranahan, 1993). Growing private affluence is not always accompanied by commensurate improvements in local environmental conditions. Alternatively, where poverty persists, local environmental conditions can contribute to a vicious cycle of ill health and economic decline. To make matters worse, the poor often pay higher prices than the affluent for less convenient water, the use of less sanitary toilet facilities, and smokier fuels (Cairncross and Kinnear, 1992; Hardoy et al, 1992; Soussan et al, 1990). In many disadvantaged neighbourhoods, environmental improvement is itself a critical aspect of poverty alleviation.

It may be tempting to diagnose these environmental problems in disadvantaged settlements as simply reflecting the lack of infrastructure and household services. Defining the problem in terms of a solution that many cannot afford is inappropriate, however, unless public funds can make up for the private shortfall. While an emphasis on piped water connections and sewerage systems may be a useful means of drawing a small unserved minority up to standard, when the majority is unserved the same emphasis is likely to concentrate resources on the relatively well off. This can again be illustrated with the examples of Accra, Jakarta and São Paulo.

In São Paulo, the expansion of water supplies and sewers to *favelas* (informal settlements) and other low income settlements has had a major impact on some of the poorest São Paulo dwellers (Briscoe and Steer, 1993; Munasinghe, 1992). During the 1980s, the share of *favelas* with piped water supplies increased from 32 per cent to 99 per cent, and the share with sewerage systems increased from 1 per cent to 15 per cent (Briscoe and Garn, 1995). While this expansion was predicated on political and economic change, and a broader attempt to formalize low income settlements, the fact that providing water and sewers is a relatively clear goal helped give it political potency, and the fact that the majority already had these services ensured that the expansion did reach the poor. Even in São Paulo, however, sewers built to what could be termed the industry standard would have been too costly to expand so rapidly, and the standard means of offering services would have been inappropriate in low income areas. The 'condominial' system, which involved both technical and organizational adaptations, provided a cheaper alternative, which was offered in a manner more responsive to the needs of low income areas (Briscoe and Steer, 1993). While the technical aspects of the condominial system did not involve new engineering principles, the deviation from the industrial standard and the political process through which it gained support were both critical to its expansion.

In Jakarta, the expansion of piped water and sewers is less central, partly because Jakarta is poorer and partly because even relatively affluent households are likely to rely on wells and aqua privies rather than piped water and sewers (Surjadi et al, 1994). The sanitation system operates with relatively little direct involvement by the government. The piped water situation depends on the salination of the groundwater.[8] In the unsalinated areas, four out of five households use well water even for drinking, and any effort to expand household connections will almost certainly primarily affect the well-off. In the salinated areas, on the other hand, almost everyone depends, either directly or indirectly, on piped water at least for drinking. Only 31 per cent have household connections, however, and even if expansion is rapid, the beneficiaries of new household connections will be primarily the well off for some years to

---

8) In international literature, the salination of the shallow wells in Jakarta is often referred to as an example of the effects of excessive abstraction. However, this link between salination and abstraction has not actually been established.

come. For the poorer majority, a more important issue with regard to the piped water system is how to increase the available supply of piped water in such a manner as to limit rent dissipation (or abnormal profits) in the water resale market.[9] Currently, vendors charge up to ten times the utility price for water and those who control sales from public hydrants make excess profits (Lovei and Whittington, 1993). Attempts to increase competition have not been very successful (Crane, 1994) and it unclear whether the high prices are really the result of monopoly pricing, of more technical limits on the water supply which would also drive the price up in a competitive market, or of some combination of the two. What is clear is that a narrow emphasis on household water connections will not address the problems of the poor, and crude attempts to punish vendors are likely to decrease water supplies and raise the market price of water for low income households still further.

In Accra, increasing centralized household service provision is also unlikely to reach those who need it most. As in Jakarta, articulated sewers are virtually insignificant. The government and the local communities are involved in supplying sanitary facilities, and the utility plays an important role removing human waste, but most of the toilets in low income areas are communal or at least widely shared. As in the salinated parts of Jakarta, everyone depends upon the piped water system, but only about 35 per cent of the surveyed households had indoor piping. About 24 per cent had private standpipes, 8 per cent used communal standpipes and 28 per cent obtained their drinking water primarily from vendors (Benneh et al, 1993). While indoor piping is only slightly more common than in the salinated areas of Jakarta, the alternative supplies of piped water are more prevalent, and the mark-up for vendor water is far less, even taking account of the higher delivery costs in Jakarta.

As these examples illustrate, centralized household water and sanitation services are less relevant in poor neighbourhoods, and especially in the poor neighbourhoods of poor cities. Much the same applies to other household environmental services, such as door-to-door waste collection and the provision of clean fuels. For example, the enormous sums that have historically been spent subsidizing electricity have had at best a marginal impact on the cooking fuel patterns of poor urban households (McGranahan and Kaijser, 1993). In any case, in many countries around the world the public sector is under pressure to retrench rather than expand. Especially in Africa, where cities have been growing rapidly and the economic plight of the public sector is often most severe, a general

---

9) Rent dissipation can occur when, for example, users or vendors expend resources queuing for water or otherwise attempting to achieve sectional preferment.

crisis in urban services developed in the 1970s and is still being felt (Stren and White, 1989). Financially strapped central governments and local municipalities are not in a position to decide to expand public services to individual households in disadvantaged areas.

Not only have the state-run utilities received considerable criticism in recent years for failing to deliver local environmental services effectively (Briscoe and Garn, 1995), but many environmentalists have noted that most centralized environmental service systems are themselves environmentally destructive at a broader level (Niemczynowicz, 1993). In considering alternatives, however, it is important to keep in mind that the attraction of these systems in the past was not that they were considered technically optimal, but that they transformed an extremely complex network of interconnected environmental problems into a set of largely independent, centrally manageable systems that could be technically controlled. Clean water is piped into homes and waste water is piped out. Faeces are immediately sealed off from air and insects, and flushed away with the waste water. Solid waste is bagged, placed in closed containers and then carted away. Wires carry electricity into every room, where it can be cleanly converted into heat, light or mechanical drive. Utilities and municipalities are left to manage the potentially polluting energy conversions, dispose of large quantities of liquid and solid waste and find new water supplies. In affluent people's homes and neighbourhoods, however, it can seem as if environmental amenities are like any other commodities – goods a household or individual purchases in the pursuit of wellbeing.[10]

In poor neighbourhoods where centralized household services are largely absent, households are more likely to have to share water sources, sanitary facilities and waste disposal services. Local environmental problems are not only more severe but also tend to reinforce each other to create a complex of interrelated environmental hazards. Bad sanitation can lead to contaminated groundwater, faeces finding its way into the solid waste, onto the open land, into the drainage ditches, and generally into contact with other people. Flies breed in the human and solid waste and can contaminate the food. Solid waste finds its ways into the drains, causing accumulations of water where mosquitoes breed. The possibilities of microbe contamination in food makes thorough cooking important, but cooking with smoky fuels exposes especially women and children to hazardous pollutants. The mosquito coils and pesticides used to combat mosquitoes add to the air pollution and chemical hazards.

---

10) The distinction between individual and household priorities and decisions can be critical (Rakodi, 1991), but is not explored in this chapter.

Under such circumstances, it is clear that individuals and households cannot choose a cleaner home and neighbourhood environment, as they might choose a normal 'good' (McGranahan, 1993). Their environmental problems arise mostly from other people's choices and actions. By and large, it is other people's faeces that are a threat, other people's waste that clogs the drains, other people's water where the mosquitoes are breeding, and so on. Children, who are those most affected by faecal-oral diseases, often move freely from house to house in the course of their play, reducing the importance of the child's own home environment still further (Pickering, 1985). In crowded settlements, even smoke from wood and coal, typically fuels of the relatively poor, can easily become a neighbourhood problem that residents cannot avoid (Terblanche et al, 1993). Problems relating to water supplies,[11] sanitation, food contamination and insect infestation are even more clearly intertwined, and people's actions are even more clearly interdependent.

Economists have long been aware that anonymous markets are not efficient institutions for handling such problems, which involve public goods, externalities and common property (Dasgupta (1993:143) provides a discussion of these and related concepts in the context of poverty.) In poor neighbourhoods, pest control is usually an example of a spatially delimited *public good*. A lower pest population typically benefits all local residents, regardless of whether they contributed to the control efforts. Thus, in an anonymous free market, people would have insufficient incentive to contribute to pest control. An *externality* arises when, for example, one household's pit latrine contaminates someone else's well water, and the polluting household does not take this damage into account. In this case, the market does not provide the polluter with sufficient incentive to desist. *Common property* problems can arise when a neighbourhood's marginal lands and waterways are used without restraint and allowed to degrade. The common feature of all these examples is that individuals acting independently do not have the incentive to manage the environment properly.

These somewhat overlapping concepts of public goods, externalities and common property are frequently applied to large-scale environmental problems, often to justify government interventions, including taxes and subsidies. However, numerous institutions and organizations

---

11) The benefits of water are closer to those of 'normal' commodities than those of sanitation and waste disposal, and a more commercial orientation is sometimes promoted on the grounds that household water supplies provide predominantly private benefits (Briscoe and Garn, 1995). This does not apply to the disadvantaged neighbourhoods being discussed here, though it may apply to more affluent neighbourhoods which should indeed benefit from a more commercial approach.

other than the government and private enterprises can and do play a role in environmental management, especially at the local level.[12] Ranging from the nuclear households to extensive kinship networks, from CBOs to international NGOs, from recreational clubs to political parties, and from environmental associations and women's groups to orthodox religious organizations, the significance of these institutions in environmental management is increasingly being recognized. Where centralized household services are absent, such institutions are especially critical. Indeed, a good part of the variation in local environmental conditions across poor neighbourhoods probably reflects their different configurations of local institutions.

Large variations in both environmental conditions and institutional configurations are themselves characteristic of unserved neighbourhoods. The much debated differences in the quality of service provided by private versus public sector utilities pales into insignificance compared to environmental and institutional differences which can be encountered even within a single low income neighbourhood. In a recent participatory assessment of local environmental conditions in a *kampung* in Jakarta, residents could compare the extent to which different waters smelled, were sticky or irritated the skin and, for example, contrasted the yellowish well water near an old swamp, the blackish, oily well water in another part of the neighbourhood, and the 'good' quality water from a deeper well sunk by the manager of a public toilet and bathhouse. Similarly, sanitary facilities ranged from pour flush aqua privies, to drop toilets, to no toilets, and from single household facilities, to shared facilities, to pay toilets owned by a local entrepreneur.[13] The residents' local environmental and health problems are closely interrelated, but are by no means homogeneous.

The prevalence of local externalities and public goods, the importance of local institutions and the high level of diversity all underline the importance of local participation in designing and implementing improvements once the possibility of providing standard household-level services is ruled out. At the same time, how such institutions operate locally depends very much on how the state functions at higher levels, and the services' centralized utilities do provide for the more disadvantaged neighbourhoods. The problems of these neighbourhoods are

---

12) Non-governmental institutions and extra-market negotiations are central to institutional economics, as well as to anthropologists, sociologists and political scientists.

13) The participatory appraisal was carried out by Save the Children, Jakarta, as part of a study of methods of household and community-level environmental assessment. These examples are taken from a summary in a report to the UNCHS/World Bank/UNDP Urban Management Programme by Charles Surjadi and Rahmadi Purwana.

often compounded by the fact that standard utility services are oriented towards providing services to well defined households, rather than negotiating with and serving ill-defined groups of households and communities.[14] Moreover, the engineers who dominate utilities are naturally loath to treat the manner in which their services are employed, and consequences they cannot directly control, as reflecting on their own performance. For almost a century, since household services became the norm in affluent cities, the professionalism of environmental engineers has been based on the premise that providing environmental amenities is a technical matter, best undertaken at a remove from politics and public negotiation. Changing this attitude is difficult and in some circumstances could have unfortunate consequences. Means must be found to make utilities more responsive to the complex needs of low income communities.[15] How this is best achieved, however, is likely to vary from place to place. Often it may be more appropriate to support intermediary institutions which can articulate local demands, rather than expecting the utilities themselves to foster participation.

Just as unserved neighbourhoods are likely to face local externalities and public goods problems analogous to those of the larger scale environmental problems, so also the need to understand environmental processes, so evident with respect to the large-scale environmental problems, is heightened at the local level by the absence of public services. Knowledge of both scientific principles and local specificities are important. Perhaps the most obvious gaps are more in communication than in knowledge *per se*. Local residents are often unfamiliar with basic environmental health and ecological principles, which, while they may not be important to someone living in a fully serviced home, can be critical to those who must fetch and carry water, build their own latrine, cook over smoky fires and implement their own pest control. Similarly, government officials are often woefully ignorant of conditions and practices in low income settlements which, while they may not be important if the government is simply providing standard services, can be critical if the government is to play an enabling role.

In addition to these communication gaps, both scientists and local residents face considerable uncertainty in their own areas of relative

---

14) Many poor urban households live in informal settlements that do not have a secure legal basis. Utilities are understandably apprehensive about investing in infrastructure within such settlements, and in some cases are expressly forbidden from providing any services directly.

15) Some utilities in Northern countries are making significant efforts to adapt their services to the needs of lower income households, which is a positive sign even if these needs are far less complex since individualized household services are maintained (Beecher, 1994).

strength. For example, scientists know a great deal more than laymen about the processes through which faecal-oral diseases are transmitted, but leading experts can only guess that food contamination accounts for somewhere between 15 and 70 per cent of diarrhoeas (Esrey and Feachem, 1989) and do not know whether flies are a major or relatively insignificant transmission mechanism (Chavasse et al, 1994). This uncertainty reflects both the inherent complexity of the subject, but also the dearth of serious and well funded research efforts attempting to break new ground in this field. Alternatively, local residents can learn a great deal about their own local environment in a relatively short time through participatory research efforts (Mitlin and Thompson, 1995). As regards more formal local knowledge, traditional schooling provides very little in the way of education on local environmental problems and, even using existing teaching techniques, could cover such issues far more thoroughly.

For far too long household environmental problems, such as inadequate water and sanitation, were portrayed as part of an old agenda which had simply not been completed. Now, the development establishment is actively constructing new approaches for addressing water supply, sanitation and environmental sustainability in the South (Serageldin, 1994). However, it is still common to portray the local environmental problems of the poor as part of a relatively 'easy' agenda, the more serious challenge arising from the broader sustainability issues (Serageldin, 1994:25). It would be more accurate to say the local environmental problems of the poor are relatively 'easy' to misdiagnose or ignore.

For many years it was received wisdom that problems of household water and sanitation were public health issues, which the private sector with its commercial orientation could not be expected to address. While the critique of the private sector was based on experience, the implicit assumption that the public sector could be relied on to address these problems has proved presumptuous. Now, it is common to argue that a more commercial orientation to the pricing and delivery of environmental services, and more generally shifts back along the public–private axis, will help provide the poor with better environmental services. In the words of a recent paper on water supply, sanitation and Agenda 21 by two senior World Bank officials (Briscoe and Garn, 1995): 'If financing policies can be "got right", all of the other key sector issues – involvement of users, the assignment of responsibility for different actions to "the appropriate level", the development of accountable institutions, appropriate standards, technology and service selection – will more readily fall into place.'

There are three major problems with this view once one moves away from the simple world of household services and into neighbourhoods where services are shared and water and sanitation conditions are closely intertwined with a wide range of other local environmental problems. First, it is far from clear how financing policies are to be 'got right,' despite a multitude of examples of how they can be 'got wrong'. It is particularly difficult to see how local finances are to be generated without having first determined, for example, how the users who share the environmental amenities will be involved, and how responsibilities will be assigned. Second, neither water nor sanitation form coherent sectors whose key issues can be defined. It is the expensive, and in many cases unaffordable, infrastructure that allows water and sanitation to be sectoralized. Third, even accepting that the financing could be solved and the other sector issues defined, the problems of participation, accountability and the like are not going to fall into place. Indeed, the financial crisis of Southern utilities is more a symptom than a cause of the lack of participation and accountability.

CONCLUSION

A focus on sustainability implies a concern to avoid practices which, while perhaps superficially acceptable in the short term, undermine future possibilities. As such, sustainability is not as central to the environmental problems of the urban poor as it is to those of the affluent. In the more disadvantaged neighbourhoods, the environmental burdens are more local, more immediate and a more direct threat to health: the problem is not so much that these burdens cannot be sustained as that they ought not be sustained. There are systematic tendencies for sustainability to become more of an issue with respect to the more diffuse, delayed and indirect environmental burdens of affluence. Even within what is conventionally designated as the South, these tendencies are evident. Thus, the results of recent case studies indicate that regional sustainability issues are more pressing in Jakarta and São Paulo than in Accra, and within Accra the household-level problems are clearly worse in low-income neighbourhoods, while city-wide burdens are more evident in the lifestyles of the affluent. São Paulo, the most affluent and largest of the three cities, has a greater concentration of polluting activities, but has also made more progress in controlling city-level pollution.

While environmental sustainability may not be a priority concern, poor urban neighbourhoods do often face complexes of environmental hazards, which, far from being simple problems to be overcome with technology transfer or more efficient markets, require political mobilization and scientific and institutional innovation. These environmental hazards can include, for example, insufficient and poor quality water, poor sanitation, microbial food contamination, local accumulations of solid waste, insect infestation and smoky kitchens. In the absence of household-level environmental services, such hazards become closely interconnected and create externalities, public goods, common property problems, problems of decision-making under severe uncertainty and other problems more commonly associated with large-scale environmental burdens.

History has shown that under normal circumstances commercial pressures do not motivate the private sector to provide adequate environmental amenities in low-income areas. It has also shown that under normal circumstances political pressures do not motivate the public sector to provide low income neighbourhoods with adequate environmental amenities either. Real improvements are likely to come not from shifting responsibilities back and forth between public and private sectors, but from measures that make actors in both sectors more responsive to environmental concerns, especially local concerns.

References

Amis, P (1995a) 'Employment Creation or Environmental Improvements: A Literature Review of Urban Poverty and Policy in India', *Habitat International*, 19 (4), pp 485–97

— (1995b) 'Making Sense of Urban Poverty', *Environment and Urbanization*, 7 (1), pp 145–57

Amuzu, A T and J Leitmann (1994) 'Accra', *Cities*, 11 (1), pp 5–9

Anton, D J (1993) *Thirsty Cities: Urban Environments and Water Supply in Latin America*, Ottawa, International Development Research Centre, 197pp

Bairoch, P (1988) *Cities and Economic Development: From the Dawn of History to the Present*, London, Mansell Publishing, 574pp

Bapat, M and N Crook (1984) 'The Environment, Health and Nutrition: An Analysis of Interrelationships from a Case Study of Hutment Settlements in the City of Poona', *Habitat International*, 8 (3/4), pp 115–26

Beecher, J A (1994) 'Water Affordability and Alternatives to Service Disconnection', *Journal American Water Works Association*, 86 (10), pp 61–72

Benneh, G, J Songsore, J S Nabila, A T Amuzu, K A Tutu, Y Yangyuoru and G McGranahan (1993) *Environmental Problems and the Urban Household in the Greater Accra Metropolitan Area (GAMA) Ghana*, Stockholm Environment Institute, Stockholm

Berman, S (1991) 'Epidemiology of Acute Respiratory Infections in Children of Developing Countries', *Reviews of Infectious Diseases*, 13 (6), pp 455–62

Bradley, D, S Cairncross, T Harpham and C Stephens (1991) *A Review of Environmental Health Impacts in Developing Country Cities*, Urban Management Program Discussion Paper no 6, World Bank/UNDP/UNCHS, Washington DC, 58pp

Briscoe, J and H A Garn (1995) 'Financing Water Supply and Sanitation under Agenda 21', *Natural Resources Forum*, 19 (1), pp 59–70

Briscoe, J and A Steer (1993) 'New Approaches to Sanitation: A Process of Structural Learning', *Ambio*, 22 (7), pp 456–9

Cairncross, S and R G Feachem (1993) *Environmental Health Engineering in the Tropics: An Introductory Text*, John Wiley & Sons, Chichester, 306pp

Cairncross, S and J Kinnear (1992) 'Elasticity of Demand for Water in Khartoum, Sudan', *Social Science and Medicine*, 2, pp 183–9

Chavasse, D C, U Blumenthal and P Kolsky (1994) 'Fly Control in Prevention of Diarrhoeal Disease' (letter to editor), *The Lancet*, 344, pp 1231

Chen, B H, C J Hong, M R Pandey and K R Smith (1990) 'Indoor Air Pollution in Developing Countries', *World Health Statistics Quarterly*, 43, pp 127–38

Chivian, E, M McCally, H Hu and A Haines (eds) (1993) *Critical Condition: Human Health and the Environment*, MIT Press, Cambridge, Massachusetts, 244pp

Crane, R (1994) 'Water Markets, Market Reform and the Urban Poor: Results from Jakarta, Indonesia', *World Development*, 22 (1), pp 71–83

Dasgupta, P (1993) *An Inquiry into Wellbeing and Destitution,* Oxford University Press, Oxford, 662pp

Douglas, I (1983) *The Urban Environment,* Edward Arnold, London, 229pp

Douglass, M (1989) 'The Environmental Sustainability of Development', *Third World Planning Review,* 11(2), pp 211–38

Esrey, S A and R G Feachem (1989) *Interventions for the Control of Diarrhoeal Diseases among Young Children: Promotion of Food Hygiene,* WHO/CDD no 89.30, World Health Organization, Geneva

Ewald, P W (1993) 'The Evolution of Virulence', *Scientific American*, April, pp 56–62

— (1994) *Evolution of Infectious Disease,* Oxford University Press, New York, 298pp

Graham, N M H (1990) 'The Epidemiology of Acute Respiratory Infections in Children and Adults: A Global Perspective', *Epidemiologic Reviews*, 12, pp 149–78

Grossman, G M and A B Krueger (1995) 'Economic Growth and the Environment', *Quarterly Journal of Economics*, 110, pp 353–78

Hamlin, C (1990) *A Science of Impurity: Water Analysis in Nineteenth Century Britain*, Adam Hilger, Bristol, 342pp

Hardoy, J E, S Cairncross and D Satterthwaite (eds) (1990) *The Poor Die Young: Housing and Health in Third World Cities*, Earthscan Publications, London, 309pp

Hardoy, J E, D Mitlin and D Satterthwaite (1992) *Environmental Problems in Third World Cities,* Earthscan, London, 302pp

Harpham, T, T Lusty and P Vaughan (eds) (1988) *In the Shadow of the City: Community Health and the Urban Poor*, Oxford University Press, Oxford, 237pp

Holtz-Eakin, D and T M Selden (1995) 'Stoking the Fires? CO_2 Emissions and Economic Growth', *Journal of Public Economics*, 57, pp 85–101

Huttly, S R A (1990) 'The Impact of Inadequate Sanitary Conditions on Health in Developing Countries', *World Health Statistics Quarterly*, 43 (3), pp 118–26

Jackson, T (ed) (1993) *Clean Production Strategies*, Lewis Publishers, Boca Raton, Florida, 415pp

Jacobi, P (1995) *Environmental Problems Facing the Urban Household in the City of São Paulo, Brazil*, Stockholm Environment Institute, Stockholm

Ladd, B (1990) *Urban Planning and Civic Order in Germany, 1860–1914,* Harvard University Press, Cambridge, Massachusetts, 326pp

Leitmann, J (1993) *Rapid Urban Environmental Assessment: Lessons from Cities in the Developing World (Volume 2: Tools and Outputs)*, Urban Management and the Environment no 15, World Bank, Washington DC

Lovei, L and Whittington, D (1993) 'Rent-Extracting Behavior by Multiple Agents in the Provision of Municipal Water Supply: A Study of Jakarta, Indonesia', *Water Resources Research*, 29 (7), pp 1965–74

Luckin, B (1986) *Pollution and Control: A Social History of the Thames in the Nineteenth Century*, Adam Hilger, Bristol, 198pp

McGranahan, G (1993) 'Household Environmental Problems in Low-Income Cities: An Overview of Problems and Prospects for Improvement', *Habitat International*, 17 (2), 105–21

McGranahan, G and A Kaijser (1993) *Household Energy: Problems, Policies and Prospects*, EED Report no 19, Stockholm Environment Institute, Stockholm

McGranahan, G and J Songsore (1994) 'Wealth, Health and the Urban Household: Weighing Environmental Burdens in Accra, Jakarta, and São Paulo', *Environment*, 36 (6), pp 4–11, 40–5

Mitlin, D and J Thompson (1995) 'Participatory Approaches in Urban Areas: Strengthening Civil Society or Reinforcing the Status Quo?', *Environment and Urbanization*, 7 (1), pp 231–50

Moser, C O N (1995) 'Urban Social Policy and Poverty Reduction', *Environment and Urbanization*, 7 (1), pp 159–71

Mosley, W H, J L Bobadilla and D T Jamison (1993) 'The Health Transition: Implications for Health Policy in Developing Countries', in D T Jamison, W H Mosley, A R Measham and J L Bobadilla (eds) *Disease Control Priorities in Developing Countries*, Oxford University Press for the World Bank, Oxford, pp 673–99

Munasinghe, M (1992) *Water Supply and Environmental Management: Developing World Applications*, Westview Press, Boulder, Colorado, 447pp

— (1993) *Environmental Economics and Sustainable Development*, World Bank Environment Paper no 3, World Bank, Washington DC

Niemczynowicz, J (1993) 'New Aspects of Sewerage and Water Technology', *Ambio*, 22 (7), pp 449–55

Oliveira, C N E and J Leitmann (1994) 'São Paulo', *Cities*, 11 (1), pp 10–14

Pickering, H (1985) 'Social and Environmental Factors Associated with Diarrhoea and Growth in Young Children: Child Health in Urban Africa', *Social Science and Medicine*, 2 1(2), pp 121–7

Rakodi, C (1991) 'Women's Work or Household Strategies?', *Environment and Urbanization*, 3 (2), pp 39–45

— (1995) 'Poverty Lines or Household Strategies? A Review of Conceptual Issues in the Study of Urban Poverty', *Habitat International*, 19 (4), pp 407–26

Rismianto, D and W Mak (1993) 'Environmental Aspects of Groundwater Abstraction in Dki Jakarta: Changing Views', *Report*, Jakarta, 13pp

ROG/UNDP/UNCHS (1989) *Environmental Study of Accra Metropolitan Area*, Final Report, Town and Country Planning Department, Accra Planning and Development Programme, Accra

Satterthwaite, D (1993) 'The Impact on Health of Urban Environments', *Environment and Urbanization*, 5 (2), 87–111

Schell, L M, M T Smith and A Bilsborough (eds) (1993) *Urban Ecology and Health in the Third World*, Cambridge University Press, Cambridge, 287pp

Schofield, C J, R Briceno-Leon, N Kolstrup, D J T Webb and G B White (1990) 'The Role of House Design in Limiting Vector-Borne Disease', in J E Hardoy,

S Cairncross and D Satterthwaite (eds) *The Poor Die Young*, Earthscan Publications, London, pp 189–212

Selden, T M and D Song (1995) 'Neoclassical Growth, the J Curve for Abatement, and the Inverted U Curve for Pollution', *Journal of Environmental Economics and Management*, 29 (2), pp 162–8

Serageldin, I (1994) *Water Supply, Sanitation, and Environmental Sustainability: The Financing Challenge*, World Bank, Washington DC, 35pp

Shafik, N T (1995) 'Economic Development and Environmental Quality: An Econometric Analysis', *Oxford Economic Papers*, 46, pp 757–73

Shapiro, A-L (1985) *Housing the Poor of Paris, 1850–1902*, University of Wisconsin Press, Madison, 224pp

Smith, K R (1993) 'Fuel Combustion, Air Pollution Exposure, and Health: The Situation in Developing Countries', *Annual Review of Energy and the Environment*, (18), pp 529–66

Smith, K R and Y S F Lee (1993) 'Urbanization and the Environmental Risk Transition', in J D Kasarda and A M Parnell (eds) *Third World Cities: Problems, Policies, and Prospects*, Sage Publications, London, pp 161–79

Soussan, J, P O'Keefe and B Munslow (1990) 'Urban Fuelwood: Challenges and Dilemmas', *Energy Policy*, (July/August), pp 572–82

Stren, R E and R R White (eds) (1989) *African Cities in Crisis: Managing Rapid Urban Growth*, Westview Press, Boulder, Colorado, 335pp

Surjadi, C, L Padhmasutra, D Wahyuningsih, G McGranahan and M Kjellén (1994) *Household Environmental Problems in Jakarta*, Stockholm Environment Institute, Stockholm

Terblanche, A P S, I R Danford and C M E Nel (1993) 'Household Energy Use in South Africa, Air Pollution and Human Health', *Journal of Energy in Southern Africa*, (May), pp 54–7

UN (1995) *World Urbanization Prospects: The 1994 Revision: Estimates and Projections of Urban and Rural Populations and of Urban Agglomerations*, Report no ST/ESA/SER.A/150, United Nations, New York, 178pp

UNDP (1995) *Human Development Report*, United Nations Development Programme, New York

UNEP/WHO (1988) *Assessment of Urban Air Quality*, Report, World Health Organization, Geneva, 100pp

Wallgren, B (1994) 'The Principles of the Ecocycle Society', in S E A Council (ed) *On the General Principles of Environmental Protection*, Ministry of Environment and Natural Resources, Stockholm

White, R R (1994) *Urban Environmental Management: Environmental Change and Urban Design*, John Wiley & Sons, Chichester, 233pp

Wohl, A S (1983) *Endangered Lives: Public Health in Victorian Britain*, Methuen, London, 440pp

World Bank (1992) *World Development Report: Development and the Environment*, Oxford University Press, New York, 308pp

— (1993a) *Water Resources Management*, A World Bank Policy Paper, World Bank, Washington DC, 140pp

— (1993b) *World Development Report: Investing in Health*, Oxford University Press, New York, 329pp

Wratten, E (1995) 'Conceptualizing Urban Poverty', *Environment and Urbanization*, 7 (1), pp 11–36

Chapter Five

Sustainability and Sustainable Cities

Cedric Pugh

ABSTRACT

The meaning that is attributed to such terms as 'the environment', 'sustainability' and 'sustainable cities' is frequently wide ranging and not precisely defined. Nevertheless, environmental issues have been moving towards the top of social and political agendas at local, regional and international levels since the mid-1980s. At international levels this was marked by the United Nations Conference on Environment and Development (UNCED), Rio de Janeiro, June 1992. Since the Rio de Janeiro international meeting, both policy makers and professionals have been addressing questions of 'meaning', 'conceptual basis', 'policy' and 'implementation' associated with the environment, sustainability and sustainable cities. This chapter provides a review and interpretation of the significant concepts, principles and developments. It reveals both the continuities of intellectual ideas and the ways disciplines such as economics are changing in the process of bringing the environment into their scope. This review of the relevant issues also indicates policy developments in the implementation of the idea of 'sustainable cities', and it brings to significance some critical commentaries on the roles of institutions and markets. In its explanation and reviews of concepts, meaning and implementation, this chapter connects environmentalism to basic theory in economics and in institutions. The theory is introduced and elaborated in a developmental way, and some of the more abstract explanations are set out in the notes and annex sections at the end of the chapter.

INTRODUCTION

The intellectual literature on sustainability and its application to cities has burgeoned during the 1990s, and internationally significant policies and programmes have commenced. One example of policy and programme development is in Dar es Salaam, Tanzania, where since 1991 the United Nations Centre for Human Settlements (UNCHS) (Habitat) has entered into agreements with the Tanzanian government under the 'Sustainable Cities Programme' in the joint UNCHS–World Bank–UN Development Programme (UNDP) Urban Management Programme (UMP). The commencement of applied policies has more significance than its indication of the relevance of environmentalism. It also enlarges the process whereby some high-minded but ill-defined ideas in the cause for environmentalism become operationally useful, with the associated intellectual principles becoming more concrete and clearer within operations. In fact it is enlightening to examine the transformations of ideas in the relationships between theory and advocacy on the one hand and policy and practice on the other.

The relationships between theory, advocacy and practice are seldom straightforward. They require explorations and exposition in both historical and conceptual scope to establish meaning, principle and relevance. And, in order to secure a focus upon the essentials, it is appropriate to be selective in the issues and questions which could be explored in an inherently wide ranging subject. For present purposes, the questions which form the framework and thematic intent of this chapter are selected as:

- In the early phases of post-1990 relevance, what is to be understood by the ideas of sustainability and their application to urban living conditions, especially for developing countries?
- How have the principles in environmentalism been influencing changes in conceptual ideas in economics and other social sciences? Also, what principles are being selected from the inherited theories and findings in social science for developing specialization in environmental studies within urban studies?
- With sustainable cities in the early phases of applied policy development, what are the first phase characteristics of policy and practice?
- In historical context, modern environmentalism enters an international political arena of dominant economic and political liberalism: but the policy implications of environmentalism have some basic requirements for markets, governments, bureaucracies, non-governmental organizations (NGOs), community-based organizations (CBOs) and households. Having these two conditions in mind,

it then becomes relevant to consider the prescription and practice of environmentalism within late twentieth-century liberalism. What are the main compatibilities and potential conflicts?

The discussions are organized around the foregoing thematic statements and questions. They commence with a broad historical and conceptual review of the idea of sustainability. Urban relevance is introduced into the broader notions of sustainability. This is followed by some expositions and commentaries on the first phases of practice in cities in developing countries. From this perspective it is then possible to identify the major emerging issues. Emerging issues usually point up some fundamental matters of theory and practice which were not contemplated in earlier advocacies and policy documents, for example in the Agenda 21 document of the UNCED meeting in 1992. Thus, the discussions turn towards some theory and some 'lessons from experience' in the economic and institutional requirements of modern environmentalism.

THE HISTORY

Environmental issues first significantly entered the UN agenda in 1962, and at that time they were mainly related to relevance and conditions in the industrialized countries. But by 1972 – marked by the Stockholm Conference on the Human Environment – environmental issues became internationalized, bringing developing countries into significance.

The significance amounted to much more than just adding other countries to the environmental agenda. It signified that the agenda and the route to solutions required global as well as localized and regionalized perspectives. The very nature of environmental issues brought to the fore the economic and political relationships between the industrialized and the developing countries. Globalized environmental interaction certainly had internationalized spatial relevance: but it also raised issues associated with the unequal conditions in which wealthier and poorer nations enter an increasingly dominant international political economy. International cooperation became a necessity, and the agenda would include the economic, political and social relations among nations at different stages of economic development.

Internationalization was not the only feature of added complexity to environmentalism. What is to be understood and pursued in policy as 'the environmental' has also been changing since 1972. In the context of the OPEC crises of 1973/4 and 1979/80, the matter of energy use and efficiency rose in importance among the various elements that are 'environmental'. However, in a short time of a decade or so, other elements of 'environmental' significance also had claims for greater attention. Collectively these various elements – examples being ozone layer depletion, degradations of natural resources among the rural poor in some developing countries, and vulnerabilities of life and death in squatter settlements in cities in developing countries – all, in effect, brought environmentalism into increased importance. Also, it became obvious that the changing set of complex issues could not be addressed simply from a bounded and compartmentalized notion of 'the environment'. Most of the major elements within the changing set are inextricably linked in cause–consequence–feedback relationships with economic development, with patterns of wealth and poverty, with 'survival' and 'profligate' conditions of economic production and consumption, and with the way humans organize their societies and develop institutional relationships in economics and politics. All of this has implications in applying notions of sustainability to economic development and to cities. In varied proportions and in contrasting contexts, nations, sub-global regions and national regions and localities have configurated mixtures of production, consumption, affluence and poverty, and they always fall within characteristic and varied patterns of institutions, organization and governance. A wide ranging multipurpose agenda of 'environmentalism' also indicated some necessities to adjust and reform institutional, organizational and governmental conditions.

The aforementioned Stockholm conference led to the founding of the United Nations Environment Programme (UNEP) in December 1972. Thus UNEP has had some two decades to develop its roles, its international persuasions on environmental issues, its collaboration with national governments, its programmes and its theory and practice of environmentalism. International organizations such as UNEP can be understood and interpreted through 'regime theory' (Grieco, 1993; Karns, and Mingst 1990; Williams, 1994). Regime theory views international organizations as mediation between general principles (for example environmentalism) on the one hand and influence upon implementing organizations such as governments, bureaucracies and (environmental) agencies on the other. They secure their legitimacy and authority from their mandates, their activities and their success in persuading some consensus in the development of ideas, practices, reforms and effective results. The activities of UNEP include publications, international meetings, securing international agreements on environmental matters, the provision of technical aid and monitoring services, and related work. For recent contextual relevance, UNEP has collaborated with various UN agencies, the World Bank and the International Monetary Fund (IMF) in broadcasting the idea of sustainability. It has also been instrumental in the preparations, in the agenda setting and in the programmatic possibilities arising from the UNCED Rio de Janeiro meeting in 1992. As indicated in earlier discussion, the case for the environment has represented changing concepts and content, with UNEP being both a promoter and a reactor to change. As an expression of regime theory, UNEP has created sets of rules, implicit norms, and procedures which influence relationships among organizations and nations, along with informal cooperation and regularized activities. For example, UNEP collaborates with the UNDP and the World Bank in formulating and developing the global environment facility (GEF), which addresses problems in global warming, biodiversity, ozone depletion and the pollution of international waters. UNEP focuses on scientific monitoring and the promotion of international environmental law, influencing national policy developments among nations.

In the 1990s UNEP and the UNCHS have moved into closer organizational linkage and collaboration. This both reflects and promotes the relevance of conditions in human settlements as having environmental impact and importance. Among the relevant conditions are the particularly important ones of insanitary conditions in large proportions of low-income settlements in cities in developing countries, air pollution from some manufacturing processes and motor vehicle emissions into the atmosphere. Consequently, the cause for environmentalism has simultaneously included the 'green' agenda (for nature) and the 'brown' agenda (for the elimination of adverse urban health impacts). The 'brown' has some causal consequences for the 'green'. As the 'brown' agenda led to greater attention in intellectual thinking and policy making on environmental agendas, so the meaning of sustainability widened and deepened. In the context of human settlements the idea of sustainability had to cover a range of economic, political and financial issues. It was not simply a matter of correcting physical environmental adversity. Sustainability had relevance to such matters as the costs and benefits of correction, the managerial and financial capability of localized government agencies to maintain viable systems of public finance to resource environmental improvement, and the economic development of cities. Also, since the localized and wider governance of cities was usually multi-institutional, issues of jurisdictional coherence and localized cooperation became important. The application of the idea of sustainability portended more than it seemed, and certainly a growing complexity in the evolution of environmentalism.

The idea of sustainability had fundamental importance in the 1987 Brundtland Report (WCED, 1987). 'Sustainability' accelerated the change in thinking in environmentalism. For example, relevance was extended to 'renewable' and 'substitutable' resources, as well as to the earlier attentiveness to 'exhaustible' resources. This kind of change in thinking widened the environmental sphere in intellectual and practised economics: concerns and applications had to be related to economic development as a whole, not just to efficiencies in energy-related resources. Changes in thinking also contributed to the growing realization that a new international impetus was required in environmentalism. The Norwegian prime minister, Brundtland, who had headed the World Commission on Environment and Development (WCED), along with other political leaders, herself became an active advocate for significant international focus. Consequently, UNEP undertook preparations for a UN conference, supported and mandated by UN resolution 44/228 in 1989. Thus, the idea of sustainability had a significant international forum, set for the 1992 UNCED meeting in Rio de Janeiro. The conference would have a 'prepared' and an 'added' agenda. The prepared agenda would consist of the range of elements that were significant in the expression of environmentalism in the late 1980s. These elements would include such considerations as:

- climatic change;
- increased pollution;
- matters relating to soil, agriculture and forestry;
- plants in a changing environment;
- oceans as a habitat and a resource;
- energy use and its effects;
- industry and the environment;
- conservation and wildlife;
- toxic chemicals and hazardous wastes;
- health problems in 'brown' and 'green' agendas;
- human settlements in their environmental significance;
- information, education and publicity on environmentalism;
- policy and management in environmental improvement;
- legal reform and the environment; and
- monitoring and assessment of environmental performance.

Clearly the prepared agenda contained diverse, wide ranging and complex elements. 'Sustainability' could be set as the unifying basis, especially as substantial physical and economic interdependence prevailed among the various elements. At Rio de Janeiro an 'added' agenda came into prominence, and itself significantly influenced the way sustainability was to be institutionalized and pursued as an international political activity. Leaders from developing countries were ready to argue the cause for economic development and for social justice between the 'first' and the 'third' worlds in the allocation of the costs and burdens implied by international environmentalism. Third World leaders took a strong position against 'environmental neocolonialism'. Comparative inequality, poverty and national affordabilities were brought to heightened relevance, with consequences for post-Rio developments and programmes in environmentalism.

The foregoing indicates the drawing together of the scientific, the political and the evolving historical in environmentalism and sustainability. The merging of these aspects is also implied by some of the elements on the 'prepared' agenda for the UNCED meeting. Items such as education, legal reform, economic reform and conditions of life in human settlements are significantly tied to theoretical and pragmatic political economy. Environmentalism was in essence a political economy with scientific, technical, economic, social and political relevance. It would thus be controversial, in conflict with other social and international priorities, and it would have a fluctuating attention in accordance with the changing dynamics of policy issues in national and international political agendas. At the intellectual levels of developments in theory, techniques, ideas and research, it is not surprising that the intellectualism of environmentalism is inextricably mixed into social, historical and political processes. These are precisely the circumstances that are reasoned and explained in the modern philosophies of science and social science: Kuhn (1970) created a 'growth of knowledge' theory which is based upon the interrelationship between the intellectual, the social and the historical. Environmentalism is a prime example of this, and the 1992 UNCED meeting was especially significant for taking this kind of interpretation.

The UNCED meeting established some important things in environmentalism, including some for urban policy and for human settlements. First, it created a significant document and report (Quarrie, 1992). Second, some general principles were set for ongoing international, national and intellectual agendas on environmentalism. These are expressed in Agenda 21, the report, with its advocacies and informational content. Agenda 21 was to be regarded as a 'comprehensive programme for sustainable development', an 'investment in the future' and a preliminary statement of the 'environmental rights' of citizens throughout the world. Third, in the elements in environmentalism each had an argued rationale, a statement of policy relevance and an indication of necessary actions and activities. Fourth, UNCED was used as a basis for follow-up and monitoring on the progress of Agenda 21. The follow-up and monitoring was brought under the authority of a (new) UN Commission on Sustainable Development, created in 1993. The commission would cooperate with UNEP, which had developed its role primarily as a 'coordinator and catalyst' among relevant UN agencies, environmental groups, environmental professions and national governments. The monitoring of Agenda 21 would consolidate the coordination and catalyst roles. Finally, from the perspective of relevance in this chapter, Agenda 21 contained policy-relevant statements on human settlements. These were in Chapter 7 of Agenda 21, but other chapters, for example on poverty, health, legal reform, education and economic instruments were also relevant to human settlements.

'Promoting Sustainable Human Settlement' was the heading to Chapter 7 of Agenda 21. The chapter argued that all countries had reason to address their urban development needs with environmentalism aforethought in their reviews of policies, institutions and programmes. Information was set out on average government expenditure ratios on social and urban allocations relative to total public-sector spending. Some prevailing international initiatives were revised, including the Global Strategy for Shelter (GSS), the UMP and the Healthy Cities Project (HCP), with intent to bring sustainability more conspicuously into these initiatives. The discourse in Chapter 7 recognized the relevance of multi-objective and multi-institutional realities in human settlements, accordingly promoting the ideas of institutional partnerships, citizen participation and innovative approaches in urban planning and urban economic development. Also, much was made of creating international networks among cities to promote 'good practice' in urban sustainability and to achieve 'good governance' in general and for environmentalism. The application of 'sustainability' was identified in housing, urban management, land policy and land management, infrastructure, energy and transport, and disaster-prone areas. In subsequent discussions of recent relevant research some of the principles and dilemmas in the agenda on human settlements are clarified and brought to relevance in policy development.

Although Agenda 21 had some coverage on demography, inter-national trade and anti-poverty policies, some post-1992 events have been heightening the significance of these aspects of 'sustainability'. World summits have occurred or been scheduled for population and development (Cairo, September 1994), social welfare and unemployment (Denmark, 1995) and human settlements (Habitat II, Istanbul 1996). The summits will all include considerations of poverty-related environ-mentalism and relevance to economic development. In the process, 'sustainability' will widen and deepen, become more complex and attract new intellectual ideas into its scope and application. Also, international trade has become more significant, consequent upon the North American Free Trade Agreement (NAFTA) between the USA, Canada, and Mexico in 1993. NAFTA contains negotiated provisions on environmental standards in economic production, all within the political aim to try to make for 'fairer trade relations' between industrialized and developing countries. This will make such controversial considerations of wider relevance in trade, particularly in the work of the World Trade Organization (WTO), which commenced activities in 1995, authorized by the Uruguay round of GATT. The significance of Agenda 21 has also been taken up by the international private sector. In 1993, the International Chamber of Commerce created the World Industry Council for the Environment (WICE). WICE is comprised of some 90 of the world's leading companies with aims to promote environmental issues and to seek good policy solutions, with links to the relevant UN agencies and the OECD. In its first phases of policy development, WICE has set up task forces on cooperation in environmental technology and on trade-relevant environmental issues. All of this is indicative of the themes argued in this chapter, centrally that 'sustainability' has evolution, change and a growing complexity.

SUSTAINABILITY AND SOME APPLICATIONS

As suggested by Houghton and Hunter (1994), in application the idea of sustainable development can range from 'strong' to 'weak' versions. Strong versions would be based upon environmentalism as fundamentalism. They would include an approach to economic development that commenced from a position of uncompromised restraint on the use of some resources, for example on those resources regarded as necessary 'environmental capital'. That would lead to basic reformulation of production, consumption and ways of life. A weaker environmental political economy would, by contrast, emphasize the adaptation of the status quo, this being argued as feasible, realistic and adequate. Such reforms as are implied by the weaker political economy would include re-regulation of economic activity, the use of taxes and incentives to modify production and consumption, attention to property rights to achieve some conservation and protection, and the introduction of impact assessments with related fees where development impinged adversely on environmental capacity. All of these possibilities in reform could be applied to human settlements, though with some likely conflicts of interest and difficulty in achieving effectiveness in some jurisdictions. Also, with circumspection, it would be recognized that the necessary packages of reforms would take some time and experience in 'learning by doing'. This would be particularly so in some countries in the transitions from socialism to market-based economies and among developing countries where the inherited institutions and legal systems have gaps, some

characteristic unwieldy features, and a lack of civic association attached
to environmentalism. These matters have been well argued by McAuslan
(1994) taking a perspective on urban-related legal reform. Societies have
to learn the application of environmentalism to policy, to economic
instruments and to the formulation and revision of relevant law. They
also have to develop their indigenous relevance, with the importation of
external institutional arrangements seldom working to good effect.

In application, the idea of sustainability raises the significance of
distributional equity in the direction of benefits and in the obligations to
bear the costs. Earlier discussions revealed this relevance at the UNCED
meeting in 1992. However, the dimensions of distributional equity
include more than the international relations between rich and poor
nations. They have relevance among social groups within nations, and
they have localized–regionalized significance. Some of this significance
has spatial dimensions. The spatial dimensions have two crucial
elements. First, the poor are generally more adversely affected by environmental deterioration than other groups. Second, environmental
conditions have more or less impact in spatial terms. For example, broad
spatial impacts emanate from motor vehicle emissions in urban contexts,
less broad (though still significant spatially) from many industrial air
pollutants, and more localized intensities from insanitary squatter and
slum housing and environmental conditions. The social and spatial
aspects are often interactive in causal and consequential ways. From distributional and economic perspectives, in formulating policies for
adjustment and correction some notion and application of the principle
of 'compensation' becomes relevant. In application, compensation could
be used for those who are required to restrain their resource use where
this has adverse third party consequences. And, it has relevance to the
conditions for survival among groups living in extreme poverty. Finally,
the question of environmentalism has intergenerational relevance to a
greater extent than in many other spheres of public policy. Pigou (1932),
who was one of the leading authors in developing the subject of 'welfare
economics', established the significance of 'myopic' characteristics in the
workings of industrialized economies. 'Myopia' is the relegation of long-
to short-term economic (and political) results: this can occur in both
capitalist and socialist political economies.

The spatial application of sustainability has brought land use and
spatial planning into significance for development and reform. Substantial rather than peripheral reform is implied. Some expressions of
town/urban planning do not take either economic development or
environmentalism as their central and interrelated purposes. In other
words, they often have only loose or fortuitous reference to 'sustainability' as this would be understood, for example in Agenda 21 of the

UNCED report. This means that 'environmental rights' (and limitations) have to be formulated and directly written into land policies for both urban and rural application. In fact, the 'rural' and the 'urban' are less separable under economic and environmental sustainability. Environmental cause–consequence relationships, and their spatial effects, do not observe rural and urban boundaries, however these are specifically defined. And, especially for developing countries, the transition towards modernization has economic interdependence between agricultural, industrial, and urbanized aspects of modernization. For example, Fei, Ranis and Ohkawa (Fei and Ranis, 1964; Fei et al, 1985) established a theory and statistical reasoning to explain why such countries as South Korea and Taiwan achieved an effective symbiosis in agricultural change. These countries formulated economic policies that expanded markets for cash crops, thus simultaneously reforming property rights in land aimed at increasing productivity. Land policy reforms broke the negative elements in (absentee) landlording in landlord–tenant relations and substituted positive elements aimed at limiting disincentives in rent contracts and allocating 'land to the tiller'. Consequently, the agricultural sector provided flows of saving, investment and finance, which contributed to the necessary high capital requirements of urbanization. Environmental agendas will similarly be dependent upon reforms in property rights and maintaining incentives for developmental growth and appropriate capital investment in infrastructure and environmentally friendly technology.

Although these discussions of sustainability in application have not been comprehensive, they have been sufficient to indicate that the relationships between economic development and the environment are fundamental in causal and consequential interdependence. This leads on to the ways in which economics may change it its scope and its conceptual foundations with environmental matters having a direct impact. Also, economists are being led into the adaptation of inherited ideas in orthodox theories and techniques. The relevant scope is wide, with particular significance to macroeconomic and structural adjustment reforms, to market-state interaction, to the contradictory 'private' and 'public' elements[1] in environmental improvement, to the valuation of environ-

---

1) 'Public elements' in goods and services are explained in the theory of public finance. The literature in public finance in the 1950 to 1970 period deepened and elaborated principles of externality and 'public goods' from their earlier discussions in nineteenth-century economic theory in continental Europe and by Pigou (1932). Some of the major 1950–70 contributions were made by Buchanan (1968), Buchanan and Tullock (1962), Musgrave (1959), Olson (1962), and Samuelson (reprinted in Houghton 1973). Also, see footnotes 3 and 5 below, along with the annex which elaborates Coase's theories.

mental benefits, to property rights and to techniques for assessing the environmental impact of development. These matters are elaborated below, with attention to conceptual issues.

CONCEPTUAL SIGNIFICANCE IN ECONOMICS

The foregoing commentaries have shown that the very idea of sustainability has necessarily led to some basic rethinking of the environment and its relationship to the economy. Thus it is not surprising that economics as a discipline has commenced some reconceptualization and extension of its basic principles. Also, as will be discussed, economists have been finding large significance in applying some inherited principles to the environment. Since 1987 intellectual work has been going on in economics and the natural sciences to develop 'building blocks', which will contribute to establishing a more comprehensive theory of the environment. Some of the building blocks include the aforementioned attention to relevant matters in property rights, in the relationships between markets and institutions, in assessing the incentives and disincentives that are economically unfriendly to the environment, and to altering the way economists view 'nature' and use it in their theoretical constructs. Orthodox economics has often regarded environmental resources as 'given' (ie exogenously derived in theory building) and thereby not being brought into full explanation and significance. New work on environmental economics (for example Turner and Pearce, 1990; Pearce and Warford, 1993) changes all this. Instead of economists adopting linear models of inputs–processes–outputs, they are now more perceptively aware of feedback loops connecting economic systems and natural environmental systems. The feedback loops are based on systems' interactions, change and nonlinear conceptualization. 'Resources' are thus understood as comprising more than labour, capital and land. The appraisal of capital can include the physical (for example machines), the human (for example education and health) and the environmental (for example renewable, substitutable and exhaustible resources). One important aspect of sustainability is to maintain stocks of physical, human and environmental capital. More than this, the creation of effective reform in property rights and institutions can be regarded as investment activity, creating effectiveness in sustainable development.

The rethinking can be used in various applied techniques and methods of appraisal. For example, cost-benefit analysis, which has a long history of application to urban development, can be adapted for incorporating 'environmental capital' into its rates of return calculations.[2] It can also be extended from social efficiency appraisals to evaluations of the distributional impact of environmental costs and benefits among the poor, the rich, and also with spatially bounded classification of impacts. Also, some recently developed techniques for appraising development impacts upon the urban infrastructure can be extended to environmental applications. One such technique is 'development impact extraction'. This operates by defining a 'carrying capacity' in the prevailing systems of urban infrastructure services, and then calculating the impact of a development proposal on the costs and benefits to the community (Johnson, 1990). Such calculations can then be used as a basis for levying 'extraction fees' for financing relevant development and redevelopment of infrastructure to maintain adequate levels of capacity and service provision. Although 'environmental capacity' is less readily defined than in some aspects of 'infrastructure capacity', the technique has some possibilities. It can also be regarded as a way of achieving financing that is not wholly dependent upon limited government budgets, for the developers and the users of the development project pay the relevant costs.

As a final example, reference can be made to the technique of attributing value to the several 'characteristics' or 'factors' that make up (bundled) aggregated value. In housing, various characteristics such as design, location, tenure and social functioning are contributory to the price or value, but each characteristic is hidden in its relative contribution to total value. The relevant technique is the compilation of 'hedonic indices', applying statistical regression or factor analyses. This technique can be extended to environmental measurement and appraisal. Jimenez (1982) did this in squatter settlements in the Philippines, calculating the separated values of sanitation, water, drainage and related services. He found that residents reported lower values than might be expected, leading Jimenez to the conclusion that information and education on the value of these utilities may be needed in some environmental upgrading programmes. Information and education is an important part of environmental change because the economics of information suggests that prevailing knowledge in communities is often asymmetrical, biased and distorted by political and economic processes (Eggertsson, 1990).

---

2) Edwin Chadwick (1800–90) was a major public health reformer in early industrial Britain. He used a cost-benefit analysis to argue that water and sewerage systems would produce social benefits by reducing the social costs of sickness and premature death, thereby raising economic production and productivity (see Finer, 1951; Finn, 1965; Lewis, 1952). Cost-benefit analyses greatly expanded after 1960, with urban applications in slum clearance, the rehabilitation of housing, transport, social housing, and environmental conditions.

As was mentioned, the increased significance of sustainability also has implications for the use and development of some inherited theories and ideas in economics. The relevant theories and ideas are many and varied, including adaptations in cost-benefit analyses, techniques for measuring consumers' valuations of environmental conditions, the dilemmas in reconciling private and social costs and benefits, and using regulatory frameworks and taxation to modify markets for environmental purposes. Some of this is in continuity of earlier discussion and will be further elaborated in the next section on research findings in post-1990 studies of environmental conditions in cities in developing countries. For present purposes, focus is given to some general theories and ideas that have overall significance for the particulars of adapting such things as cost-benefit analysis, the valuation of environmental conditions, and so on. Overall significance can be identified in pursuing the question of which theories and principles in economics provide explanatory power and relevance in formulating policies and actions in blending market, state and household roles for environmental improvement. The essence of environmental improvement is that it requires multi-institutional application, and that individualism and inappropriate approaches to seeking organized cooperation can have positive or negative results in the environment. This is inherently complex. Complexities are several and varied. Considerations of efficiency and social justice are intertwined; the benefits from good environments are delayed to medium- and long-term delivery; and, owing to the 'public goods' nature[3] of some of the benefits and asymmetries in information, individuals often undervalue the benefits. Thus, much depends upon creating good policy frameworks and implementing policy within carefully designed institutions and organizations.

Economic theory can address some of the inherent complexity. Coase (1960) gave attention to organizational form and state–market relationships where private and social costs and benefits diverge. The theory of 'merit goods' developed by Musgrave (1959:13–14) and Head (1974)

---

3) 'Public goods' are goods that have benefits that are captured by the wider society rather than just by individuals. They have some inherent dilemmas. Private producers cannot always recover their costs because pricing is either unfeasible or the transaction costs of imposing costs are very high, resulting in production and resource allocation impediments. Also, individuals acting in their own self interest will often understate their benefits (ie distort their expression of preference). This can arise because individuals may 'free ride', acting on the mistaken but 'rational' assumption that others will express their preferences, bear the costs of provision and consequently supply the social benefits which would occur from the 'externality' or 'publicness' inherent in the goods. Examples include elements of health, education and environmental conditions. Also, see footnote 1, above, with its references to the founding theorists, and the annex notes on transactions costs.

provides explanation and justification for modification of private and market choices where the mixed complexities of 'public goods' elements, distorted individual preferences and social equity characterize goods and services. Also, the post-1950 theory of state roles and public choice has both positive and cautionary significance in the blending of market and state roles. On grounds of both theory and performance, market and state roles can variously lead to success or failure, according to circumstances. In other words, markets can fail the environment and so can states. Whether success or failure occur largely depends upon how well policies, property rights, institutions and organizations are designed and operated. Coase's theories and principles are relevant to matters of good design and implementation in these matters. The overall perspective of the theories of Coase, Musgrave, Head and the post-1950 political economy of state–market relations can be summarized in a set of statements:

> *First*, Coase (1960) recognizes that goods with social benefits and 'publicness' (ie they have externality third-party consequences in the enjoyment of benefits) pose dilemmas for their optimal provision. Some goods with these 'externalities' can be partially provided through markets, but sometimes goods with social costs (for example pollution) will be oversupplied and those with social benefits (for example a clean environment) undersupplied relative to optimal levels of provision. In some cases the sub-optimality can be corrected by rearranging property rights through the market to increase production where there are wanted social benefits and to decrease it where there are unwanted social costs. Appropriately formulated property rights and legalities can lead to bargained outcomes among producers (and sometimes among producers and consumers), with the outcomes reflecting the market 'internalization' of social costs and benefits. But where 'externality' affects large numbers, as is the case in many environmental conditions, the private bargaining possibilities may be limited because self interest (see footnote 3) distorts or impedes private preference and bargaining. Thus, resolution is then deflected either to non-market institutions such as government and organized social groups, or to some blending of multi-organizational roles, including market participation. It is a question of achieving social cooperation through an appropriate division of labour and coordination among a variety of institutions and organizations. In Coase's theory this means the selection of institutions and organizational form on the basis of achieving efficiency in transaction costs. Transaction costs are the costs of formulating, monitoring and enforcing agreements in formal or informal relational contracting. In such spheres as land development and environmental improvement, relational contracting can

be very complicated and highly involved, though necessary for
effective results. For relevance to the environment and sustainability, Coase's theories place emphasis on creating appropriate
property rights and assessing the relative effectiveness and efficiency of alternative social arrangements in multi-institutional
conditions (for further elaboration and detail of Coase's theories
see Annex at end of this chapter).

Second, although economic theory and comparative performance in different economic systems suggests that large roles for
individualism and the private sector are justified, economic theory
contains some limited justification for overriding individualism in
some circumstances. 'Merit goods' theory as developed by Musgrave (1959:13–14) and Head (1974) has particular relevance to
sustainability and the environment. Some of the physical processes
in environmental conditions, for both degradation and improvement, are slow, long-term and difficult to isolate in terms of exact
causes and consequences. That is to say, the merits from improvement and the demerits from degradation are not fully enjoyed or
suffered until the long term, sometimes amounting to decades.
Also, they have distributional relevance of a special kind because
environmental change is linked to poverty, affluence (see discussions below) and intergenerational significance. These realities
combine with the 'public goods' (and 'bads') elements in environmental change, with consequences for preference distortion under
individualism. Thus, the 'merit goods' theory suggests that some
justifications exist for modifying individualism, or sometimes
overriding it, for reasons of social effectiveness and social efficiency. Modification can occur through consultative and educational processes, by way of state regulation and sometimes
through professionally legitimated activities in relationship with
government roles. Merit goods theory brings learning and leadership to relevance in preference formation and in changing
adversely distorted preferences in individualism.

Third, two contradictory tendencies can be observed in the
political economy of state and market roles. Both markets and
states produce 'welfare' and 'diswelfare': it makes sense to argue
from theory and from comparative economic performance among
nations that market failure (or success) and government failure (or
success) can coexist. In broad evaluation, orthodox economic
theories of the state simultaneously reason that state roles are
(contingently) justified where some externalities exist, owing to
market failure, and that state roles can lead to diswelfare from
politicians and bureaucrats pursuing sectional interests and their
own interests, rather than pursuing the general public interest.
Also, in some jurisdictions, the political element in 'political
economy' will tend to support institutional arrangements that
consolidate distributional advantage to privileged groups (i e 'rent-

seeking' behaviour) rather than the enhancement of production and competitive productivity. Levine (1992) has collected a set of articles on the theory of government roles and government failure. Having regard for the contradictory elements in the orthodox economic theory of the state, at the broad level this implies that we should not be excessively optimistic on the economics and politics of liberalism (for elaboration, see Pugh, 1994). For the pursuit of environmental improvement, the implications are for care in designing and implementing multi-institutional and multi-organizational application. As revealed in the statements on Coase's theories and 'merit goods' principles, complexity is involved in multi-institutional roles, and coherent bounded limitations applies to both market and state roles. The import of this will take on more specific meanings in subsequent discussions of the progress in applying 'sustainability' to the reform of some cities in developing countries.

Coase, Musgrave and Head have formulated basic economic theories that have their primary relevance to microeconomics, property rights and selecting effective institutional conditions. However, since the early 1980s economic reform has centred around macroeconomic matters, including stabilization and structural adjustment. The macroeconomic reforms for structural adjustment have some microeconomic and sectoral relevance, especially in their pursuit of market liberalization, export-led growth, privatization and reviews of public sector budgeting. Policies for structural adjustment and stabilization have been widespread in Latin American, sub-Saharan African and (some) Asian countries. This obviously raises to significance the question of what sort of impacts such reforms have on environmental conditions and sustainability. This question has received theoretical and analytical attention from Munasinghe and Cruz (1995). These authors argue contingently that, because the reforms remove distortions, in general it can be expected that there will be both economic and environmental gains. But, as indicated, the argument is contingent. Unintended harmful effects can arise from the expansion of uncorrected social costs (for example pollution), from specific cutbacks in environmentally relevant public sector budgets, and in introducing economic reforms without first reviewing institutional conditions to ensure environmentally friendly effects. As would be expected, Munasinghe and Cruz (1995) advocate the formulation and use of 'action impact matrices' to coordinate macroeconomic and environmental reform.

The foregoing discussions have brought to heightened significance some new and inherited principles in economics. Those with major implications include Coase's theories of relational contracting and property rights, the 'merit goods' theory developed by Musgrave and Head, general political economy of state–market relationships, and review of macroeconomic impacts. These matters will be taken forward into further discussions below on the progress of research in sustainable cities, in a review of multi-institutional conditions in environmental policy, and in concluding commentaries on political economy in environmentalism. The discussions and themes developed to this juncture show that environmentalism has complexity not only in its science of cause and effect issues, but also in the ways appropriate institutions and economic reforms are designed and operated. Institutional and economic conditions are associated with theories of transaction costs, information costs, property rights, social costs and benefits, public goods, merit goods, regulation, principal–agent relationships and ways to use incentives to promote environmental improvement or disincentives to break negative relations between the environment and economic development. In fact, it is the aptness of policy spheres such as the environment, poverty, urban development, health and housing that is bringing these wide ranging and formerly fragmented theories into cohesive and interdependent relevance. A new literature reflecting the cohesion and the relevance is emerging (for example see Eggertsson, 1990). As reasoned by Kemeny (1992), urban studies can progress along methodologically sound lines and interpretations when they are properly connected to basic theoretical developments in social science subjects such as economics, sociology, politics and anthropology. Since the early 1970s, urban studies have been all too frequently disconnected from developments in basic theory. Good policy and principle in environmentalism require strong theoretical foundations.

IDEAS AND RESEARCH IN SUSTAINABLE CITIES

The case for an urban scale of analysis of sustainability is quite straightforward:

- Cities are enormous sources of consumption, waste and environmental relevance.[4]
- Cities in developing countries produce over 60 per cent of GDP;

---

4) As noted by Houghton and Hunter (1994), for statistical relevance, cities of over 1 million population have average daily resource use and waste of 625,000 tonnes of water, 2000 tonnes of food, 950 tonnes of air pollutants, 500,000 tonnes of waste water, and per capita domestic wastes of 0.7–1.8 kg in industrialized countries and 0.4–0.9 kg in developing countries.

some 40 per cent of the world's population is urbanized, 72.6 per cent in industrial countries and 37.6 per cent in developing countries; and some 65 per cent of the world's cities are 'coastal' with its heightened environmental significance in waste and global warming.

- Urban demographic growth is rapid in developing countries, and associated with a present period of time marked by important phases in the demographic transition. The demographic transition is characterized by changing, time-based relationships between fertility and mortality rates. In phase one, fertility and mortality rates are high, stable and in balance. Phase two sometimes has increased fertility rates and always has reduced mortality rates associated with modest improvements in nutrition and medicine. Population increases, and the more so in phase three as mortality reduces further from improved health and fertility rates fall, but less rapidly than mortality rates. Finally, in phase four the likely changes are that fertility rates reduce (from educational, cultural, urbanized lifestyles, and gender-associated social change, especially in women's roles) and stable conditions emerge. Developing countries are variously in stages two and three, with a few in stage four (for example Singapore). Urbanization is especially associated with stages two and three, including rural–urban migration, and some dependence upon informal sector employment. Environmentalism becomes increasingly relevant because developing countries become poised for widespread industrialized growth, some of which is environmentally adverse.

- Urbanization also has some positive aspects with relevance to environmentalism. It is associated with changed lifestyles and attitudes, including lower fertility rates and aspirations for improving standards of living. Cities are at the heart of the technological revolution, including possibilities for improving technological and economic applications to environmental problems. As cities become more productive and economically sophisticated some environmental adversities diminish, but others become more problematical (see the discussions below). Also, although structural poverty is significant in many Third World cities – much of which is associated with insanitary living conditions – the poor can be a source of action and labour to improve unsatisfactory environments.

The environmental conditions of cities consist of much more than can be derived from mounting up relevant statistics of waste, of trends in consumption, and of demographic growth (see footnote 4). The effects of environmental conditions – both the benefit and cost effects – have impacts upon human development indicators, such as health and education, on human economic productivity, on whether adverse outcomes in resource use are reversible, and on the environment outside the boundaries of cities. Some of the environmental matters in cities also have relevance to important intangibles, such as appreciation of architectural, historical and cultural values. Also, environmental conditions have become of increasing political and economic relevance in some countries, especially in middle-income developing countries such as Brazil. For example, in 1992 the state government of São Paulo launched a $4 billion programme of environmental improvement in the Tietê river, which is one of the most polluted in the world (Foster, 1994). Pollution comes from factories and mass squatter settlements: daily discharges to the Tietê are 1000 tonnes of organic waste and 3 tonnes of untreated inorganic waste, including chemicals and heavy metals. The programme aims to halve the pollution by 1996 and to restore 'biologically dead' sections of the Tietê back to life by 2005. These environmental problems have been politically unattended since their appearance in the 1950s, but by the 1990s environmental politics has led to some response, with critics ready to discern whether the programme will be effective or symbolic.

Urban environmental issues vary in accordance with stages of economic development and situational circumstances such as relationships to poverty and affluence and to patterns of consumption and living conditions. This can be conceptualized and explained in terms of the idea of an 'environmental transition', as suggested by McGranahan and Songsore (1994). The 'environmental transition' is given graphical expression in Figure 5.1, below. In stylized oversimplification, Figure 5.1 illustrates that brown agenda insanitary residential living is associated with neighbourhoods and low stages of development/income. As income level rises, then these brown agenda issues affect lower proportions of the urban population. Manufacturing industry increases as development and income levels of cities improve: this often leads to water and air pollution (for example as indicated in the earlier reference to São Paulo). The impacts are city-regional and intensified in some neighbourhoods. Finally, an 'environmental transition' has general air pollution associated with motor vehicle emissions in some cities that experience specific climatic conditions (for example Mexico City). This arises from consumption patterns and production where there is dependence upon motor vehicles. As illustrated in Figure 5.1 the three 'stages' or 'representations' have some spatial and stage-of-development overlap. Although the illustrated 'environmental transition' has conceptual and interpretative usefulness, it is, as suggested above, an oversimplification. With modern concentrated economic development and the economic restructuring of cities, the three stages will increasingly occur simultaneously.

Policies can either reduce or increase the intensity of the problems. Finally, although generalization has some relevance, cities and their 'environmental profiles' are highly varied in characteristics and the specific policy attentions that are required. And, even as cities advance in their stage of development, low-income groups, substandard housing conditions and insanitary living conditions will continue to have relevance to policy and environmental agendas.

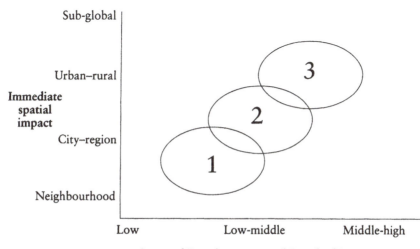

Stage of Development and Level of Income

Key: (1) Sanitation, access to potable water, squatter settlement and health-associated brown agenda issues such as malaria, respiratory disease diarrhoea, contagious diseases; (2) Industrial pollution in water and particulate air pollution (for example sulphur dioxide); (3) Air pollution associated with motor vehicle emissions and city-regional climate conditions (for example carbon dioxide).

Figure 5.1 *The 'environmental transition' stage of development and spatial impacts*

The earlier (pre-1993) literature was characterized mainly by reviews of environmental problems and the proposal of some initial concepts to interpret urban environmental conditions. Both independent researchers and multilateral and bilateral aid agencies contributed ideas and evaluations. Hardoy et al (1992) exampled the widespread environmental adversity in urban areas in developing countries, with detail on the damaging effects in disease, life and death. They also significantly demonstrated that low-cost technological solutions were available in latrines, sewerage systems and drainage for improving squatter and slum settlements. It was policy and resource allocating mechanisms that were inadequate, not appropriate technology. Mikesell (1992) reviewed the theory and practice of economics, emphasizing the relevance of principles such as public goods, property rights, natural resources as capital, and the long-term implications of resource allocation to education, health and the environment. At root, Mikesell's work brought significance to those theories reviewed in earlier discussions, including those formulated by Coase, Musgrave and Head.

The ideas and principles from multilateral and bilateral aid agencies are both significant for their intrinsic intellectual qualities and because they are associated with international loan and technical advice programmes. The United States Agency for International Development (USAID) has provided ideas, experimentation and innovation for urban-related programme development. Its review of urbanization and the environment (USAID, 1990) was based upon the notions of the 'carrying capacity' of urban environments, and 'buffer capacity' at the interface of urban and rural environments. These are conceptually useful ideas, relevant to assessing 'capacity' in relation to scientifically-derived measurement, social costs, air and water pollution, and urban–rural interdependence. Also, USAID collaborated with city and county organizations in the USA to inaugurate and review privatization programmes in waste disposal in Third World cities. The reviews (ICMA, 1992) established some important lessons from experience with case studies and experiments. These were that state/government roles have importance in successful privatization, and that institutionally-loaded reform has central significance. Government roles include designing and monitoring contracts with the private sector, increasing environmental commitment in political and administrative institutions, and strengthening accountabilities in delivery systems and operational programmes.

The World Bank undertook a strategic review of urban policies in the late 1980s and published its directions for the 1990s in 1991 (World Bank, 1991). The main thrust of the World Bank's policies was towards linking urban and macroeconomic development, but environmental relevance was included. This was carried forward and elaborated in some in-house reviews in 1991–3 (Buckley and Heller, 1992). It was noted that policy and loan programmes were shifting from project-related relevance to sector and urban-wide significance in finance, in structural adjustment in urban economies, and in the way these were shaped in regulatory and institutional frameworks. In short, property rights, institutionally-loaded reform, multi-institutional development and related matters were rising in importance alongside the earlier attention in the World Bank to macroeconomic reform and microeconomic efficiencies in markets.

Environmentalism, infrastructure services, poverty alleviation pro-grammes and such like were raising the importance of state–market relationships with recognition that improved performance in both the state and market activities were relevant to these policy spheres. The ideological advocacies for the superiority of either the state or the market, as reflected in some intellectual debates in the 1970s and 1980s, were being increasingly seen as creating a false dichotomy. As argued by Meier (1991) and Klitgaard (1991), the major policy agendas in the Third World in the 1990s required appropriately blended state, market and other roles.

Environmental research became more elaborate and sophisticated after 1992. Independent researchers began reporting their findings from empirical and conceptual work in cities in developing countries. Follow-ing the 1992 UNCED meeting in Rio de Janeiro, the multilateral aid agencies deepened their research and programme development. As indi-cated in the introductory discussions, the jointly collaborated Sustainable Cities Programme by the World Bank, the UNDP and the UNCHS com-menced in Dar es Salaam in 1991. This was part of the UMP for the years 1986 to 1995. The UMP is a programme of technical assistance, of raising awareness of the need for urban reform, and for capacity building among relevant institutions and organizations. Policy papers were pub-lished under the auspices of the UMP, with a number of these having direct and indirect relevance to environmental improvement. Also, the World Bank was increasingly pressed by international lobby groups (for example Greenpeace, '50 Years is Enough') on environmental, social and developmental issues.

The Stockholm Environmental Institute undertook comparative envir-onmental studies in cities in developing countries, with surveys of living conditions in low-income living areas and reviews of characteristic environmental problems at different stages of economic development. In the first research study Benneh and his coauthors (Benneh et al, 1993) reported their findings from surveys of low-income settlements in Accra, Ghana. Diseases were widespread, arising from inadequate water and sanitation provisions, insect infestation, and indoor smoke pollution associated with cooking. However, improvement occurred where CBOs organized households for self-help environmental improvements. House-holds were seen as the central institution in community-based approaches to neighbourhood environmental improvement. Individual-ism could be changed in favour of necessary group cooperation, but public authorities also had important roles in the improvement of infra-structure. The second reporting of research findings (McGranahan and Songsore, 1994) dealt with comparative environmental conditions in Accra, Jakarta and São Paulo. As discussed earlier, interpretation was

provided through the concept of environmental transition, relating varying environmental problems to levels of income, stage of development
and spatial scope. Both studies pointed to the importance of multi-
institutional approaches in environmental policy, to the synchronization
of state, market, CBO and household roles, and to innovations in policy
and delivery systems. These matters were also central in the research and
reports of international aid agencies.

The policy papers in the UMP have dealt with a range of issues. Bernstein (1993) argued for the significance of coherent jurisdictional
authority among levels of government and between environmental
administrative agencies. This was consolidated in a further report by
Dillinger (1994). Dillinger set out principles for decentralization in
service delivery and the public administration of environmental policies.
For Dillinger the prescriptively good principles included clarity in setting
functional responsibilities at different levels of government, assigning
responsibilities for raising revenues and for spending in accordance with
functional responsibilities, and installing institutional conditions to
improve efficiency and responsiveness to client groups. All of this was
advocated in a context of multi-institutional relevance, and in an
inherited general performance of inadequacy and organizational inco-
herence. Other UMP studies (Leitmann et al, 1994a, 1994b; Bartone et
al, 1994) set out manuals of practice in making 'rapid environmental
assessments', indicating the lessons from programme experience in seven
cities in a variety of countries, and providing policy-relevant evaluation.
Some of the policy-relevant evaluation was associated with approaches
adopted in the Sustainable Cities Programme in Dar es Salaam. The
evaluations argued for time-phased key elements:

- The mobilization of public support, especially among stakeholders
  in environmental improvement;
- a selection of policy instruments which would change behaviour and
  contribute to improved environments, with an awareness that some
  resolution of conflicting interests would be required;
- the development of institutional capacity;
- taking steps to strengthen service delivery, much along the lines of
  decentralization as advocated by Dillinger (1994); and
- increasing the local knowledge of environmental matters, and thus
  modifying asymmetrical information, which distorted (in adverse
  ways) economic resource allocation mechanisms and the politics of
  environmental policies.

The Dar es Salaam programme for sustainable urban development is
at the stage of prescriptive principles and advocacy: as yet, it has no

evaluation of effectiveness in institutional and policy conditions, which are complex and subject to uncertainty in effectiveness.

Much of what emerged from the UMP policy papers and post-1992 research by independent authors can be related to the themes discussed earlier that addressed issues in economics and political economy. The recommended policies and evaluations were based on the theory of property rights, principal–agent relations, social costs and benefits, public goods, transaction costs, asymmetries in information, the comparative advantages of different organizations and institutions, merit goods and principles of good governance. The theory was not detached from practice and policy. For example, the Sustainable Cities Programme was also applied to Ibadan, Nigeria. The skill and experience requirements specified for the appointment of a senior coordinating officer were expertise in public administration, development economics, planning law, community participation and conflict resolution, creating frameworks for a range of actors in the environment in order to shape urban growth and development, and introducing economic instruments to leverage environmental improvement. Both theory and executive responsibilities for sustainable cities are eclectic and complicated. The rest of this chapter addresses some of the complexity and eclecticism issues.

MULTI-INSTITUTIONAL THEORY AND PRACTICE

The discussions to this point have established the inherent complexity and eclecticism of environmentalism. One aspect of complexity and eclecticism is that applied policy usually requires a multi-institutional and multi-organizational approach. This raises the question of what sort of principles lie in the theory and practice of partnerships among institutions, including lessons from experience. The necessity for multi-institutional approaches derives from the nature of environmental problems and from formulating policies to deal with them. Environmental conditions have their cause–consequence relationships in markets, in government policies, in state agencies, in NGOs, in CBOs and in the activities of households. This is so because, as reasoned in earlier discussions, environmentalism has mixed configurations of individualism, 'public goods' elements, 'merit goods' characteristics, and both voluntary and legislative responses to seek social cooperation. Stated in this way, the topic of multi-institutional conditions is an extension of the earlier themes centred around the conceptual basis of sustainability, but with a greater emphasis on the relevance of political economy. Thus, the treatment in this section will deepen and widen the conceptual foundations and bring relevant issues of political economy to the fore.

Institutions are ways of doing things, usually reflecting formal or informal rules, norms, and influencing the boundaries and interactions between individualism and social cooperation (Hodgson, 1993). In social science studies, institutions are studied from two distinct perspectives. In sociology and anthropology, for example, emphasis is placed on such things as social bonding, the transmission of culture and social values, and the roles of institutions in continuity and change. Within economics, the pre-1970 old institutional economics (OIE) was a reaction against the neglect of social, historical and political considerations in orthodox economics. But since the early 1970s, North (1981, 1987 and 1990) and others have developed a new institutional economics (NIE). NIE offers a distinctive departure from approaches in sociology and in OIE. Institutions are understood in more abstracted terms, sometimes with 'materialist' and 'rational choice' foundations. The rational choice approach to social science is basic in orthodox economics, especially in the 'individualistic' and 'maximizing' characteristics of orthodox economics. However, the authors of NIE have created new ways of exploring the foundations of market and non-market institutions, with some departure from the 'methodological individualism' of the orthodoxies in economics. All this has relevance to environmentalism and sustainability owing to the multi-institutional context and the nature of the theory in NIE.

North (1981, 1987 and 1990) argues that institutions will exist as important additions to markets when 'transaction costs' are high in the creation and monitoring of agreements. He develops Coase's theories (see Annex notes for explanation) centred on the conditions when transaction costs are so high as to block spontaneous market outcomes. This means that attention has to be given to rearranging property rights to achieve better results by lowering transaction costs, or to designing nonmarket institutional conditions that can be justified in terms of achieving better outcomes at comparatively cheaper transaction costs than alternative institutional arrangements. Such institutional arrangements that could be considered include regulation, direct state provision of relevant goods and services, privatized provisions under state contracting and monitoring, and cooperative action in NGOs and CBOs. In multi-institutional contexts, the significance of the Coase and North theories arises in relational contracting among different organizations, in partnerships, in intergovernmental and inter-agency relations, and in the activities of CBOs and NGOs. The theories are also relevant to formulating and implementing policy. In environmentalism, the central reasons why care in institutionally-loaded reform in policy making is important derive from the mixed 'private' and 'public goods' nature of the environment. From earlier discussions this mixed nature of environmental goods and bads is closely bound up with social costs and benefits, asymmetries in information, merit goods principles, and principal–agency relationships. The mixed private–public goods nature of environmental conditions poses some characteristic dilemmas.

The major dilemmas revolve around the question of how to get social cooperation where individualism and private behaviour would, if left to themselves, generate social costs in the environment or preclude environmental improvement. An example will clinch what is involved. An individual household in an insanitary squatter settlement may prefer a sanitary environment and be willing to pay for this by self-help or in a tax, but is unable to influence a change because the potential private actions could not significantly bring about improvements. In fact, the public goods nature of the improvement (and the lack of improvement) might be similarly perceived by other households, resulting in probable nonaction. This 'free rider and prisoners' dilemma' is at the heart of the divergence between individual and social interests.[5] The dilemma can be broken by some form of social cooperation, which could be achieved by a CBO organizing households collectively into self-help, mediating between households and policy makers and between government environmental and infrastructural agencies. These possibilities also have some reasoned support in the theory of how social cooperation can arise in circumstances of the free rider and prisoners' dilemma (see Axelrod, 1984; Nutt and Backoff, 1992; Sugden, 1986). Social cooperation is more likely when a number of households or individuals have a long-term interest in resolution and when the environmental 'bad' (or 'good' from the removal of the bad) is subject to continual repetitive experience. Also, leadership, initiative and social entrepreneurship are necessary: sometimes the initiative comes within public policy interventions. Problems associated with free rider and prisoners' dilemmas are clearly maintained where leadership and policy are inadequate and where the

---

5) The 'free rider' problem is explained in footnote 3, above. 'Prisoners' dilemma' matters are an extension of the free rider problem. In essence individuals will gain most benefit where they cooperate with each other, but sometimes the mechanisms for social cooperation are not in place or individual self interest overrules cooperation where 'free riding' is possible. The prisoner is in a dilemma of whether to confess, to inform on accomplices, or to maintain silence under questioning by police in a suspected crime. The police treat with each prisoner separately as individuals seeking confession and informing on accomplices. All suspects would be advantaged as individuals by maintaining silence, but each is uncertain as to whether others will inform on them to obtain lower sentences. Prisoners' dilemmas arise in such urban examples as housing and neighbourhood improvement because individual property values rise with least individual cost when others improve but the individuals do nothing. That is, they free ride. The environment has these prisoners' dilemmas by virtue of the 'publicness' of its nature. Also, see the annex detailing the principles of transactions costs and institutional arrangements to secure social cooperation.

potential beneficiaries have no long-term interest in resolution, or the probability of continual sufferance or benefit is low.

The foregoing principle can be further elaborated by reference to the association between short- and long-term interests in land-associated environmentalism. Panayatou (1993) explains how 'brown' and 'green' agenda issues are related to property and tenure rights in land. Insecurity of use or tenure can lead to environmental degradation and suboptional use of land because it induces uncertainty and disposition to short- rather than long-term perspectives. Conservation and environmental improvement are better served by legal or *de facto* security of occupancy and tenure. For urban relevance, this implies the elimination of social practices that harass and evict households in squatter settlement and, instead, introducing reforms for the regularization of tenure. Regularization is a policy whereby public authorities acquire private land (or transfer public land) and sell the tenure rights to occupants. Such policies work best when they are also associated with loan finance, infrastructure servicing and reasonable methods of cost recovery in public and private finance. They operate more effectively with the sorts of principles for coordination and decentralization in local environmental governance advocated by Dillinger (1994), as discussed earlier. This places emphasis on coherence in the assignment of roles, finance and delivery systems in intergovernmental inter-agency partnership and the general framework of multi-institutional relationships.

Coherence and effective partnering in multi-organizational contexts are not assured or guaranteed. From the basis of both theory and experience in practice some dilemmas arise. At the level of theory, these include 'free rider and prisoners' dilemma' issues, which can lead to divergence between self-interested individualism and the necessary conditions for social cooperation (see Annex at the end of this chapter). From the practice of community development over a period of some 40 years a variety of problems have become apparent. These include contested authority and conflict between representative democracy in government and partnerships in urban programmes (Marris and Rein, 1972), the usurping of power for opportunistic self interest by some groups in the politics of partnerships and principal-agent relationships (Marris and Rein, 1972), and some marginalization and fragmentation in the end results, with consequent ineffectiveness among low-income groups (UNCHS, 1993). Although some 'lessons from experience' can lead to a broadening of adequate or good performance, inadequacies can be recurrent and at risk in many projects. For example, evaluations of post-1986 community development programmes under UNCHS housing and neighbourhood projects in Sri Lanka, Zambia and Bolivia reveal the following. In some countries the projects lack coherence because significant gaps exist in the development of national and local-regional urban policies, insufficient attention has been given to the necessary research and monitoring of partnerships, and implementation has been approached rather casually, without regard for some of the sorts of risks and dilemmas referred to earlier in this paragraph (DANIDA, 1994). Clearly, it is necessary to develop a clear and well-informed theory and practice of community development in housing and neighbourhood improvement programmes.

A starting point for the theory and practice of useful community development would begin with the following principles. First, it is necessary that key political and administrative leaders want the programme and are prepared to put in commitment, resources and the necessary time for negotiation and coordination in multi-institutional contexts. Second, NGOs and CBOs with professional and policy interests in community development will undertake policy reviews and redirections based upon evaluations and the need to revise policies based upon social change and social realities. For example, this has been the case in the Ford Foundation's Urban Poverty Programme (UPP) in East Africa. In the years 1984 to 1988 the Ford Foundation undertook in-depth evaluations to set the UPP on a course for sustainable development from the late 1980s and through the 1990s. The foundation found that gaps occurred in civic association, in localized research support for CBOs and localized government, and that risks were apparent for low-income groups because political, administrative and informational impediments retarded progress (Hokans, 1988; Howard, 1984). Accordingly, the Ford Foundation emphasized medium-term capacity building, ie for skill formation, social and political advocacy and improved governance, and for effecting a change from fragmented community development to something that was 'integral' in the sense of multi-organizational coherence. Third, as is evident from experience with economic and social programmes in internationally relevant policies, policy makers in developing countries will have a higher probability of success if prior attention is given to the implementation of policies (Thomas and Grindle, 1990). This is so because otherwise groups whose interests are adversely affected by reforms and social change will probably organize and oppose change within the processes of implementation. Finally, overall design of the vertical and horizontal aspects of multi-institutional coordination can become more coherent if the principles advocated by Dillinger (1994), as discussed above, are followed. But, in some instances, overall systemic coherence of organizations and institutions will be either limited or impossible. This does not mean that nothing can be done: some process coherence can come from leadership, persuasion and negotiation, all aimed at bridging or reducing institutional blockages and impediments.

Consideration for the household has been given insufficient attention by policy makers and community development professionals. Households are the intermediary spheres through which top-down economic and environmental programmes are processed and acted upon, and they directly connect with community-based and income generation elements in bottom-up applications of policy. In environmental initiatives in low-income living areas, households are being persuaded to change their attitudes, to give time and labour to programme and policy development, and to work for both their own and the wider community's interests. Benneh et al (1993) found that households were central in the potential for success or failure in 'brown agenda' housing and environmental improvement. This means that household policies (and research) are in need of formulation and development. Households have social, economic and political functions. The economic functions include divisions of labour among women, men and children. (Although children's roles in education are within Agenda 21 of the UNCED report, their work contributions have been ignored.) Households have to determine, largely through intra-household bargaining, their allocations to consumption, saving, housing outlays, and so on. Under various post-1985 international policies, households are 'required' to generate income, to save and spend it in prescriptively useful way (though within a context of some freedom) and to pay for significant proportions of basic needs goods. Also, households produce some 'at home' goods and services, including housing and environmental improvements, meals, house-keeping services and self-help in education and entrepreneurship. In developing countries self-help can be enhanced by public policies and resource allocations in health, education, housing and environmental spheres. Age- and gender-sensitive policies can influence the improvement in the social roles of children and women. The economics of households has a long and fragmented history, but since 1955 the subject has received greater attention from economists and economic anthropologists (Amsden, 1980; Apps, 1981; Babb, 1981; Becker, 1981; Bender, 1967; Bossen, 1981; Clark, 1958; Folbre, 1988; Hansen, 1980; Hull, 1968; Norris, 1988; Pugh, 1990.) Household economics has huge significance for environmental policy and sustainability.

In concluding this section, it is relevant to examine policy and multi-institutional coherence in a city-region as a whole. This can be done by drawing on some exemplary principles and practices. Rabinovitch (1992) provides exposition and commentary on the development of urban and environmental policies in Curitiba, south Brazil. The city-region's population grew from 500,000 in 1965 to 1.6 million within an economic development and planning framework since the mid-1960s. The step-by-step progressive development of economic and spatial policy has been:

First, in the 1960s public transport axes, in the form of express busways, were planned and constructed. Intensive land development was located along the axes, with feeder roads and less intensive land uses coordinated with these, located in the 'wedges' between the axial lines. In effect, it was a linear-formulated planning scheme.

Second, in the 1970s an industrial sector was developed some seven miles from the city centre, and accessible in low-cost time-access along the axial routes.

Third, in the 1980s some environmental content was further developed, with linked city-wide to neighbourhood relevance. This included green spaces, self-help improvements in squatter settlements, and various economic incentives to involve the poor in waste management and solid waste collection. For example, the poor are paid 'bus voucher' tickets for taking garbage to central collection points. Also, attention is being given to reducing pollution in the city's Iguaza river basin.

The foregoing has occurred as a result of the leadership of the city's mayor, Jaime Lerner, from 1970 to 1974 and again from 1979 to 1983. The city's Research and Urban Planning Institute has also been instrumental in formulating policies, which have been unconventional, innovative and effective. Along with Singapore (Pugh, 1985), Curitiba has a multi-institutional approach to economic, spatial and environmental policy, which is unified and coherent. Localized governance has been simultaneously 'market friendly', developmentally oriented and pragmatic in bringing institutionally-loaded reform and economic development in relationship to each other. Some of the underlying theoretical principles have been readily available for about 30 years, but are seldom practised and not brought to the fore in the relevant urban and environmental literature (for example, see the ideas of Lauchlin Currie (1961) and Sandilands (1990)). Currie's ideas and theories provide explanation for the widespread benefits that can be derived from adopting spatial policies that structure cities around linear axes and multi-centering. This relieves pressures on an otherwise mono-central radial form, which concentrates intensities of land values and consequently leads to price-access problems, especially in housing and social infrastructure. Also, Currie argued persuasively that excess labour could be readily employed in low-income housing, construction and infrastructure development. Currie's theories and ideas can be extended for modern post-1990 relevance to sustainability and brown agenda matters.

CONCLUSIONS

The discussions have ranged widely, covering the changing conceptualization of sustainability, the broad history of environmentalism, with
focus upon the 1992 UNCED meeting and its Agenda 21, and the way
sustainability is deeply intertwined with economic development, markets
and institutional conditions. Themes and arguments have revolved
around four questions, set out in the introduction to the chapter. These
questions sought understanding to the meaning of 'sustainability', to the
influence of post-UNCED impacts on the way economics and other
social sciences are changing or elaborating their theoretical constructs,
and the general political economy of sustainability in its late twentieth-
century context. In the light of the discussions, some summarized and
reflective answers can be given to the questions.

First, some of the early phases of developing the intellectual content of
sustainability have made substantial progress. The building blocks in
developing theory, principles and technique have changed some thinking.
For example, economics has extended its notions of 'capital' to include
environmental resources, variously as exhaustible, renewable and substitutable in economic development. Its conceptual foundations have to
deal with feedback loops from environmental conditions, as well as
deploying its more conventional linear, input–output framework of
thinking. Techniques, such as cost-benefit analyses, have been adaptable
for application to some appraisal of environmental conditions, with possibilities for measuring social impact and the distributional incidence of
costs and benefits among different groups. Some inherited theories of
social costs, property rights, asymmetrical information, transaction costs,
and the relationships between markets and institutions have heightened
significance in environmentalism. However, the underlying ideas for sustainability have come not only from pure intellectual thought: they have
also been influenced by the social and political context. Inequalities
between the industrialized and developing nations, and the roles of international organizations, have been influencing the concepts and direction
of 'sustainability'.

Second, sustainability and environmentalism are not tightly bounded
either as concepts or in their social, economic and political contexts.
They are influenced by changing priorities in the national and international economies. For example, international trading relations in such
things as NAFTA raise issues of 'fair trading' relating to environmental
standards imposed on industry in different countries. Such issues will rise
in significance within the auspices of the newly created WTO, which will
have broader responsibilities than GATT, which will be absorbed in the
WTO. More generally, environmentalism has to compete with other

priorities on national and international political agendas. But it does have some stronger post-1992 advocacies and applications in the UN and the World Bank, some of this in response to more organized international lobby groups for social and environmental causes.

Third, sustainability has an interactive relationship with theoretical and pragmatic political economies in the wider context. It has some influence on the general direction of political economy in national and international settings. And, it is influenced by the broader and dominant political economies in the late twentieth century. The dominant late twentieth-century political economy has been liberalism and the 'new political economy' (NPE). This dominant political economy has some underlying characteristics in market–state relationships and notions of 'good governance'. These characteristics are elaborated in the discussions that follow.

The foregoing indicates the relevance of more than attaching findings to questions set in the introduction. In pursuing the questions and their relevant thematic arguments, the chapter itself is a discourse and a method of study. Also, the notion of sustainability has some general overall significance. What is the theory and practice of a 'sustainable city', and how is this to be related to a broad conceptual framework?

As discourse and methodology, the writing is policy economics, interpreting sustainability in terms of developmental change, the relevance of markets, the theory and practice of institutions and some historical context. Colander (1994) argues that policy economics necessarily has to draw on the evolution of theoretical developments in mainstream 'positive' economics, but adopts a different methodology. Whereas 'positive' economics is concerned with creating basic theory, with drawing testable hypotheses from that theory, and with undertaking sophisticated empirical tests, policy economics has regard for institutions, history and principles of selection in drawing on theory and concept for explanation. Thus, both 'positive' and 'policy' economics are relevant to sustainability and environmentalism, by virtue of their interdependence and their separate contributions. This is further consolidated below, in the overall conceptual issues and the nature of sustainability as political economy.

One useful way of looking at urban environmental matters is through the concept of *urban income*. Consider income as comprising two sources. The first source is *prior* income, derived from earnings, wages, profits, rents and social security or intra-household allocations. This, of course, is characteristically inegalitarian in state–market societies and is related to stage-of-development and macroeconomic conditions, including economic fluctuations. For many developing countries, relevance is associated with high volumes of poverty and the nature of the informal sectors during demographic transitions. Second, view *urban income* as derived from welfare or diswelfare in terms of the price-access to urban (dis)amenities. Urban (dis)amenities would include price-access to infra-structure and utility services such as potable water, sanitation and so on. It would also include the various brown agenda environmental condi-tions of disease, health, quality of life and related effects from neighbour-hood sanitary conditions, various sorts of water and air pollution, and wider regional and global environmental matters (see earlier discussions on the 'environmental transition'). Viewed in this way, *urban income* interacts with prior income, modifying the welfare, the efficiency and the distributional effects of that prior income. The modifications can add to or subtract from welfare, and they can have socially- and spatially-related effects on the distribution of costs and benefits among different groups. The aim of environmental policy is, of course, to add to welfare, efficiency, and to do so in equitable ways. As argued earlier, this depends on the effectiveness of policies, institutions and the relationships of markets to states, NGOs, CBOs and households. To some extent, the *urban income* can be measured and monitored in appraisals such as those previously referred to, including hedonic indices, cost-benefit and development impact extraction techniques.

The idea of *urban income* is inherently a notion of political economy. Environmentalism falls within late twentieth-century liberalism. Late twentieth-century liberalism contains both economic and political elements. The economic elements include both micro- and macro-economics. Microeconomics falls under the widening internationalization of market-friendly policies, often brought under the term 'enablement'. 'Enablement liberalism' is about some deregulation of markets and the acceptance that markets tend to have greater potential for efficiency and growth than other institutions. But 'enablement liberalism' does not mean that the state has unimportant roles. Although in some contexts 'enablement' is practised as the substitution of markets (for example in privatization) for some earlier state involvement in production, generally the state has important roles in the creation and enforcement of property rights and in institutionally-loaded reform. As indicated in earlier dis-cussions, in sustainability the institutional framework is often multi-organizational, with synchronized market, state, NGO, CBO and house-hold roles. The macroeconomic elements of liberalism have evolved from experience in the 1980s, and especially with the external debt problems among Latin American and sub-Saharan African countries. The macro-economic orthodoxies of the late 1980s include anti-inflation monetary and fiscal policies, liberalization in international trade, 'realism' in exchange rates, curbs on the growth of public expenditure, and matching tax collection to plans for public spending. The economic elements were sometimes imposed under the conditionalities of the IMF and World Bank loan programmes for macroeconomic stabilization and structural adjustment.

The political elements of late twentieth-century liberalism have been evolving in reaction to the post-1988 demise of state socialism and experience of 'bad governance' in some countries. Thus 'good governance' is argued as pursuing economic 'enablement', as having transparency, probity and clear accountability in governance. 'Good governance' is more or less associated with democratization, having relevance among some developing countries and in countries in the transition from state socialism to state–market capitalism. As I have argued elsewhere (Pugh, 1994), the economics and politics of the liberalism has some excessive optimism and it moves within a spectrum of 'minimal state' neoliberalism to 'medium state' expressions of social and environmental significance. The neoliberalism was aimed at rapid withdrawal of state roles in production and in restricting 'welfare state' expression. It was current in the early 1980s, but changed in the later years of the 1980s, with concerns for poverty and environmentalism being significant. Attitudes to the state became more positive, with intellectuals (for example Klitgaard, 1991; Meier, 1991) arguing for blended state–market roles and for the improvement of both markets and states. Excessive optimism is relevant because liberalism often assumes that the pursuit of efficiency, good governance, and the amelioration of social problems are readily reconcilable. The earlier discussions on the complexity of multi-institutional conditions in top-down and bottom-up environmental policy applications revealed the relative risks of success and failure. Accordingly the pragmatic political economy of liberalism has to address mixed success and failure, and the possibilities of synchronizing potentially conflicting institutions with each other, including all institutions with markets. Theoretical political economy is the NPE. As described above, the NPE has economic and political elements attempting to develop appropriate relationships in 'enablement' frameworks. Environmentalism falls within the NPE; it has been significant in the evolution of the NPE from narrower neoliberalism towards a broader 'medium state' liberalist argument; and it deepens the internationalization of a dominant political economy. Environmentalism has, then, to be evaluated in terms of a changing NPE and its comparative expressions in countries with varying webs of institutions, cultures and approaches to governance.

Finally, what is a 'sustainable city' in terms of the thematic arguments developed in this chapter? First, consider the negative aspects of meaning. Sustainable cities are not economically self sufficient cities; they are not paradigmatic expressions of low technology or simple organizational form; and their economic processes will sometimes encroach upon exhaustible resources, but with more acknowledgement and 'reason' than in the past. A sustainable city will organize its multiple institutions towards 'environmental friendliness'. This will be expressed in policy making, in institutional reform, in the growth of appropriate information (and the reduction of distorted and asymmetrically biased information), and all of this will be expressed in a wide range of interdependent public policies and economic activities. The 'environment' cannot be pursued in only a bounded 'environmental policy' because it is subjected to impact from other social, economic and political policies. Over a period of time, sufficient to redirect processes and to reform institutions, the sustainable city will have much reduced health risks in neighbourhoods (ie the sanitary question and appreciation that bad environments can be detrimental to long-term mental health) and in city-regional water and air pollution. It will cause less environmental damage to its region and to the international economic environment. The sustainable city will have economic growth, some directed by environmental considerations; it will express both efficiency and social justice, but with some continuing tensions between these objectives; and it will be conscious of good theory and practice in other city-regions. Good practice has principle, pragmatism and reformed spatial policies. Curitiba and Singapore are examples of good practice, but as in all cases, with scope for further improvement. The sustainable city may be paradoxically possible within 'medium' expressions of environmentalism, and less likely under uncompromised attempts to create a pure environment. Pure environments imply strong authoritarianism and some neglect of other relevant social objectives. They can end up with increased poverty, with inequality and with the suppression of basic freedoms. These may be politically and economically unsustainable.[6]

ANNEX: THE COASE THEORY AND ITS EXTENSION IN THE NEW INSTITUTIONAL ECONOMICS (NIE)

In his theory of social costs and benefits (ie the economics of externality) Pigou (1932) had shown that some third party consequences of consumption and production could lead to divergence between private and social interests. In order to correct for overproduction where social

---

6   The author gratefully acknowledges comments and suggestions on an earlier version of
     this chapter by Professor Trudy Harpham. Responsibilities for any errors or misconceptions remain with the author.

costs prevailed and underproduction where social benefits prevailed, Pigou recommended that government apply externality-specific taxes and subsidies. This was a method of 'internalizing' accountability of the externality within the market. It has relevance to public policies in environmental issues. However, Coase (1960) argued that Pigou's solutions are incomplete and bypass some of the essential matters of principle. The essential matters of principle are:

- Where an economic activity 'A' interferes with an activity 'B' (for example by imposing social costs), reciprocity is at issue. Essentially it is a question of whether the extra production from A is more or less highly valued than the loss of production in B. Reciprocity leaves grounds for bargaining, negotiation and compensation, providing that the legal rights are secure for the adversely affected party to pursue the liability of the perpetrator for compensation.
- Bargaining, negotiation and the pursuit of liability are not costless. They involve the occurrence of transaction costs in reaching and enforcing agreements. The transaction costs can be sufficiently high as to block correction. And, where the externality is significant, affecting large numbers, corrective action can be inhibited by the free rider and prisoners' dilemma problem (see footnotes 3 and 5).
- In view of the foregoing, Coase argues that it does make a difference as to the way legalities are established (Coase, 1960:16): 'In these conditions the initial delimitation of legal rights does have an effect on the efficiency with which the economic system operates. One arrangement of rights may bring about a greater production than any other. But unless this is the arrangement of rights established by the legal system, the costs of reaching the same result by altering the combining rights through the market may be so great that this optimal arrangement of rights and the greater production which it would bring may never be achieved.'
- Sometimes the circumstances of high transaction costs and economic externality require multi-institutional conditions or some substitution of market provision by administration. Thus, for Coase, this implies an assessment of the relative costs and benefits of alternative organizational and institutional arrangements. Coase gives the example of land development where economic externality is often significant: a large tract of land owned by a single company can achieve reconciliation of the relevant adverse and beneficial interactions among elements in a development without the necessity for bargaining. Transactions and bargaining costs rise with fragmented ownership and operation. A single operator or developer can acquire the legal rights of all parties.

- Bargaining, partnership arrangements and such like often involve highly complicated relational contracting. In the words of Coase (1960:16–17): 'Where contracts are peculiarly difficult to draw up and an attempt to describe what the parties have agreed to do or not to do (for example the amount and kind of smell or noise that they may make or will not make) would necessitate a lengthy and highly involved document, and, where, as is probable, a long-term contract would be desirable; it would be hardly surprising if the emergence of a firm or extension of the activities of an existing firm was not the solution adopted on many occasions to deal with the problems of harmful effects.' However, Coase goes on to say that in some of the potentially harmful effects from pollution and inappropriate land development, regulation and administrative agency may be appropriate. Harmful effects can be reduced by restrictive covenants, large-scale real estate development within effective institutional arrangements, and relational contracting. Coase takes economics beyond attention to factors of production as input resources, to factors of production as rights, including rights to pollute or to refrain from polluting.

Coase's theories have been elaborated and extended in NIE. NIE has four main elements. First, the principles of transaction costs, negotiation, relational contracting and maladjusted costs in institutional arrangements have been developed by North (1981; 1987; 1990) and Williamson (1975 and 1985). Williamson sees a firm as an efficient alternative to excessive relational contracting by consumers and producers in markets. Firms reduce the transaction costs of consumers who otherwise seek to organize elements of production by self-help to secure the goods and services they need. The argument can readily be extended to institutionalized public and social responsibilities in environmental goods and bads. North produces arguments to show that institutional conditions can be either positive or negative in their impact upon economic growth and societal functioning, this also, being readily applicable to the principles of 'sustainable cities'.

Second, the NIE has connected the presence of imperfect and asymmetrical information with Coase's theories of transaction costs and social costs. Against some assumptions in orthodox (neoclassical) economics, Akerlof (1970), Alchian and Demsetz (1972) and Stigler (1961) reveal that information can be costly, asymmetrical, distorted and subject to uncertainty. This means that in some spheres, including matters to do with the environment, information needs development and correction. Informational change can influence the political economy of markets and public policy.

Third, the NIE contains a deepening appreciation and understanding of property rights for guiding decision-making within economic activity. Mistaken specifications and arrangements in law can lead to misallocations of resources and the overproduction of public bads or the underproduction of public goods. The potential applications to environmentalism are in the improvement of squatter settlements, in land tenure and in air pollution. As argued in this chapter, security of tenure in squatter settlement can encourage environmental and housing improvement.

Fourth, as elaborated by Ostrom (1990) in her theoretical approach to common pool resources, and with extensive case study work, in stable communities it is sometimes possible to achieve spontaneous social solutions in balancing the supply and appropriation of environmental resources. For example, village communities in Switzerland have created rules, committee structures, monitoring arrangements and remedies for breaches of rules over pasture, forestry and related environmental sources. Successful spontaneous social-political arrangements depend upon a number of features, including designing the rules to take account of the specific circumstances in common pool resources, achieving congruence between provision and appropriation, installing effective collective choice arrangements, developing monitoring and sanctions conditions, and creating conflict resolution provisions. Ostrom's research indicates the importance of institutional as well as market developments in sustainability.

References

Akerlof, G (1970) 'The Market for "Lemons": Quality, Uncertainty and the Market Mechanism', *Quarterly Journal of Economics*, 84, pp 488–500

Alchian, A and H Demsetz (1972) 'Production, Information Costs and Economic Organization', *American Economic Review*, 62, pp 777–95

Amsden, A (1980) *The Economics of Women and Work*, Penguin, Harmondsworth

Apps, P (1981) *A Theory of Inequality and Taxation*, Cambridge University Press, Cambridge

Axelrod, R (1984) *The Evolution of Co-operation*, Basic Books, New York

Babb, F (1990) 'Women's Work: Engendering Economic Anthropology', *Urban Anthropology*, 19 (3), pp 277–302

Bartone et al (1994) *Towards Environmental Strategies for Cities*, Paper 18 Urban Management Programme, World Bank, Washington DC

Becker, G (1981) *A Treatise on the Family*, Harvard University Press, Cambridge, Masschusetts

Bender, D (1967) 'A Refinement of the Concept of the Household: Families, Coresidence and Domestic Functions', *American Anthropologist*, 169, pp 483–503

Benneh, G, J Songsore, J Nabia, A Amuzu, K Tutu, Y Yangyuoru and G McGranahan (1993) *Environmental Problems and the Urban Household in the Greater Accra Metropolitan Area, Ghana*, Environment Institute, Stockholm

Bernstein, J (1993) *Alternative Approaches to Pollution and Waste Management: Regulatory and Economic Instruments*, Urban Management Programme, Paper 3, World Bank, Washington DC

Bossen, L (1981) 'The Household as Economic Agent', *Urban Anthropologist*, 10 (3), pp 287–305

Buchanan, J (1968) *The Demand and Supply of Public Goods*, Rand McNally, Chicago

Buchanan, J and G Tullock (1962) *The Calculus of Consent*, University of Michigan, Ann Arbor

Buckley, R and M Heller (1992) *Implementing the Urban Agenda of the 1990s*, Urban Development Division, Infrastructure and Urban Development Department, World Bank, Washington DC

Clark, C (1958) 'The Economics of House-Work', *Bulletin of the Oxford Institute of Statistics*, 20 (2), pp 205–11

Coase, R (1960) 'The Problem of Social Cost', *Journal of Law and Economics*, 3 (1), pp 1–44

Colander, D (1994) 'The Art of Economics by the Numbers', in R Backhouse (ed), *New Directions in Economic Methodology*, Routledge, London

Currie, L (1961) *Operatión Colombia: Un Programa Nacional de Desarrolla Económica y Social*, Cámara Colombiana de la Construcción, Baranquilla

DANIDA (1994) *Evaluation Reports: Volume I, Main Report: Volume II, Country Reports (Zambia, Sri Lanka, Bolivia)*; DANIDA, Danish Ministry of Foreign Affairs, Copenhagen

Dillinger, W (1994) *Decentralization and its Implications for Urban Service Delivery*, Urban Management Programme, Paper 16, World Bank, Washington DC

Eggertsson, T (1990) *Economic Behaviour and Institutions*, Cambridge University Press, Cambridge

Fei, J and G Ranis (1964) *Development of the Labour Surplus Economy: Theory and Policy*, Irwin, Homewood, Illinois

Fei J, K Ohkawa and G Ranis (1985) 'Economic Development in Historical Perspective: Japan, Korea and Taiwan', in K Ohkawa, G Ranis and L Meissner (eds), *Japan and Developing Countries*, Blackwell, Oxford

Finer S (1951) *The Life and Times of Sir Edwin Chadwick*, Methuen, London

Finn, M (ed) (1965) *Chadwick's Report on the Sanitary Conditions of the Labouring Population of Great Britain, 1842*, Edinburgh University Press, Edinburgh

Folbre, N (1988) 'The Black Four of Hearts: Towards a New Paradigm of Household Economics', in D Dwyer and J Bruce (eds), *A Home Divided: Women and Income in the Third World*, Stanford University Press, Stanford

Foster, A (1994) 'Green River Rising', *Financial Times*, 6 July 1994, p 20

Grieco, J (ed) (1993) *The International System and International Political Economy*, vol 1, Edward Elgar, Aldershot

Hansen, K (1980) 'The Informal Sector as a Development Issue: Poor Women and Work in Lusaka, Zambia', *Urban Anthropologist*, 9, (2), pp 199–225

Hardoy, J E, D Mitlin and D Satterthwaite (1992) *Environmental Problems in Third World Cities*, Earthscan, London

Head, J (1974) *Public Goods and the Public Sector*, Duke University Press, Durham, North Carolina

Hodgson, G (1993) 'The Renewal of Institutionalism', in G Hodgson (ed), *The Economics of Institutions*, Edward Elgar, Aldershot

Hokans, J (1988) *Urban Poverty Programming in East Africa: A Focus on Local Governance for Urban Community Development*, Inter-Office Memorandum, 2 May 1988, Ford Foundation, New York

Houghton, G and C Hunter (1994) *Sustainable Cities*, Jessica Kingsley, London

Howard, C (1984) *Program Statement for Urban Community Development*, Ford Foundation, New York

Hull, C (1968) *The Economic Writings of Sir William Petty*, Kelley, New York

ICMA (1992) *Privatizing Solid Waste Management Services in Developing Countries*, Proceedings Paper, Seminar Sponsored by Office of Housing and Urban Programs, USAID, Washington DC

Jimenez, W (1982) 'The Value of Squatter Dwellings in Developing Countries', *Economic Development and Cultural Change*, 31, pp 739–52

Johnson, T (1990) 'Development Impact Extractions: An Alternative Method of Financing Urban Development in Less Developed Countries', *Third World Planning Review*, 12 (2), pp 131–46

Karns, M and K Mingst (eds) (1990) *The United States and Multilateral Institutions: Patterns of Changing Instrumentality and Influence*, Unwin Hyman, Boston

Kemeny, J (1992) *Housing and Social Theory*, Routledge, London

Klitgaard, R (1991) *Adjusting to Reality: Beyond State versus Market in Economic Development*, ICS Press, San Francisco

Kuhn, T (1970) *The Structure of Scientific Revolutions*, 2nd edn, University of Chicago Press, Chicago

Leitmann, J (1994a) *Rapid Environmental Assessment: Lessons from Countries in the Developing World, Vol 1, Methodology and Findings*, Urban Management Programme, Discussion Paper 14, World Bank, Washington DC

— (1994b) *Rapid Environmental Assessment: Lessons from the Developing World, Vol 2, Tools and Outputs*, Urban Management Programme Paper 15, World Bank, Washington DC

Levine, M (1992) *The State and its Critics*, vol I, Edward Elgar, Aldershot

Lewis, R (1952) *Edwin Chadwick and the Public Health Movement*, Longman, London

McAuslan, P (1994) 'Law and Urban Development: Impediments to Reform', *Cities*, 11 (6), pp 402–8

McGranahan, G and J Songsore (1994) 'Wealth, Health and the Urban Household: Weighing Environmental Burdens in Accra, Jakarta and São Paulo', *Environment*, 36 (6), pp 4–45

Marris, P and M Rein (1972) *Dilemmas of Social Reform*, 2nd edn Pelican, Harmondsworth

Meier, G (1991) *Politics and Policy Making in Developing Countries: Perspectives on the New Political Economy*, ICS Press, San Francisco

Mikesell, R (1992) *Economic Development and the Environment*, Mansell, London

Munasinghe, M and W Cruz (1995) *Economywide Policies and the Environment: Lessons from Experience*, World Bank Environment Paper Number 10, World Bank, Washington DC

Musgrave, R (1959) *The Theory of Public Finance*, McGraw Hill, New York

Norris, D (1989) 'Household Survival in the Face of Poverty in Salvador, Brazil: Towards an Integrated Model of Household Activities', *Urban Anthropologist*, 17 (4), pp 299–321

North, D (1981) *Structure and Change in Economic History*, Norton, New York

— (1987) 'Institutions, Transactions Costs and Economic Growth, Economic Inquiry', 25 (July), pp 419–28

— (1990) *Institutions, Institutional Change and Economic Performance*, Cambridge University Press, Cambridge

Nutt, P and R Backoff (1992) *Strategic Management of Public and Third Sector Organizations*, Jossey-Bass, San Francisco

Olson, M (1962) *The Logic of Collective Action*, Harvard University Press, Boston

Ostrom, E (1990) *Governing the Commons: The Evolution of Institutions for Collective Action*, Cambridge University Press, Cambridge

Panayatou, T (1993) *Green Markets: The Economics of Sustainable Development*, ICS Press, San Francisco

Pearce, D and J Warford (1993) *World Without End: Economics, Environment and Sustainable Development*, Oxford University Press, Oxford

Pigou, A (1932) *The Economics of Welfare*, 4th edn, MacMillan, London

Pugh, C (1985) 'Housing and Development in Singapore', *Contemporary Southeast Asia*, 6 (4), pp 275–307

— (1990) 'A New Approach to Housing Theory: Sex, Gender and the Domestic Economy', *Housing Studies*, 5 (2), pp 112–29

— (1994) 'The Idea of Enablement in Housing Sector Development: The Political Economy of Housing for Developing Countries', *Cities*, 11 (6), pp 357–71

Quarrie, J (ed) (1992) *Earth Summit 1992: The UN Conference on Environment and Development*, Regency Press, London

Rabinovitch, J (1992) 'Curitiba: Towards Sustainable Urban Development', *Environment and Urbanization*, 4 (2), pp 62–73

Samuelson, P (1973) 'The Pure Theory of Public Expenditure', 'Diagrammatic Exposition of Public Expenditure Theories', and 'Pure Theory of Public Expenditure and Taxation', reprinted articles in R Houghton (ed), *Public Finance*, 2nd edn, Penguin, Harmondsworth

Sandilands, R (1990) The *Life and Political Economy of Lauchlin Currie*, Duke University Press, Durham, North Carolina

Stigler, G (1961) 'The Economics of Information', *Journal of Political Economy*, 69, pp 213–25

Sugden, R (1986) *The Economics of Rights, Cooperation and Welfare*, Blackwell, Oxford

Thomas, J and M Grindle (1990) 'After the Decision: Implementing Policy Reforms in Developing Countries', *World Development*, 18 (8), pp 1163–81

Turner, K and D Pearce (1990) *Economics of Natural Resources and the Environment*, Harvester Wheatsheaf, Hemel Hempstead

UNCHS (1993) *Public–Private Partnerships in Enabling Shelter Strategies*, UNCHS, Nairobi

USAID (1990) *Urbanization and the Environment in Developing Countries*, Office of Housing and Urban Programs, USAID, Washington DC

WCED (Brundtland Commission) (1987) *Our Common Future*, UN, New York

Williams, M (1994) *International Organizations and the Third World*, Harvester Wheatsheaf, Hemel Hempstead

Williamson, O (1975) *Markets and Hierarchies: Analysis and Antitrust Implications*, Free Press, New York
— (1985) *The Economic Institutions of Capitalism: Firms, Markets, Relational Contracting*, Free Press, New York
World Bank (1991) *Urban Policy and Economic Development: An Agenda for the 1990s*, World Bank, Washington DC

Chapter Six

Urban Sustainability and Social Cohesion

Peter M Townroe

There is a widespread consensus among researchers and policy commentators that the affluent lifestyle of the richer nations of the world cannot continue without there being consequences of environmental degradation, in land, sea and air.[1] Present technologies are inadequate to prevent this, even if they become effectively deployed, with supporting investments in pollution prevention. At the same time the rapid industrialization and urbanization in the poorer nations of the world in the late twentieth century are both beginning to add very significant further pressures on the ecosystems of the planet earth. These pressures are set to mount considerably in the first decades of the twenty-first century (World Bank, 1992). It is already clear that rising material living standards across the world are causing irreversible changes to the natural environment, locally and globally (Pearce et al, 1990). What is not so clear is how undesirable these changes may be seen to be. Do the environmental changes lessen the net sum of human health and happiness when taken alongside the undoubted benefits of many of the attributes of rising material living standards?

It is not my intent in this chapter to address this leading all-encompassing question on environmental sustainability. Rather, it is to consider a single aspect of the linkage that seems to exist between environmental sustainability, economic sustainability and social sustainability; and to

---

1) This chapter is a development of a paper entitled 'Social Exclusion in the Sclerotic City', prepared for a conference on 'Social Exclusion in Europe: Urban and Labour Market Dimensions', Centre for Regional Economic and Social Research, Sheffield Hallam University, June 1995.

focus this consideration on the city, both in the more industrialized and the less industrialized nations.

The core argument here may be characterized as follows. The rich urban lifestyles of 'the West', which are in fact found among the middle and upper classes of poorer nations as well as encompassing nearly all households in the richer nations, are surrounded by considerable uncertainties. For individuals and for families, there are uncertainties as to the continuity of income and of related employment. There are uncertainties of continuity of access to services, particularly to health care and to assistance in old age. And there are uncertainties in respect of social cohesion, with concerns for family support, exposure to criminal activity and for community participation. Arguably, it is the very nature of the economic system that yields such significant material benefits to this large minority of the population of the world that contributes to these uncertainties. The marketplace, both locally and globally, benefits from flexibility and rapid change and an absence of continuity. And material consumerism, it is often asserted, yields attitudes that are individualistic as well as hedonistic, with a consequent lower priority given to actions and energies directed at the wider social good (see for example Lash and Urry, 1987).

These 'uncertainties of the rich' pose fundamental problems for policy initiatives intended to secure 'environmentally good behaviour'. It is of course tempting for politicians and their electorates in the more affluent cities of the world to ignore the environmental consequences of their urban lifestyles, other than in cases where they become threatening to health (in air pollution, in trace chemicals in the food chain, in the disposal of wastes, or whatever). And even if dangers of this nature, which are classed as 'environmental', are widely recognized, there is a temptation to push what are deemed to be the necessary policy responses onto imposing controls on company behaviour and onto national and international treaties and agreements. The basic materialist consumerist behaviour of households and individuals is barely addressed. For example, policies to raise the price of fuels in the interests of energy efficiency, and hence resource conservation and reductions in emissions, are resisted. Also, household commodities are designed for a cost effective delivery of this or that service to the owner, and with little or no thought to final destinations once the service is no longer required in that form other than to a land-fill site. Policies that effectively reduce the direct material standards of living of households and individuals are not vote winners. And the politicians anyway find that their advisers have difficulty in demonstrating the environmental gains of seemingly desirable policies.

Our understandings of both the short- and the long-term environmental consequences of the various aspects of the present urban material consumerism are very inadequate. And yet any prospect of retreating to an earlier and less environmentally damaging phase in the history of human urban living is unrealistic. To change behaviour now, in the light of what is known now, requires an extremely difficult exercise in political judgement and political leadership in each nation and each city. Certain freedoms will need to be curtailed, key prices raised, new prohibitions introduced – all in a difficult to specify environmental interest. And many of these sorts of policies will hold back or damage the economic competitiveness of cities and nations in their trading relations with other cities and nations, unless, that is, there is some harmonization of policy initiatives between cities and across international boundaries, and also unless capital and labour and the supporting infrastructure in the cities concerned are able to be sufficiently flexible and innovative to refocus the urban economy to maintain its trading position. From that flexilibility and innovation there is the ability to yield gains in areas of real income expenditure of households that do little or no environmental damage to set alongside the losses imposed by the policies introduced in the interests of environmental 'good behaviour'.

The argument therefore is that, put simply, urban environmental sustainability requires urban economic sustainability. This linkage is addressed further in the next section of this chapter. The argument is then taken further to include an explicit social dimension. Changes of the last four decades in the international economic system have posed problems in maintaining the economic competitiveness of many major industrial cities, and hence in providing a potential base for politically less threatening policies designed to enhance environmental sustainability. At the same time, the corporate and public sector policies, in terms of flexibility, innovation and investment in the production activities of the urban economy that are required for urban economic sustainability, pose problems for the social sustainability of the city. There is a linkage through the changing nature of employment and income generation which, it may be argued, introduces a threat to social cohesion. This is highlighted in the literature surrounding what has come to be termed social exclusion. The nature of social exclusion in interacting with the economy of both growing and static cities is considered below.

SUSTAINABILITY AND FLEXIBILITY

The environmental impact of late twentieth-century cities is immense. This is true of cities both in rich nations and in poor nations. The characterizations of the impact may be somewhat different in the two cases, but in both cases impacts arise from the production side and the consumption side of the urban economy.[2]

In outline, a city economy requires inputs of food and water, of energy supplies, and of materials. Each of these is taken from the natural environment and is processed to a greater or lesser degree before the supply reaches the city gates. The real and potential impacts of the extraction of minerals and energy resources are well rehearsed in the literature; the environmental impacts of both the 'primitive' agricultures of poorer nations and the chemical fertilizer rich agricultures of richer nations are also becoming well understood.[3] Before supplies reach the city further impacts arise from stages of processing perhaps taking place in rural areas or in other cities, and of the associated transportation requirements. The chain of stages from the original source of supply may be lengthy.

Within the urban economy two processes then take place in the use of these inputs, both of which yield environmental impacts. Both may challenge the precepts of environmental sustainability. The supply side or production area of the local economy has three dimensions in using the inputs. The first is simply a distribution dimension, taking the inputs from the city gate and making them available for sale in whatever form local markets, whether corporate or household, may demand. The second dimension involves further processing of the inputs within the boundaries of the city, adding value in a material transformation of one kind or another. The resulting products are then sold within the city. The third dimension parallels the second but is directed at sales elsewhere, in other cities, contributing to the economic base of the city in question. Each of the three dimensions has environmental consequences, for land, water and air, within the boundaries of the city and then beyond.

A similar picture comes from the consumption side of the urban economy. Households purchase goods and services which have used natural resource inputs of one kind or another, both involving production (i e transformation) processes within the city or similar processes in other cities and then taken in as imports to the urban economy in question. The resource inputs within these goods and services are not sold on, but they remain in the environment, to remain as artefacts or to become wastes of various kinds or to degrade and decay in various ways.

A distinction is normally made between consumption and investment. However, in thinking of the use made of the resource inputs arriving at

2) Evidence from many sources is discussed at length in Houghton and Hunter (1994). See also Hardoy, Mitlin, and Satterthwaite (1992).
3) See, for example, Lutz and Young (1992), Pearce and Turner (1990), Pearce and Warford (1993), OECD (1994a) and OECD (1994b).

the city gate it is useful to consider additions to the capital stock of the city also as a form of consumption, albeit resource consumption. This capital stock is held in the corporate production sectors in the form of buildings, machinery or vehicles, and in the public or privately owned infrastructure sectors in the form of roads, sewers and utility supply facilities. There are environmental impacts involved in the processes of introducing additions to this capital stock of the city. There are then impacts from the use of the stock and from its ageing and progressive deterioration.

As already suggested, both the supply and the demand sides of the production and consumption sides of the city economy have environmental consequences for the natural environments from whence its resource inputs are derived. There are then consequences experienced within the city boundary. There are then 'downstream' consequences experienced outside the city from the production and consumption activity – solid wastes for disposal, pollutants in the local rivers, air contaminants blown to other locations and so forth.

The outline in the previous five paragraphs is familiar to anyone concerned with the environmental consequences of economic activity.[4] The reason for setting out this particular urban picture, however, is threefold. First, it is a way of emphasizing that the underlying processes involved are similar for cities in poorer nations as for cities in richer nations. Secondly, it points to the obvious limitations of city based environmental policies, desirable as they may be: there is the need for complementary policies that impact at the national and international levels. And thirdly, it underlines the complementarities and the trade-offs between the economic and the environmental aspects of cities. However, the complementarities and trade-offs then extend to the social aspects of cities. So there can be a three way set of relationships in characterizing sustainability.

Relationships between the economic and the social life of a city are direct, involving questions of income distribution, employment and the provision of public services, as well as indirect, involving the culture and heritage of the city, the provision for political involvement and voluntary association of all kinds and the support for education and learning. Similarly, the relationships between the economic life of the city and its local and wider environment are direct and indirect, involving, as Munasinghe (1993:2) suggests, questions of resource use, pollution and

---

4) The discussion is a variant on the standard materials balance approach, which stresses that the mass and energy that enter production and consumption will eventually end up as residuals.

biodiversity and resilience. There are also direct and indirect relationships between the social life of the city and its local and wider environment, seen in attitudes and consequent valuations of the natural environment and of negative environmental externalities associated with both production and consumption; and also seen in attitudes towards policies of limitation and restraint on environmentally damaging behaviours. This raises political questions of popular participation, leadership and consensus, as well as the difficult to articulate question of intergenerational equity.

Any notion of sustainable development seen from the perspective of life in a city at the end of the twentieth century is therefore not only complex but conflict ridden. Both this complexity and this conflict are perceived by many policy makers and commentators as posing new and more severe threats to urban social cohesion. Much of this writing has focused on the urban groups that have become characterized in being excluded from the mainstream of society. The attributes of this exclusion make for a lack of social and economic flexibility in the urban society and economy, with consequences for environmentally damaging behaviour and nonacceptance of the spirit and ethos of environmental policy measures. A useful metaphor for an urban society which seems to be facing a loosening of the bonds of its social cohesion is to see that society as characterized by a form of sclerosis. The rigidities implied by this term can then also be used to view the low levels of flexibility in the urban economy when the economy is subject to external change; and, indeed, used to view the difficulties urban societies have in coming to terms with emerging environmental realities.

The capabilities of the city as a man-made entity are restricted by the existence of a sclerosis in its social and economic life. In the sclerotic city there are dysfunctions which, over time and if not corrected, will reduce the average standard of living and the quality of life of households, even while the marginal benefits therefrom remain positive. Tendencies towards sclerosis in this sense are present in cities that are relatively static in terms of real income growth and/or increases in resident population. They are also present in cities that are much more dynamic, with increases in income and rising populations. In other words, tendencies towards the consequences of socioeconomic sclerosis are found, but in contrasting ways to be explored below, in cities that are typical of the First World as well as in cities that are typical of the Third World. In both the static and the dynamic cities a relationship can be suggested between this urban sclerosis and the presence of socially excluded groupings within the urban population; and hence of threats to sustainability.

PRESSURES FOR CHANGE

In both the characterizations of the static city and of dynamic city which are used here it is useful to be aware of four underlying dynamics of change at work: new technology, evolving patterns of trade with other cities, changes in social organization and developments in cultural attitudes. Even in a city which is relatively static in terms of its population and without improvement in per capita or household income, these four forces for change are present, both endogenous and exogenous in their origins.

The first of these, new technology, will impact upon both the production and the consumption sides of the urban economy. Production methods change with the inventiveness of the work force and as lessons are learnt from elsewhere, associated with capital investment and with an evolution in related labour skills. Similarly, technologies in consumption will change, in both individual households and in social infrastructures and services, with a feedback effect into the input markets of the suppliers of these technologies, whether they be locally based or located in other cities.

Technological change is a major contributor to changes in the patterns of trade *between* cities as well as to the patterns of buying and selling *within* a city. Modifications in the nature of goods and services on offer, and in their supply prices, interact with consumer responses to change the trade flows; and hence the flows of income into and out of the city and the demands made upon the local labour market and the local supporting infrastructure services. The city economy will need to respond both to the availability of new technologies and to the competitive effects of evolving trade demands to be able to sustain current levels of per capita income: the idea of urban economic sustainability (for example Nijkamp, 1990).

Dynamic cities will tend to reorganize themselves as they grow, as in most organisms. The urban society and its associated economy have to meet the new challenges presented by the forces of rising incomes and/or rising populations. This will involve 'civil society', in all of its facets, but also changes in formal and informal social organizations of all kinds. Indeed, many of these organizations have an internal dynamic of their own, as participants learn and invent and modify. And this will occur within a static city also, less externally imposed perhaps for each organization than in the contrasting dynamic city but nevertheless still evolving over time.

An important source of pressure for change in the social organization of the city, alongside new technologies and changes in trade, and rising income and population where relevant, will be developments in the understandings, outlooks, attitudes and values of its inhabitants. Cultural change in the late twentieth century, worldwide, seems to be faster than at any time in world history. Whether it is as profound as in certain past epochs is still an open question, but there is no doubt that no city in the world now escapes new sources of influence on social attitudes and values as they flow around the globe on the back of the international media of communication (see for example Waters, 1995). This source of change, in the static and the dynamic city alike, demands a response: in the urban economy, in social organization and in civil polity. It also, like the three other sources of change referred to here as being present in both the static and the dynamic city, has consequences for the natural environment; and for the phenomenon of social exclusion.

THE POLITICAL ECONOMY OF URBAN SCLEROSIS

Where is sclerosis, an economic and social sclerosis that may hinder moves towards more sustainable economic, social and environmental lifestyles, to be found in urban society? The answer can come from five directions, taking what may be termed a process view of urban society as subject to the forces of change referred to above. The first source of rigidity, of a hardening of the urban arteries, comes from the urban economics textbook – *market failure*. This is a pejorative description of situations in which the efficiency with which markets allocate resources is impeded by inadequate information, for example, or by an asymmetry in power on the supply or demand side of a particular market. In the urban economy this may be seen most clearly in the market for land.

Market failure will result in a loss of potential productivity – values of outputs per units of inputs, of whatever kinds. A *misallocation of capital* is a contributor to this and, while an aspect of market failure, may be taken as a second source of sclerosis. The financing of capital investment involves, necessarily, judgements about the future. This, also necessarily, is very different when the environment of the capital project in question is subject to strong underlying changes through the anticipated life of the project. The urban economy is dominated by investments in buildings and transport and service infrastructures. These structures typically have a very long life and, once in place, are exposed to fundamental changes in the demands placed upon them. Their lifetime efficiency in use is difficult to guarantee and there is therefore a cost attached to uncertainty. Part of that cost arises from the interdependency of different structures at different points in their economic lives. An unwise investment decision, in an economic or a social sense, in one of these structures can have very long-run adverse consequences.

Major capital projects both within the static city and within the dynamic city involve a political process as well as a commercial judgement. Whether the land use planning system within the city be one of discretionary provision or of area-wide zoning, whether services are provided communally or by privately owned organizations, the state intervenes in the processes of change. We can therefore point to potential *political barriers* to the acceptance and facilitation of change, a political sclerosis as a source of rigidity, dampening energies and evolution.

The operation of political barriers depends, of course, on the formal (and informal) powers of politicians and how these powers are influenced by the citizenry. These powers also have to be implemented through governmental entities of various kinds. This suggests a further source of sclerosis: *bureaucratic restraint.* The barriers arise here from the way organizations within the city, both in the state system and within the private and voluntary sectors, react to imposed change and are capable of generating change. Their processes and procedures exhibit rigidity, in the sclerotic city, relatively to similar organizations in other cities.

The final source of sclerosis arises from the structure of these social organizations – an *institutional blockage.* The allocation of powers and responsibilities, the access to resources, the openness of the rules and systems of each organization to modification and change can open up opportunity, or close it down. The arteries harden. And an important, but not sole, influence on this institutional rigidity will be the part that the state plays in the life of the city. The state, in the collective interest, has to act as a ringleader to life in the city. It is the source of laws and regulations limiting activity, as well as being the provider of important institutions offering key goods and services. There is a necessary rigidity in these activities, in these roles, even though nothing is for ever. But the institutional blockages can hold back necessary change.

SOCIAL EXCLUSION AND SOCIAL SUSTAINABILITY

The term 'social exclusion' has been used to denote groups of individuals in a society who can be regarded as 'excluded' by virtue of one or more dimensions of non-involvement or participation in that society (for example Rainwater, 1992). This exclusion may be by unforced choice, either by individuals acting alone or by membership of groups that see themselves as 'outside society'. For the individual, this exclusion may be reflected in a lack of participation in social groupings, in a lack of interest in social events, possibly in a very personal feeling of being an outcast, of being estranged. For the group, the feeling is of being a minority, perhaps a minority that is in some sense in social or political conflict with the wider society, a minority that feels itself to be oppressed or a victim of injustice, or a minority that has chosen to follow a different path to the future from its host society, setting off to build on different values and aspirations.

The use of the term 'socially excluded' has, however, been used much more commonly to denote a different form of exclusion, not by unforced choice but by imposed circumstance or by the attitudes and behaviour of others.[5] Here there are groups of individuals and households who would wish to feel themselves to be full participating members of the wider society, but who find that because of their income level, their race, their physical or mental disability, their lack of education, their place of residence, that this is not possible. Here also there is a difficult distinction to be made: those who *feel* that this full participation is not possible, ie where there is an opinion about perceived attitudes and barriers imposed by others; and those who actively test the barriers, to find themselves in some sense repulsed by the wider society, without successful routes of political, social or economic redress.

'Social exclusion' therefore has dimensions of inactive citizenship attached to it, and dimensions of a lack of mobility past a range of socio-economic barriers, both in terms of opportunity and in terms of achievement – hence the use of that dangerous term 'the ghetto'. At a more functional level, the term can be taken to denote a *lack of access* at a level regarded by the wider society to be both normal and appropriate to the key offerings of society – in education, health care, housing and recreational facilities. Social exclusion can result therefore from a lack of access to these offerings, even when they are made available by the wider society through non-market channels. In other words, functional social exclusion need not necessarily be the result simply of low income employment or of a lack of employment in the local labour market. The term 'socially excluded' could be applied to certain individuals or households with above average incomes and in seemingly secure employment, even though this is not normally the case.

Exclusion may be seen as a process, not as a state, like poverty. The Commission of the European Communities (1989) has seen social exclusion as affecting 'at risk' populations, such as the elderly, the low

---

5) This has been the thrust of the policy concern of the European Union towards the poor and disadvantaged within the European community: a total of some 50 million people within the total community population of 330 million who have a per capita income of less than half their national average, the basis of the 1984 council decision for the Second Social Programme. See Commission of the European Communities (1989 and 1993).

skilled, the long-term unemployed, the school failures, single mothers with children, those living in large public-sector or shantytown housing areas on the fringes of cities, or recent immigrants. The exclusion is characterized by isolation, by being outside networks of sociability, with consequent feelings of guilt, humiliation and absence of self-confidence. Clearly the routes to reintegration for individuals are many. A key vehicle lies in the workings of the urban labour market. The next two sections of this chapter turn to the labour market, both in static and in growing cities, remembering that the reality of social exclusion and failing social cohesion is more complex and multicausal than is implied by considering the labour market alone.

SCLEROSIS IN THE STATIC CITY

The static city here has no growth in population or in real per capita income. It is, however, subject to technological change and to changes in the activity mix within its economy. Indeed, since each city exists within a hierarchy of mutually competing cities, change is necessary for continuity if not for survival. The city economy in its widest sense has to be an evolutionary self-adjusting system. The sustainability of the urban economy requires a minimal capacity of the given city to compete, to maintain its relative per capita income in the face of marketplace competition for both the factors of production and for the goods and services that result from productive activity within its borders.

The urban economy therefore has to flex. This has never been more true than in the late twentieth century. International trade barriers have been progressively lowered over the past 50 years, transport costs have fallen, finance capital is geographically mobile, and patterns of consumption have become progressively more homogenous within an ever widening portfolio of choice of goods and services. The urban economy of the static city has to find the capacity for continual regeneration. This is much more than a stepwise rebuilding after an adverse exogenous shock. It is ongoing. It will be pulled along in part by new demands from the consumption side of the urban economy: new tastes in households, new capabilities in service providers. These new demands will both lead and follow the production side of the economy. The latter will respond with new goods and services, or with more cost effective ways of producing existing goods and services. If not, imports from other cities will rise, local incomes will fall and the population will decline through out-migration. Simultaneously, the production side of the economy must maintain its performance in exporting to other cities, or again local incomes will fall and out-migration will take place.

The possible barriers to the required processes of continual regeneration were those indicated in the section of this chapter on the political economy of urban sclerosis. These are the sources of sclerosis which hold back economic flexibility. The rigidities of market failure and the inefficiencies of misallocations of capital are dominant in the economic as compared with the social arena of the city. But the other sources of sclerosis, political barriers, bureaucratic restraints and institutional blockages, also have consequences for the urban social life and social forms as well as for the local economy.

Unconstrained market forces, for all the reasons set out in introductory economics textbooks, to a greater or lesser degree misallocate resources on criteria of efficiency and badly serve criteria of equity. This is particularly true in the market for investment goods. The capital stock of a static city changes only slowly. Much of this stock is product or process specific. The ability of one item of past investment to be modified, abandoned or replaced interlinks with other changes in other investments, where there is frequently a lack of synchronicity in appropriate financial timing. The facilitating role of urban infrastructure is critical.

Similarly, alongside the flexibility required in the production process from the capital stock there is a need continually to re-evaluate the use made of the pool of labour skills in the city. And in the static city, modified by in- and out-migration it is true, this pool changes only slowly. There are therefore three requirements from the labour force. First, that new entrants have the education and skill training appropriate to the demands of the urban economy. Second, that the education and training before entry provides the basis for subsequent flexibility. And third, that flexibility is ensured by ongoing training and skill updating, and by a preparedness by workers to use their skills flexibly. An inadequate performance by the city, in educational institutions as well as by employers, in any of these three requirements prepares the way for low incomes and/or exclusion from the labour force by significant groupings of citizens. As an example, in the past 20 years the British labour market has moved more towards an American-style labour market, and away from the characteristics found in many continental European nations (Beatson, 1995):

- part-time working has increased;
- self-employment has increased;
- female participation has increased (but with a greater likelihood than now to work on a part-time or temporary basis);
- working hours have increased (since the mid-1980s);
- job demarcation has been reduced;
- time limited contracts have increased;

- labour migration has increased (but has then been blocked by a static housing market since 1990);
- more elements of pay are directly linked to performance, as wage bargaining has become more decentralized;
- wage differentials have widened, in favour of the better educated and more highly skilled; and
- the average number of years spent in formal education by entrants into the labour force has risen.

What are the consequences for social cohesion and social exclusion? Perversely, there are pressures that can result in aspects of exclusion from both the greater flexibility in the labour market and from its rigidity. Lack of flexibility from the demand side of the market, be it for reasons of ignorance or prejudice or an unwillingness to invest in training and retraining, can result in the marginalization of groups of workers, seen in the statistics of the long-term unemployed. A lack of flexibility in the supply side of the labour market can have a similar result when the flexibility is about willingness to change industries, to change occupations, to move geographically, to undertake training or to switch to a lower paid job. That said, at the same time, a high degree of flexibility can put great pressures on individuals and families: in the journey to work, in unsociable working hours, in a lack of job and/or income security, in general uncertainty. These same pressures can result in social withdrawal to a very individualistic lifestyle, and to a lack of community involvement as a form of social exclusion. This could be regarded as a self-inflicted exclusion, but it is the structure and operation of an unregulated labour market that is encouraging it.

A very different form of threat to social sustainability than that arising from the labour market can arise from a different arena of urban sclerosis – the arena of health, education and welfare. In this arena provision in the static city of the more developed nations is typically undertaken through a mixture of public sector, private sector and voluntary sector agencies. All agencies may be subject to sclerosis from institutional blockage – from a failure to update themselves to reflect changing circumstances as well as changing client expectations and attitudes. Rigidity may also come from political restraints on change and from imposed bureaucratic rules and requirements. The result may be that inequities arise over time in the allocation of resources to different social groups, while certain individuals find that their needs are not served by any of the agencies in the city. The needs are then met by migration to another city; or the individual or group is forced back onto what may be inappropriate self-help, which results in the situation for them and for society becoming worse rather than better.

SCLEROSIS IN THE DYNAMIC CITY

In the dynamic city the assumptions of no growth in population and no growth in income are removed. Depending on the rapidity of these two aspects of growth, great change is then forced upon the city. At the same time, changes arising from new technologies and changes in the activity mix arising from developments in trading relationships with other cities will continue to be imposed upon the economic and social fabric of the city. What is now added to the story in respect of social cohesion to that of the static city?

As the average household income rises in terms of real purchasing power, there is no reason to suppose that an automatic trickle down will keep different groups across the city-wide distribution of income in step with one another. Even if the groups were kept in step in relative growth terms, their incomes would diverge in absolute terms. But processes of economic growth, unless associated with redistribution policies, have a tendency to widen rather than narrow income distributions. In a sclerotic dynamic city, the relative inequalities may be particularly marked, with particular consequences for all forms of sustainability.

Rising income reflects changing comparative advantage in intercity trading and a rising productivity of both the capital stock and the labour force locally. The sclerotic effects are seen in different rates or rapidity of response by different agencies and providers in the city to the additional and new demands being made upon them by the higher levels of income present. The higher levels of income will be seen in both the company and the home; and, depending upon the buoyancy of revenues from the local taxation system, will be seen in the public sector also. The rising expenditures place new demands for producer goods and services and for consumption goods and services. A flexible city economy will then respond. But a sclerotic city will find barriers to change, barriers within the market processes or in the hard and soft infrastructures of the city.

Urban sclerosis, from whatever source, holds back the rate of growth of city per capita and per household income to below what it might otherwise have been. It also compounds the difficulty of ensuring that all citizens and households share in the rising prosperity, with the clear result that some individuals and groupings either feel themselves to be socially excluded or are forced into a form of exclusion by a new inability to participate in the evolving labour market, or to purchase or to have access to consumption goods from both the public and the private sectors. Their relative position in the city economy and society is worsened by the rising prosperity of the city majority. Inflexible institutions and bureaucratic procedures, not only of the local state but also of the private and voluntary sectors, do not respond adequately to the new context of higher income, so one or more local minority grouping thereby suffers in an exclusionary sense.

Rising incomes can make a further, deeper impact on the city. This may be characterized as secular consumerism, or attitudes and values that work against inclinations towards community involvement and active social intercourse. Secular consumerism also works against a preparedness to accept responsibility for behaviour that causes longer-term environmental damage. The wider social good is neglected and progressively fails to be understood. Civil society in general suffers, and particular groupings feel themselves to be more and more marginalized. There is damage to the environment both within the city and 'upstream' and 'downstream'.

In many nations of the developing world, in both those that are regarded as being 'middle income' as well as those that are certainly poor on a per capita basis of their gross national products, the major pressure on the social environmental and economic fabric of their cities comes from population growth (United Nations Population Fund, 1991). Growth rates in resident populations of 6 or 7 per cent per annum, giving a doubling time of ten or twelve years, are to be found in many cities, large and small (UNCHS, 1987). The host nations of these cities are well into the phases of economic and demographic transition that put maximum pressure on market responses, on the need for state regulation and institution building and on requirements for a flexible and educated labour force. High rates of population growth alone mean a very skewed age distribution of city residents and a high proportion of in-migrant residents, from other cities but especially from the countryside.[6]

In a situation of high population growth, with or without rises in real incomes, but with changes in technologies in production and consumption, maximum pressure is put upon city governance, broadly defined (Mohan, 1994). The city government, however structured and however much answerable to the national government, finds itself faced with an avalanche of demands for additional housing, water and sewerage services, education, health care, policing, fire services and gas, telecommunications and electricity hook-ups (Gilbert and Gugler, 1992). Access to employment opportunities requires costly expansions to the transport infrastructure, a demand coming simultaneously from industry and commerce needing to move goods and to purchase services. The demands made by the newcomers in all of these areas come on top of

---

6) Policies for education and training and for employment restructuring are discussed in the *World Development Report* (World Bank, 1995: Chapters 5 and 17), with many examples taken from developing nations. The winners and losers from economic change are discussed in the same report (World Bank, 1995: Chapter 16).

demands from existing residents and businesses for additional or improved services, or at least a demand to hold the status quo. But growth makes the status quo problematic. Traffic is congested, utilities become overloaded, queues lengthen for services, all forms of pollution worsen. Low level or limited demands from very large numbers of incomers get in the way of meeting the rising demands and expectations of established households and companies.

CONCLUSION

Three attributes of late twentieth-century cities, both in more developed and in less developed nations, are inextricably linked together. These are the economic vitality of the urban economy, the environmental sustainability of the city lifestyle, and the exclusion of groupings within the citizenry from full participation in the social, economic, political and cultural life of the city.

Such a bold statement invites the immediate response of 'Yes, of course', quickly followed by 'But what do you mean by "economic vitality", "environmental sustainability", and "social exclusion"?' This chapter has partially addressed this question, but note the language of the statement. It is starting to slide into the anthropomorphic: 'vitality', 'sustainability' and 'exclusion' are all terms that can be applied to an organism, including that of the human body. The city may be seen in such organic terms, as an entity of great complexity and with an interdependency of its many component parts. It may be seen as a system, but also as an organic entity capable of repair and renewal when damaged, and characterized by adaption, reproduction and growth over time. The energies of its citizens provide a basis for protraying the city as a living being.

Whether in the context of a rising and progressively richer resident population or not, the linkages between the ongoing sustainability of a city economy, the wider natural environment, and urban social cohesion are far from clear. In putting forward suggestions as to such linkages there is a danger of slipping into economic determinism. Similarly, there are dangers in using a medical metaphor like sclerosis to describe the apparent inabilities of a city to respond to economic and social change in such a way as to result in what may be regarded as the social exclusion of groupings within the citizenry. And yet, there are patterns of causation to be unravelled, and metaphors have their place in reaching an understanding. This chapter has pointed to possible attributes of sclerosis in the economy and society of a city: a hardening of the urban arteries, being the conduits of the creative energies of the city. Rigidities in market processes and in the institutional, bureaucratic and political contexts of the marketplace result in threats to sustainability.

References

Beatson, M (1995) *Labour Market Flexibility*, Research Series No 48, Employment Department, Sheffield

Commission of the European Communities (1989) 'Medium Term Community Action Programme to Foster the Economic and Social Integration of the Least Privileged Groups', *Bulletin of the European Communities*, Supplement 4

— (1993) 'Combatting Social Exclusion', *Social Europe*, 2, pp 33–6

Gilbert, A and J Gugler (1992) *Cities, Poverty and Development*, 2nd edn, Oxford University Press, Oxford

Hardoy, J E, D Mitlin and D Satterthwaite (1992) *Environmental Problems in Third World Cities*, Earthscan, London

Houghton, G and C Hunter (1994) *Sustainable Cities*, Jessica Kingsley, London

Lash, S and J Urry (1987) *The End of Organized Capitalism*, Polity Press, Cambridge

Lutz, E and M Young (1992) 'Integration of Environmental Concerns into Agricultural Policies of Industrial and Developing Countries', *World Development*, 20 (2), pp 241–53

Mohan, R (1994) *Understanding the Developing Metropolis: Lessons from the City Study of Bogotá and Cali, Colombia*, Oxford University Press for the World Bank, Oxford

Munasinghe, M (1993) *Environmental Economics and Sustainable Development*, World Bank Environment Paper Number 3, Washington DC

Nijkamp, P (ed) (1990) *Sustainability of Urban Systems: A Cross-National Evolutionary Analysis of Urban Innovation*, Avebury, Aldershot

OECD (1994a) *Environmental Degradation from Mining and Mineral Processing in Developing Countries: Corporate Responses and National Policies*, Organization for Economic Cooperation and Development, Paris

— (1994b) *Agriculture and the Environment in the Transition to a Market Economy*, Organization for Economic Cooperation and Development, Paris

Pearce, D W and R K Turner (1990) *Economics of National Resources and the Environment*, Harvester Wheatsheaf, London

Pearce, D W and J Warford (1993) *World Without End: Environment, Economics and Sustainable Development*, Oxford University Press, Oxford

Pearce, D W, E Barbier and A Markendya (1990) *Sustainable Development: Economics and Environment in the Third World*, Edward Elgar, Cheltenham

Rainwater, L (1992) 'The Problem of Social Exclusion', in *Human Resources in Europe at the Dawn of the 21st Century* (conference proceedings), Eurostat, Luxembourg, pp 397–410

UNCHS (1987) *Global Report of Human Settlements*, Oxford University Press for the United Nations Centre for Human Settlements (Habitat), Oxford

United Nations Population Fund (1991) *Population, Resources and the Environment*, United Nations, New York

Waters, M (1995) *Globalization*, Routledge, London

World Bank (1992) *World Development Report: Development and the Environment*, Oxford University Press, Oxford

World Bank (1995) *World Development Report: Workers in an Integrating World*, Oxford University Press, Oxford

Chapter Seven

Sustainability and Methodologies of Environmental Assessment for Cities

Ernie Jowsey and Jonathan Kellett

Most cities have developed along lines which do not fully accord with the principle of sustainable development. They continue to be subject to constant change and growth, again usually in an unsustainable fashion; and in many cities millions of people survive *despite* their environment. Even when growth and change occurs in a planned and regulated manner the results may not be sustainable. Yet cities represent an enormous investment in terms of capital and human resources. Wholesale clearing, redesigning and rebuilding of more than very small areas is therefore not a viable option in the drive to achieve sustainability. The challenge, therefore, is to devise techniques and methods which both seek to promote sustainability and are capable of assessing the contribution to sustainability of particular policies and developments. Consideration should be given to:

- the effects of current activities on the future, for example, the continuation of insanitary housing conditions with their adverse impact upon absenteeism at work and school attendance;
- the maintenance of favourable ecological conditions, for example, by taking steps to control motor vehicle emissions which add to the volume of greenhouse gases; and
- enhancing living standards, but in ways which do not lower the living standards of future generations.

Appraisal techniques can be formulated and used to advance the cause of 'sustainable urban development', that is, in bringing together considerations of development, equity and environmental accounting. Applications can be diverse, for example, ranging from the overall pattern and form of urban settlement to specific development projects such as the installation of underground railways. Also, as elaborated in subsequent discussions, city-regions can be appraised and monitored for their overall environmental performance in health-associated risks, pollution and so on.

ENVIRONMENTAL IMPACT OF CITIES

Cities affect local, regional and economy-wide environments. At the local level, the city environment is directly affected by pollution, congestion and destruction of natural habitats. There may be increasing alienation between humankind and the natural world (Goode, 1990). City planners are now sensitive to environmental concerns. In developing countries the sensitivity to environmental concerns does not always mean that effective policies are formulated or that, even if formulated, they are adequately implemented. However, in situations where professional, political and economic conditions are conducive, sometimes some important aspects of urban development are coordinated to secure less polluted air and water, improved removal of wastes, and regard for the conservation of materials, species and desirable environments. The task is enormous: a city absorbs energy and raw materials and discharges wastes, as is illustrated in Figure 7.1.

Daily Input
200 tonnes food
1000 tonnes fuel
62000 tonnes water

City of
100,000
people

Daily Output
275 tonnes garbage
110 tonnes human
waste

Figure 7.1

And disposal costs are increasing. According to Morris (1990) in 1975 in the United States the disposal cost of a tonne of garbage in 1975 was between $3 and $5; by 1990 this had risen to between $30 and $50. For hazardous waste, disposal costs have risen by somewhere in the region of 3000 per cent. Disposal costs can, of course, be cheaper in developing countries, and in some circumstances the retrieval and recycling of waste can be turned into a profitable informal sector activity. Nevertheless, rising costs will become increasingly significant with explosive increases in populations and with good rates of economic growth. The first law of thermodynamics recognizes that matter can neither be created nor

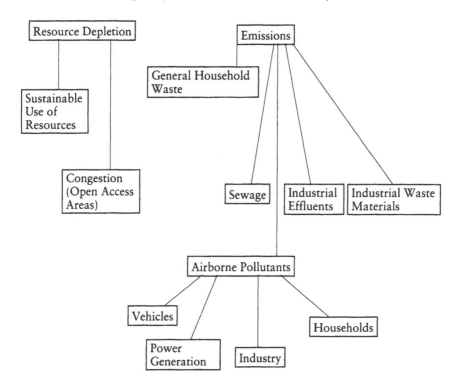

Figure 7.2 *The environmental impacts of cities*

destroyed and so this is a problem which is not going to go away. Of course recycling wastes can play an important part in reducing emissions into the environment and rapid progress has been made in the last 20 years in recycling metals, glass, paper and even the curse of the age, old motorcar tyres. But recycling can never be 100 per cent (the second law of thermodynamics). Many products are dissipated and energy cannot be recycled.

Minimizing waste generation, and optimizing the use of energy and other resources are important components of any strategy to make a local city environment sustainable. In addition, the wastes generated by processes, both domestic and industrial can, as suggested above, be used as raw materials in other processes. At a regional level, cities make increasing demands on their surrounding area for land, energy and food, and most large cities are not self-sufficient in water, often drawing from distant reservoirs. Cities are also often major industrial centres, taking advantage of scale economies, and they impact on the surrounding area

in terms of direct emissions from industry and emissions from commuter
vehicles in their journeys to and from work. Some of the pollutants can
have effects very far afield, as in the case of damage from acid rain in
Scandinavia which originates in part from the emissions from power-
generation plants in Britain. River pollution can affect downstream
ecologies hundreds of miles from its source as evidenced by recent events
on the Rhine and Danube rivers. The landscape of the region can be
affected by the city's transport links, its food requirements, its waste
disposal sites and its recreation needs.

Even economy-wide impacts may be important. Large building
projects such as an airport terminal or undersea tunnel may draw on
resource inputs from distant sources and trigger a general rise in the price
of building materials everywhere. Increased mineral extraction means
more environmental damage in the wider economy. Nuclear power
generation carries dangers which can be enormously widespread as was
proved by the Chernobyl meltdown in 1986. Even hydropower can have
unforeseen widespread effects. The decision to establish a hydropower
plant on the Kaptai river in Bangladesh had widespread social impacts.
To feed the Kaptai reservoir, the Karnafuli river was closed in 1962 and
a number of marked ecological and socioeconomic changes occurred: a
number of large lakes formed and forests and teak plantations were
cleared. A large area of Kassalong Reserve Forest had to be cut down for
the rehabilitation of displaced people. The project was welcomed by the
non-tribal people of Chittagong District, particularly those industrial
groups and urban elites who needed electricity most, but it is evident that
the decision to establish the hydropower plant by the then East Pakistan
government (now Bangladesh) did not adequately consider the social
impacts of the project (Haque, 1991).

Figure 7.2 illustrates the most important environmental impact of
cities under the headings of resource depletion and emissions which are
the two paramount issues of environmentalism. As indicated in Figure
7.2, emissions occur continually and widely in various economic
activities, including formal sector industry, informal sector production,
and in running the household economy. As revealed in other chapters in
this volume, gaps and inadequacies occur in some important infrastructure services, resulting in added environmental adversity. Also, as
elaborated in the chapter by McGranahan and his coauthors, city-regions
can experience an 'environmental transition' whereby impacts can be
classified (for example, sanitation, particulate pollutants, and greenhouse
gases) and related to levels of affluence and stages of urban economic
development. As shown in the diagram, 'resource depletion' has direct
impact upon matters such as the renewability, the substitutability, and
the exhaustibility of resources. From the perspective of relevance in this

chapter, in principle the foregoing factors can be analysed, assessed and monitored using appropriate techniques. The discussions now proceed to give exposition and commentary on appraisal techniques.

ASSESSMENT TECHNIQUES

The essential prerequisites of a move toward the development of environmentally more sustainable cities are a policy framework which overtly considers environmental issues and a range of techniques to be used in both the analysis of these policies and in informing decision making on development proposals. Policies need to be framed at a number of different levels, with some consistency running through the hierarchy. The experience of the European Union (EU) action programmes on the environment is a potentially useful model for action elsewhere. In particular, the guiding principle of the 'polluter pays' sets the agenda for the application of techniques at a variety of levels.[1] Equally the principle of considering the potential environmental implications of policies and development proposals at the outset is enshrined in EU policy and in terms of moving towards sustainability can be usefully employed elsewhere in the world by national, regional and city governments. A wide variety of techniques is available to assist in the analysis of city environments as a means of furthering public policy.

Appraisal techniques can be arranged, classified and selected according to purpose and use. In general and in comprehensive perspective, appraisal is required for city-wide assessment and monitoring, for undertaking performance audits, and for examining the specific beneficial effects, the costs, and the impacts of particular urban development projects. Figure 7.3 displays the classification in a set or 'hierarchy'.

At the top of the hierarchy is Strategic Environmental Assessment (SEA) which allows the wider policy content at central and city level to be examined in terms of its environmental implications. Relationships between the city and its surrounding hinterland may also be critically examined at this level. Below this level of analysis Environmental Impact Assessment (EIA) can be used to consider the potential environmental

---

1) The 'polluter pays principle' was adopted by the member countries of the Organization for Economic Co-operation and Development in 1985. It states that the polluter should bear the expenses of carrying out the pollution prevention and control measures decided by the public authorities to ensure that the environment is an acceptable state. This is a simple idea in its direct sense because it means that the costs are levied on the firm or group that pollutes. However, the real cost will normally be shared because costs will be raised, decreasing supply and at least part of the increased costs will be passed on in increased prices, thus reducing demand.

effects of specific development proposals and Environmental Audit (EA) used to present a picture of the existing state of the urban environment. Cost-benefit analysis feeds into both of these latter techniques in that by a variety of methods it can be used to formulate monetized valuations of environmental (ie non-market) goods and thus aid in internal policy making, for example by finding shadow prices for non-market costs and benefits.

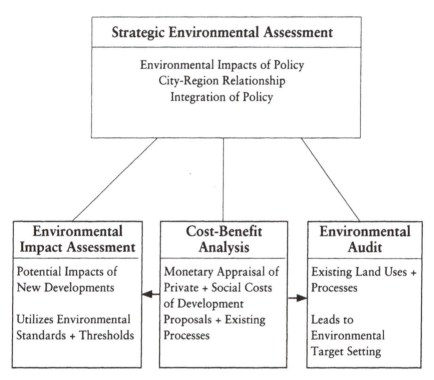

Figure 7.3   *Hierarchy of assessment techniques*

As mentioned above, the hierarchy in Figure 7.3 expresses various purposes and levels of application. Cost-benefit analysis can be used in versatile ranges of application, for example, in EIA and project appraisals. Other kinds of analyses can be used selectively to provide information in their own right or to support some elements in cost-benefit analyses. For example, hedonic pricing and contingent valuation techniques provide a breakdown of factors compressed into prices, and means of indicating the shape and form of demand curves in simulated markets. The various methods and techniques in Figure 7.3 are now given exposition and commentary.

STRATEGIC ENVIRONMENTAL ASSESSMENT (SEA)

SEA has significant relevance for the formulation and development of policies and for giving effect to the idea of sustainable urban development. Consider the nature and exampling of sector policy developments. Sector policies in energy, in transport and so on are frequently formulated and pursued without general assessments of their results in the environment, even though specific projects or programmes such as hydroelectric schemes may have some environmental evaluation. This means that though sector level policies have consequences for sustainable development, they tend to be ignored and remain unanalysed. SEAs can be designed and instituted to reveal the general advantages or disadvantages in environmental relevance. For example, energy policies will probably contain provisions for various regulations, for levels and applications of taxation, and for economic incentives or disincentives which favour some modes of energy production relative to others. Such policy frameworks have differential effects on the volumes, the physical characteristics, and the health conditions arising from particulate emissions and greenhouse gases. An SEA would aim to assess the comparative results, adding to the usually gathered economic information.

In terms of urban development this pattern tends to be repeated. Individual housing, industrial or transport projects often receive a good deal of consideration of their potential environmental effects. But there is rarely a rigorous assessment of the impacts of project decisions in one sector on another. For example, consideration of the implications of road construction or industrial development on demand for housing is only infrequently addressed by aid organizations (Hyman, 1990:210). At the city-wide level plans are often formulated which overtly consider environment concerns in relation to particular land use zones, specific policy areas or projects, but for the most part such plans have not examined the interrelationships of different policy areas in terms of their potential environmental effects or in terms of their implications for sustainable development. A clear gap exists in relation to the environmental appraisal of policies, plans and programmes at the national, regional and city levels. Let us examine the SEA system of policy appraisal further.

The main principles of such policy appraisal can be expressed, as follows:

> Systematic appraisal entails being clear about objectives, thinking about alternative ways of meeting them, and estimating and presenting the costs and benefits of each potentially worthwhile option. Used properly, appraisal leads to better decisions by

policy makers and managers. It encourages both groups to question and justify what they do. It provides a framework for rational thought about the use of limited resources.

(HM Treasury, 1991)

Of course, the principles were originally formulated to apply to policy appraisal for reasons of financial efficiency and economy in the use of resources: but they are equally applicable to the examination of the environmental implications of policy. SEA is therefore the application of policy appraisal techniques in order to assess the environmental implications of policies, plans and programmes. The question we now address is what can SEA achieve in terms of enhancing the sustainability of cities?

City governments must deal with the complex interaction between policy, the economy and the environment. Therefore, in order to ensure that sustainability is being given sufficient consideration, the following objectives (derived from Therivel et al (1992)) need to be addressed:

- alternative policy options, including the 'do nothing' option, should be given full consideration at an early time, this being the time when an agency has greater flexibility, relative to subsequent times;
- consistency is needed across different policy sectors, especially where trade-offs need to be made between objectives;
- cumulative, indirect or secondary impacts of diverse multiple activities must be considered, including their unintended consequences;
- adverse environmental impacts must be anticipated and hence reduced or prevented;
- environmental impact of policies that do not have an overt environmental purpose must be considered;
- the needless reassessment of issues and impacts at project level which could more effectively be dealt with at a strategic level, must be avoided;
- there should be a publicly available and accountable decision-making framework;
- environmental principles such as sustainability and the precautionary principle must be integrated into the development, appraisal and selection of policy options; and
- proper place must be given to environmental considerations in decision-making vis-à-vis economic and social concerns, with appreciation that in some contexts these concerns may be traded off against each other.

Thus SEA is intended to ensure that full regard is given to environmental aspects of all significant policy decisions whether concerned with land use, the economy or society. In the majority of cases the focus for such analysis is likely to be a land use plan but this is no reason to exclude budgetary plans, for example from examination by means of SEA.

The technique itself is still in its infancy, though a growing body of literature (for example Wood and Dejeddour, 1992; Therivel et al, 1992; DoE, 1993; Cuff, 1994) suggests that it is clearly related to, but different from, project level environmental impact assessment. The literature suggests that an SEA should incorporate a number of stages including for example, scoping,[2] providing a description of the affected environment, evaluating the significance of potential impacts, and examining mitigation measures. SEAs should also incorporate extra stages, notably a consideration of alternatives to the proposed policy, plan or programme, and a discussion of the boundary, either spatial or sectoral, which is to be applied in the study.

There is little documented evidence of the application of SEAs in developing countries, beyond statements of intent. The US Agency for International Development (USAID) for example has stipulated that its environmental programme will seek to address:

- relationship of renewable natural resources to economic growth and the need for a strong policy base;
- global environmental issues and climatic change;
- integration of environmental concerns in all sectors;
- complex relationships between population growth and natural resource use; and
- rapid urban and industrial growth.

The starting point for SEA development is attention to training both donor and host government professional staff. Lack of environmentally aware personnel both within donor agencies and host countries has produced fundamental failures in the past. For example, the construction of housing in Dakar, Senegal and Umoja, Kenya on unstable sites indicates the very low knowledge base from which many such projects begin (Hyman, 1990:206).

In respect of policies, plans and programmes that aim to enhance the

---

2) Scoping an environmental impact assessment is the process by which the impacts and issues which the study will address are determined. From the overall list of potential impacts, which may be extensive, a shortlist of key impacts is determined as a result of consultations with statutory agencies and the general public and by extrapolating from similar experience with developments elsewhere.

sustainability of cities two approaches to SEA seem particularly appropriate. The first concerns attempts to evaluate the environmental implications of a group of policies relating to the economy, land and resource usage. Thus, the interdependence, complementarity or contradiction between policies relating to property rights, agriculture and industry is a useful case in point. A study of Thailand (Panayatou and Sussangkarn, 1991) demonstrates that the absence of clear delineation of property rights increased incentives to exploit fragile lands, while an accompanying lack of regulation or economic instruments governing industrial development was associated with major environmental damage. The need to coordinate policies in rural and urban areas, recognizing the effects of action in one area on the other is crucial.

Secondly, analysis of the environmental implications of policy within a discreet sector such as energy, at national, regional or city level can be facilitated by SEA and reveal useful information for future policy adjustments. For example, it was common practice in the formerly socialist countries of central and eastern Europe to subsidize energy prices. Although this provided households with substantial consumer benefits, and partly acted as an anti-poverty device, it severely increased pollution levels. This adverse environmental effect arose both from distorted high-volume production and from the lack of economic incentives to introduce pollution-reduction technology into economic processes. Also, environmentally insensitive lignite was used extensively in energy production in eastern Europe (World Bank, 1993).

Methods of SEA are as yet ill-defined and diverse. General equilibrium models could be regarded as representing a useful tool in the overall process, as indeed could most models designed to test the effects of variations in policy on a range of other variables or policy areas. Probably the simplest and most common approach, however, is the matrix as illustrated in Figure 7.4.[3]

Figure 7.4 displays a range of policies on the vertical axis and a range of factors broadly relating to global sustainability, natural resources and local environmental quality on the horizontal axis. Each cell in the matrix receives a score illustrating either a beneficial, adverse or neutral impact. The advantage of the method lies in its simplicity. An examination of the completed matrix quickly reveals where the potential problem areas lie. This allows the consideration of alternative strategies and policies and their evaluation in relation to environmental impacts. And, as suggested earlier, evaluation can take place in a timely way

---

3)   Figure 7.4 is crown copyright and is reproduced with the permission of the Controller of Her Majesty's Stationery Office.

Criteria	Global Sustainability						Natural Resources				Local Environmental Quality				
	1 Transport energy: Efficiency: trips	2 Transport energy: Efficiency: models	3 Built environment Energy: efficiency	4 Renewable energy potential	5 Rate of CO$_2$ 'fixing'	6 Wildlife habitats	7 Air quality	8 Water conservation and quality	9 Land and soil quality	10 Minerals conservation	11 Landscape and open land	12 Urban environmental 'liveability'	13 Cultural heritage	14 Public access open space	15 Building quality
Policies															
1 To provide a network for open space corridors	O	✓	O	O	✓	✓	✓	O	✓	O	☑	✓	✓	✓	O
2 To concentrate residential development on an existing public transport corridor of the city	O	✓	✓	O	O	☑	✗	O	O	O	☑	✓	☑	✗	✓
3 To concentrate residential development on a new rural 'green' settlement (c 8000 population)	✗	✗	✓	☑	☑	☑	O	☑	✗	☑	✗	✓	☑	✓	✗

Context: District-wide plan for a city of 150,000 and its hinterland
Illustrative policies: 1 For open space. For fuller explanation see Figure 5.5.
2 and 3 Represent options for the location of housing

Suggested impact symbols

- O No relationship or significant impact
- ✗ Significant adverse impact
- ☑ Likely, but unpredictable impact
- ✓ Significant beneficial impact
- ☐ Uncertainty of prediction or knowledge

Figure 7.4 *The policy impact matrix*

before the practical steps of land acquisition, site availability, financial commitment and commercial decision making are commenced.

The problems attached to SEA relate largely to its nature. The emphasis on policy interactions and in many cases inter-departmental cooperation suggests that governmental structures both at national and city level may sometimes be ill-equipped to accommodate the technique. A corporate willingness to take a holistic approach to the environmental implications of policies, plans and programmes is essential to the successful application of SEA, which, as argued here, can promote urban sustainability.

PROJECT LEVEL ENVIRONMENTAL IMPACT ASSESSMENT

EIA has historical justifications and these provide some understanding of its development during the post-1970 period. Before the institutionalizing of EIA (which has been gradual and uneven), it was common for mega projects in such things as the construction of dams, new towns, large airports, and major intra-city highways to have substantial technical analyses in engineering and economics, but scarcely any consideration of environmental impact. With the increasing social and political significance of environmentalism EIAs were introduced. These can range in analytical characteristic from very generalized commentaries on potential environmental impact to thoroughgoing technical and evaluative analyses of such things as conservation of species, changes in groundwater processes, profiles of pollution and so on. The sorts of analyses which are used are varied, including cost-benefit analysis and supporting work on hedonic pricing, contingent valuation and other methods (see subsequent discussions). The roles and attitudes of the World Bank have been of particular significance to developing countries. During the 1980s the World Bank received much criticism for ignoring environmental analyses, for example, in mega dam projects in India. This led it into adopting the role of EIAs, and the 1992 Earth Summit has heightened interest in applying EIAs more generally.

EIA at the level of individual projects is much more clearly defined and accepted by both politicians and developers than is SEA. A considerable body of literature describing the technique and its applications exists (Lee and Wood, 1987; Wathern, 1988; Fortlage, 1990; Glasson et al, 1994; Morris and Therivel, 1994). The method can prove of great benefit in identifying potential environmental threats from new development and provide mechanisms for their mitigation. It should ideally be used in conjunction with SEA because by itself it is incapable of dealing with the question of alternatives to a proposed development, either in the sense of alternative sites or alternative actions, nor can it readily identify the effect of cumulative impacts. Each project is subjected to an analysis of its environmental effects, but the compounded effects over time of, for example, a number of road schemes and subsequent traffic generation, or a number of power station developments and their combined effect on air quality, are difficult to establish using EIA alone. It is in respect of individual developments that EIA comes into its own. Here it provides a rigorous and objective assessment of the likely impacts of a project before it is developed and can prove of enormous benefit in the design of measures to mitigate these impacts.

As suggested above, too often in the past, even in cities and regions in developed economies, the potential environmental effects of proposed projects have been inadequately considered. Objectivity and a willingness to consider the full range of potential project impacts on, for example, air quality, water pollution, destruction of ecosystems, contamination by pesticides and toxins are vital prerequisites of any serious environmental impact assessment. Within the EU the groundwork for just such an approach has been laid down in Directive 85/337/EEC, *On the assessment of the effects of certain public and private projects on the environment*, to which all member states have now complied. Elsewhere, progress towards this more rigorous approach to evaluating the environmental effects of projects is patchy. In China, for example, while legislation in the form of the Environmental Protection Law (1979) exists, its application often leaves much to be desired. The system contains no formal procedures for public consultation and thus must be regarded as wanting in respect of the scoping process. Also, while the process is usually adhered to, the results may not in all cases have a direct bearing on the final decision to permit or prohibit development. Elsewhere in the 1980s, particularly in several Latin American countries, the overriding political agenda has deliberately played down environmental issues. Authoritarian regimes sometimes sought to exclude the democratic process, and proved a major obstacle to effective implementation of the EIA process (Verocai Moreira, 1988). However, since the late 1980s, the reform of a number of such regimes in favour of more democratic systems, allied to the increasingly rigorous environmental requirements of aid organizations has considerably increased the scope for the application of EIA. Guidelines on project level EIA are now operated by the Organization for Economic Cooperation and Development (OECD), the United Nations Environment Programme (UNEP), the United States Agency for International Development (USAID), the World Bank and the UK's Overseas Development Administration. Furthermore, international trade agreements such as the North American Free Trade Agreement normally carry with them a requirement to impose minimum environmental standards in the interests of fair competition. As a result Mexico has sought to upgrade its environmental controls in the industrial zones of the Mexico–US border.

The vital prerequisites of successful EIA are participation, the involvement of all affected and interested parties and openness about development proposals from their initial conception. Equally important is an established and clear set of standards relating to pollution thresholds. A cornerstone of EIA is objectivity and quantification of impacts. Prediction of, for example, air pollution from an increased number of private cars within a city, requires both the expertise to forecast the level of traffic increase, relating this to increased air pollution from exhaust emissions, setting this against the existing baseline pollution level and, crucially, establishing whether the predicted situation is acceptable. Arriving at this judgement depends upon the existence of established standards. These can take various forms, ranging from measurement of pollution at the point of emission through to standards related to the eventual target of pollution (for example levels of lead in the human bloodstream or the rate of erosion by acidic rainwater of heritage buildings). Between these two points various other pollution references are possible, for example, a standard of maximum acceptable pollution in drinking water supplies can be an extremely valuable criterion against which to judge the impact of potential future developments. City governments should therefore consider closely both the need for a system of pollution standards and the most appropriate point on the pollution pathway at which to establish standards (see Figure 7.5).

Figure 7.5 provides a summarized view of the pathway that a pollutant takes from source to target and indicates the various points at which it can be monitored. There are advantages and disadvantages to carrying out measurement at different points. For example, monitoring emissions of particular gases or chemical outflows may be technologically fairly simple and easy to police but takes no account of the environment into which the pollutant is being emitted. The capacity of the environment to absorb pollution, with little or no harm to humans, flora or fauna is thus ignored. At the other end of the scale, monitoring of biological targets such as foodstuffs or the human bloodstream may give very accurate information on the effects of pollution on health but provide little clue as to the source of a particular pollutant. Also, it may only provide a signal once dangerous levels of pollution have been realized. Careful consideration should, therefore, always be made of the best point of measurement and this usually depends on the purpose of the exercise. Is monitoring being carried out to pinpoint a source of pollution, test the existing environmental quality before a new development is built, or to assess whether certain health standards or thresholds have been reached

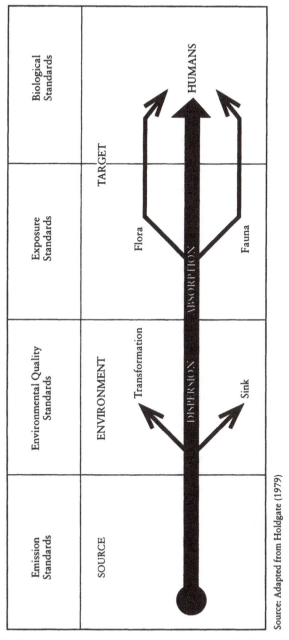

Figure 7.5   *Pollution, pathways, environmental standards and points of measurement*

or breached? We can say with certainty that all these points of measurement and stages in the pollution pathway are relevant in providing information to an EIA study.

ENVIRONMENTAL AUDIT (EA)

The framework provided by a coherent set of pollution standards and an institutionalized and democratically operated system of EIA are basic tools in the management of change and control of new developments in the interests of increasing the sustainability of cities. It must be recognized, however, that change in the form of new activities, in land use patterns, new developments, industrial processes and infrastructure represents only a small fraction of the environmental impact of an existing urban area. Most buildings and land uses have been in existence for a long time. Most activities, patterns of movement, sources of energy and industrial processes are equally well established. All have environmental effects which are in most cases not quantified, recorded or even in some instances subject to legal controls. Environmental auditing is a growing commercial field in industrialized nations and mostly focuses on the activities of individual companies which wish to ensure that they are complying with current environmental legislation and to promote their own 'green' credentials in a world of increasingly environmentally aware customers and consumers. More generally, the results of various environmental policies and economic development activities can usefully be subject to overall monitoring and review. Periodic environmental audits on a city-wide basis can achieve these purposes. More is said about this below.

In developing countries many firms may be serious polluters of the environment but have few resources to put into pollution control technology. For example, small-scale metal finishing and galvanizing firms, normally employing less than 20 persons are important to the economy of Kuala Lumpur, Malaysia. They also represent a source of contamination of local water courses. A study by Industrial Development for Environmental Action (IDEA) analysed the problem and established a project team consisting of scientists and representatives of government and the metal finishers themselves. A strategy for dealing with the problem was devised with the cooperation of all parties (Corley et al, 1991:71).

Environmental auditing can also be applied more widely by governments, particularly at the level of cities or regions. In this instance it consists of an examination of the existing state of the environment and the development of environmental policies covering a range of factors.

The scope of such a study would typically include consideration of air, water, waste, noise, energy, land, agriculture, wildlife, open space, transport and townscape. The initial stage can often prove to be the most problematic in that the data required, for example, on air quality, land use, or resource utilization may not be readily available or accessible. Where data do exist they may be out of date. Building up a complete state of the environment review may therefore be costly. Moreover, continual monitoring to assess the impact of policy change is vital if the expenditure is to prove worthwhile. The outcomes of such a review may prove extremely valuable. First, it can identify areas where immediate action is required in order to avoid major public health or environmental problems. As Harpham and Werna demonstrate in Chapter 2, environmental and health auditing can be combined. Further examples might include the cumulative effects of exhaust fumes from traffic growth, or the impending degradation of fragile ecosystems as a result of urban development or water resource exploitation. Second, a steady flow of time series data on environmental quality allied to the existence of pollution standards and thresholds allows policy to be established and environmental targets to be devised. Thus, a realistic framework for the reduction of greenhouse gas emissions from power stations burning fossil fuels may emerge from such a review. Energy policy may diversify to include increased prominence for conservation measures and the development of renewable sources of power in order to reduce fossil fuel dependence.

Intrinsic to the development of such targets and policies from the environmental review is an attempt to compare different aspects of environmental quality and value them in a common unit of account. Thus, the potential degradation of air quality can then be set against increased availability of electric power in a way which will allow direct comparison to be made. One aspect of the application of all of the methodologies discussed so far, therefore, is the basic usefulness of overall economic appraisal and some analytical endeavour to value environmental assets.

COST-BENEFIT ANALYSIS (CBA)

CBA has versatility, relevance, and useful analytical qualities for environmentalism. As suggested in earlier discussions it can be used to inform strategic environmental assessments, environmental impact assessments, and environmental audits. It also has significant possibilities for drawing together many environmental impacts into a common unit of account, usually set in economic terms. Essentially, like conventional private sector investment appraisals, it conveys information on rates of return over investment periods or cycles, on associated benefits and costs, and these indicate project justification or rejection. However, CBA has some significant differences compared with private sector investment appraisal. First, CBA takes a longer view. That is to say, the conventional time period of investment in private sector projects is in the range from 8 to 15 years, whereas CBAs are sometimes associated with social and public sector investments which have durations of up to 60 years or longer. Since environmental relevance is long term, CBA is accordingly more appropriate than private sector appraisals. Second, CBA tends to be wider than private sector investment appraisal. It is wider in the sense that it can account for (and sometimes measure) social costs and social benefits. Examples of social costs are the deleterious health effects of pollution: these sorts of things are obviously relevant to environmentalism. Third, CBA is often related to matters which are within the governmental arena, making them inherently political.

The use of CBA has expanded since the 1960s, with applications in health, education, housing, urban renewal, urban development and a range of environmental issues. The analyses are seldom free of technical, social and political controversy. Nevertheless, they can be adjusted to incorporate considerations of anti-poverty and social equity, thus adding to information on their primary purpose to assess social efficiency (ie economic returns to society). As elaborated further in subsequent discussion, issues to do with the environment also add to the need for adopting CBA. This is especially relevant in accounting for and valuing environmental assets (for example, the ozone layer, fisheries, clean air and water, and so on). Analytical progress in the valuation of environmental assets is in its infancy.

CBA is one of a range of techniques which can provide quantitative guidance to decision makers when appraising projects. It is uncontroversial to suggest that all benefits and costs should be accounted before a particular policy or project is implemented. Where CBA is contentious, however, is in its methods of attaching specific numbers or values (especially money values) to costs or benefits which many regard as unquantifiable. For example, Ranasinghe (1994) uses a loss of earnings (human capital) approach to quantify the possible future health impacts of pollutants SO_2, NO_x and particulates in Sri Lanka. In simple terms, the benefits of a project must be greater than the cost and all costs and benefits are evaluated, both private and social.

Environmental costs and benefits are often difficult to predict, however, and to quantify in physical terms. Even when quantified, the process of translation into money values is difficult because markets for effects such as loss of a scenic view or biodiversity loss either do not exist or are imperfect.

CBA is a technique which has been developed and applied chiefly in the public sector where it is used to assess projects in relation to their net benefit to society as a whole. As suggested above, CBA is an extension and development of private sector investment appraisal (which takes into account private costs and benefits) by accounting for the wider social costs and benefits. The technique proceeds in stages by identifying, quantifying and evaluating direct and indirect costs and benefits arising from a project. The main purpose is to bring a greater sense or rationality and objectivity into decision making. This includes attempts to identify and measure all costs and benefits, including indirect social costs and benefits such as pollution and the value of environmental amenity, notwithstanding the presence of difficulties in achieving comprehensive measurement. For example, consider the conventional application of CBA to the construction of a new motorway. The direct costs would include the value of materials, wages and other resources used in construction. Benefits are largely indirect, taking the form of 'shadow price' cost reductions associated with a more efficient road network. (More is said about 'shadow pricing' in subsequent discussion.) The relevant cost reductions are the value of time savings in journeys, lower rates of fuel consumption and the lower levels of injury and death in the improved road system. Dilemmas and difficulties will occur, of course, in placing economic values on injury and death. Inherently, as a form of economic project appraisal, CBA involves comparisons among alternative ways of fulfilling similar objectives. Such comparisons are achieved by assigning monetized values to all relevant costs and benefits, and deriving the net present value (NPV) of the project using discounted cash flow (DCF) analysis. Net present value (NPV) is the sum of the discounted benefits of a project minus the sum of the discounted costs or losses arising from the project:

$$NPV = \sum Bt \, (1 + i)^t - \sum C_t \, (1 + i)^t$$
> where $\sum Bt \, (1 + i)^t$ is the sum of the benefits discounted for t years and $\sum C_t \, (1 + i)^t$ is the sum of the costs discounted for t years.

If the sum of the discounted benefits exceed the sum of the discounted costs it can be assumed that the project or policy is efficient in terms of its use of resources. Discounting is necessary because the costs and benefits will accrue over a period of time and people attach less weight to a similar benefit or cost in the future than they do one in the present because of impatience or 'time preference' and the existence of positive interest rates. That is to say, the existence of positive interest rates means that, for example, £1 hypothetically saved, will accumulate higher returns at, say, 10 per cent than at 5 per cent. Then, by the principle of reciprocity, £1 in the future is worth less in the present, discounted at 10 per cent rather than at 5 per cent. Discounting, as specified in the formula above is a technical means of transforming flows of costs and benefits (including environmental flows of costs and benefits) into capital sums. In other words, it is the capitalization of a timestream of flows to a 'present value'. This has significance for environmentalism beyond its role in project appraisal: it can be used to value environmental assets.

Conventional CBA has been primarily concerned with the social and economic costs and benefits of projects. However, provided that relevant costs and benefits can be identified and assigned financial values, it is also possible to take environmental considerations into account. Environmental cost benefit analysis (ECBA) thus involves the identification, quantification and evaluation of all the environmental effects of a project. For new road construction, environmental costs such as the destruction of natural habitats and the effects of global warming due to any rise in the emission of carbon dioxide from increased levels of traffic must be evaluated if the project is being appraised from a global environmental perspective. The application of ECBA for such purposes can be extremely complex and potentially contentious since any project usually has many diverse environmental impacts and there may be disagreement over their assigned money values.

Monetized valuation of environmental effects seems to some to be anathema. Applying crude monetized values to environmental costs such as the loss of a living species seems almost immoral, but it must be regarded only as a unit of account or measuring rod in order to enable comparisons. It may not be ideal but it is all we have got. And the practice of putting values on loss of life as in the motorway example is now well-established in conventional CBA, which often uses the loss of the sum of future anticipated earnings as a measure (or people's willingness to pay (wtp) for a reduced risk of death).

The practice of attaching money values to environmental effects or services at least emphasizes that environmental services (despite the absence of conventional markets for them) are not free. The 'total economic value' (TEV) of an environmental resource consists of its use value (UV) and its non-use value (NUV) or existence value. This type of value exists because people may value an environmental asset without ever using it or even intending to use it. For example, people may value the continued existence of a particular architectural style in a preserved building, without ever intending to visit it. Further subdivisions of these types of value are possible and Figure 7.6 illustrates some possible classes of values for the preservation of a historically important building as part of a city's heritage.

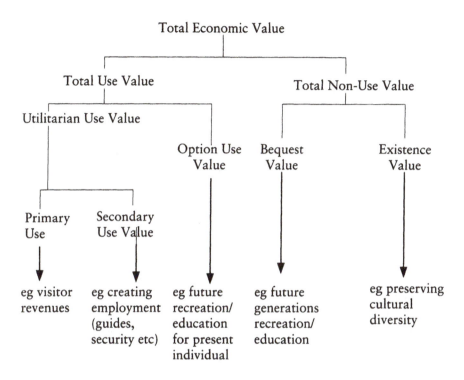

Adapted from Bateman (1995)

Figure 7.6

Environmental economics attempts to take into account both use and non-use values in ECBA using a variety of valuation methods.

HEDONIC PRICING

Urban environmental conditions are often captured in the prices of housing and other assets. However, the prices are reflecting the aggregate of diverse elements or characteristics, including location, design, proximity to transport, and positive or negative environmental attributes. It would be useful to have the information unbundled and sorted into separated values. Hedonic pricing techniques aim to achieve this. Accordingly from environmental perspectives it is possible to 'see' the values attributed to sanitary conditions, to pollution free location, to tree planting, and so on. This has policy relevance and gives some useful meaning to the idea of urban sustainable development. Hedonic pricing is highly technical, using sophisticated statistical techniques.

Hedonic valuation methods find values for the environment by considering changes in prices in surrounding markets. Very often a change in the value of an environmental asset can be assessed by changes in property prices. For example, a change in the landscape of an area can lead to a change in local house prices and the cost or benefit of the environmental change can be estimated from the change in property value. Usually such a study would use cross-sectional data from a number of different types of property at a point in time in order to eliminate the possibility of other influences occurring over a period of time. Of course a number of influences on property values would be exerting some upward or downward pressure on values and it is important to specify the variables which have an effect correctly and not to include variables which will not have an effect. It is necessary to assume that households are willing to pay more for an improvement in environmental quality and while this assumption seems reasonable in richer societies it is not necessarily true in very poor societies.

In most studies the effect of an environmental cost or benefit on property values has been observed. It is possible to control the non-environmental factors by studying a cross section of different properties with similar attributes but different environmental effects, for example, varying levels of aircraft noise. In this way a money valuation of the effect of an increase in noise levels can be found. For a detailed case study of the hedonic valuation method see Nelson (1982), which reviews nine empirical studies covering 14 different housing samples for Canada and the United States and suggests that location of a property close to major highway could reduce its value by 8 to 10 per cent. In terms of significance for urban conditions in developing countries, as discussed in the chapter by McGranahan and his coauthors, low-income households have environmental priorities for safe and sanitary living conditions. Hedonic pricing can be usefully applied to the valuation of specific neighbourhood improvements, consequently identifying priorities.

THE TRAVEL COST METHOD

The travel cost method (TCM) was developed by Clawson (1959) and Clawson and Knetch (1966). This method creates a 'shadow price' value by assuming that the costs incurred in visiting a recreational amenity, such as a city park reflect the visitors' valuation of enjoying the amenity. The amenity value of a city park will be thus assumed to be at least equal to the costs incurred to get there. Multiplying the travel cost by the number of visits will give an indication of total value provided by the park. As might be expected there will usually be a normal relationship between the costs of a visit and the number of visits made so that those living furthest away and facing the highest travel costs make the fewest visits.

This is a relatively straightforward method which is often used for valuation of recreational amenities. The TCM divides the area surrounding the site into concentric circles or 'zones'. Visitors are asked by questionnaire which zone they have travelled from and visitation rates are calculated for each zone. Of course other factors apart from travel cost may have an influence on visitation rates and so the survey will obtain data from visitors on income, starting point for the journey and number of alternative sites available, and adjustments can be made for these 'other factors'. The duration of the journey must also be included with a value placed on time. Grandstaff, Dixon and Eutrirak (1986) conducted such a travel-cost study for Lumpinee Public Park, Bangkok. The opportunity cost of retaining it as a park is high and rising because of its potential value for commercial development. Visitors' responses were used to build up a simulated demand curve for visits to Lumpinee, relating frequency of visit to total cost (in terms of time cost and travel cost). Following the principles in welfare economics (a specialist branch of economics), because there is no admission charge, all the area underneath the demand curve is accounted, this being known as 'consumers' surplus'. The method produces a valuation which is remarkably similar to that produced by the contingent valuation method applied to users of the park (see the discussions below) and considerably less than the contingent valuation method applied both to actual users and to those who did not actually visit it but who valued its existence and the 'option value' to visit it in the future.

The TCM uses information on travel costs to generate a final demand curve for a recreation facility. It is, therefore, most appropriate for those facilities where travel cost is a major component of total visit costs which may well be the case where entry to city parks is free. One major aspect of TCM is that it can be used as justification for city-regional investments in recreational areas, including these with environmental and educational relevance.

A major problem with TCM is estimating travel time costs. The costs of time spent travelling are usually estimated as some proportion of hourly wage rates, but what proportion is to be selected can be a subjective decision. It may even be possible that time spent travelling is not a disutility, but is part of the whole recreational experience, in which case a zero cost for travelling time could be justified. A further problem is that other variables such as income and age are likely to influence visit rates and these are likely to vary across the zones. Also, for some visitors the visit may be only part of a multipurpose trip, and the cost should, therefore, be shared among those places visited.

THE CONTINGENT VALUATION METHOD (CVM)

The essential purpose of CVM is to use simulation and hypothesis to derive hypothetical demand curves and economic values in circumstances where markets in environmental goods are either incomplete or do not exist in direct and readily discernible ways. This method asks consumers directly for their valuation of a specific environmental asset or effect. CVM uses survey methods to obtain individuals' willingness-to-pay for an environmental attribute or their willingness-to-accept compensation for the loss of that attribute. Empirical research has shown that willingness-to-pay valuations are consistently considerably less than willingness-to-accept valuations for reasons which may be more to do with people's psychology than economics. It may be that people value more highly the loss of something they already own, leading to a high willingness-to-accept valuation, compared with the gain of something they do not yet have. There are several possible reasons for this divergence including: 'income effects', i e richer consumers suggesting very high willingness to accept values; 'loss aversion' whereby losses are weighted more heavily than gains; survey problems because of bias in the format of the questions; and respondents acting strategically or politically by giving answers that they believe will serve their interests best (i e they misrepresent their true valuation).

Questionnaire design is always problematic and that is certainly the case with CVM valuation. Normally, a series of values are listed and respondents are asked if they are willing to pay increasing amounts (or willing to accept decreasing amounts). The starting point for values may influence the respondent, leading to bias in results, and other forms of bias may occur. Techniques can sometimes be refined, aiming to eliminate bias by asking people to assume fixed budgets, or by using alternative ways to find the same information in order to verify responses. Bias problems can be minimized with suitably designed survey instruments (Tietenberg, 1992).

CVM can be used to value environmental benefits or costs where no market exists by asking people for their estimation of value if the market did exist, i e in a 'contingent market'. As such it is a technique which can be used for valuing some environmental assets and is potentially useful, but because the respondents or valuers are providing information on a hypothetical cost or benefit it is necessary for them to be familiar with the issue and it is most likely to be useful for valuing changes in amenity, air and water quality, wildlife and biodiversity amongst a well-informed and concerned population (Winpenny, 1991). People are not always well informed on the objective benefits and costs of environmental factors and accordingly this can lead to under- or over-valuation. Favourable circumstances for consumer valuation are most likely to arise in industrialized countries, although a study of willingness-to-pay for water services in southern Haiti, a developing country, leads Munasinghe to the conclusion that 'it is possible to do a contingent valuation survey among a very poor, illiterate population and obtain reasonable, consistent answers' (Munasinghe, 1993:85-8). Accordingly, CVM has analytical and policy relevance. It can be used as information in cost-benefit analysis and for improving policy development.

PRICING METHODS

Earlier discussions referred to situations where environmental effects are not directly priced or observable in price. For example, cost-benefit analysis includes the accounting of social costs and social benefits. Social costs and social benefits arise from the operation of market processes, but occur in dispersed and hidden ways affecting third parties. That is to say, such things as the adverse health effects (with their associated remedial costs) arising from pollution are placed upon parts of the general urban population, not being confined within direct producer–consumer relationships. However, by using appropriate methods of measurement, such indirect and dispersed cost impositions can be set out in the form of 'shadow prices' (ie inferred prices). Also, it will be recalled that demand curves can be simulated in contingent valuation methods, using hypotheses and surveys to create estimates of demand in relation to price. In this section, inferential and simulated price is given more attention. The *'shadow-pricing' or opportunity cost approach* looks at the amount or value which would have to be foregone in order to preserve the environment or to restore it to its original state after it has been damaged. In an extreme case the victims of environmental damage might have to be completely relocated and these relocation costs would give a shadow price for the environmental damage. An urban industrial site may require restoration or decontamination before being used for housing or as an amenity. Restoration costs in this case are clearly observable and give a clear shadow price for the environmental damage.

Where restoration is not feasible at the original site, for example where trees are cut down or wildlife habitat is lost in a road-building scheme, it may be necessary to 'price' an equivalent alternative project elsewhere. The compensating project does not actually have to take place, but it should be clear that there would be sufficient value in the original environmentally-destructive project to pay for the alternative scheme. In other words, a 'potential Pareto improvement' should be demonstrated. 'Pareto improvements' (named after the Italian nineteenth-century mathematician and economist, Vilfredo Pareto) are gains in economic growth and efficiency, whereby there are no losers. The implausibility of this criterion has led other economists to modify it, relaxing the requirements for gain. That is to say, a 'potential Pareto improvement' requires only that in principle, hypothetically, the efficiency gains would be sufficient to compensate any losers from a policy intervention. In most environmental applications there would be gainers and losers: the 'potential Pareto improvement' asserts a principle of analytical compensation. Thus gainers could compensate losers (The 'Hicks-Kaldor Criterion'). The major problem with the compensating approach is that in some applications it simply may not be possible to replace the natural environment which is lost. Indeed some environmental assets, such as the ozone layer or the Amazonian rain forest may be regarded as 'critical natural capital'. In the context of the city economy, however, this is less likely.

The *dose-response method* assesses the impact or response of the 'dose' of pollution on production from such things as agriculture, forestry and fishing. The physical effects of the pollution must first be ascertained by laboratory or field research or controlled experiments. This must be followed by a statistical regression technique to isolate the influence of a particular variable and to exclude the influence of exogenous (ie incidental) variables. Volumes of production lost are valued at market prices (adjusted for subsidies) giving a 'shadow price' for the pollution cost. A major problem here is that the loss of production from the pollution can itself increase market prices, resulting in over-valuation of the loss. Or consumers may avoid the produce if they believe it to be contaminated, resulting in less demand and lower prices. Clearly this technique could be applied to pollution damage to buildings where this damage can be measured by costs of restoration, and to health effects where the pollution causes measurable (priced) impacts upon a local population's health. This latter possibility, however, may be difficult because of the problem of identifying the statistical relationship between the pollutant and the health effects. For less developed countries in particular, the population may suffer the ill-health without recourse to medicine, which means that an accurate 'shadow price' cannot easily be estimated. Care also needs to be taken with health issues when valuation of human life is necessary; assessments have to be made of the value of increased risk of death, which is often controversial.

A general criticism of the pricing methods is that they do not capture all value, as would be more likely in the 'valuation' methods previously discussed. They measure only prices of some related product or scheme and provide rough price estimates of environmental goods and services which might otherwise be disregarded. The pricing approaches are, however, generally easier to apply and in some cases easier to understand (and therefore to justify).

OVERALL PERSPECTIVE ON ENVIRONMENTAL ASSESSMENT

The foregoing reviews indicate that there is a wide and versatile range of approaches and techniques for environmental assessment. Moreover, the range not only assesses socioeconomic returns, cost, benefits and rankings of alternatives: it can also be used to value environmental assets in more or less useful ways. Consequently, the techniques add calculation, measurement and some objectivity in urban sustainable development. In fact, in some intellectual developments it has been possible to adapt and transform *conventional* cost-benefit analysis to *environmental* cost-benefit analysis, thus setting on course a new technical subject specialization.

Having indicated some positive aspects of technical and analytical approaches to environmental assessment, it should not be assumed that assessment is uncontroversial. It is possible to recall and summarize some dilemmas and controversies from earlier discussions. First, cost-benefit analysis is inherently full of value judgements and ethical choices in its attempts to extend the range and application of economic valuation in social costs and social benefits, in providing monetized value to environmental assets, and generally in testing the boundaries of the 'economic' and the 'noneconomic'. Second, it is necessary to heighten awareness of the relationships and problems which exist between project-level and economy-wide situations. Project analysis operates within narrow and specific terms of reference, whereas broad sectoral and economy-wide (including international as well as national units of analysis) assessment have effects which can influence the efficiency and effectiveness of projects. It is necessary to review terms of reference at project levels to incorporate the wider processes and impacts, especially in matters environmental.

Third, environmental applications of techniques such as cost-benefit analyses raise to special relevance the issue of compensation. As explained in earlier discussions, at analytical and theoretical levels the subject 'welfare economics' is couched in terms of 'Pareto' and 'potential Pareto' improvements. Whereas a 'Pareto improvement' abjures compensation because it excludes the possibilities of any losses occurring in a policy or programme intervention, a 'potential Pareto improvement' includes the (hypothetical and analytical) possibility of compensation of losses from a larger aggregate of gains. The 'potential Pareto improvement' is known in the relevant literature as the Hicks-Kaldor Compensation Criterion. However, as suggested above in matters environmental it is often necessary to move beyond hypothetical compensation in principle to a *real* provision for restitution or compensation. This point is strongly argued by Bateman (1995), giving examples of equivalent substituting of lost natural assets in development. Compensation is thus simultaneously expressive of principles of social and economic equity on the one hand and 'sustainability' on the other.

Finally, in overall perspective the earlier explanations on the discounting of futures and the capitalization of 'flow' phenomena into (present value) lump sums can be taken a step further. It is appropriate to consider the role and the specific value of the rate of discount (ie the opportunity cost rate of interest and social rate of return). High discount rates have been indicated to discount futures heavily: that is they place a relatively high value on the present rather than on the futures. Also, it will be recalled that more distant benefits in time are worth less in technical formulae than those closer to the present. Obviously this poses dilemmas for environmentalism. For example, trees are often very slow growing, or, detriments such as cadmium have very long-term adverse activity. The dilemmas arise in a context that discount rates are both theoretically and operationally derived from economic processes of saving, investment and market behaviour. This does not always represent idealized perspectives on environmental objectives, although it does represent some valuing of present priorities relative to futures. The underlying point is well put by Pearce (1991) who argues that discount rates above 1 or 2 per cent in environmental analyses imply that global climatic change would not be considered a serious problem. Thus, analyses which use discounting techniques are always implicitly saying something about future environmental valuation.

CONCLUSION

The approaches to analysis of policy, estimates of environmental effects and valuation of environmental goods outlined above are of immense potential value in the drive towards increasing the environmental sustainability of cities. In order to achieve this end it is clear that many often conflicting trends and viewpoints need to be reconciled in a transparent and democratic manner. This process itself demands a certain formalization of approach and the utilization of specific techniques. In this chapter we have attempted to show how a hierarchy of such methodologies can be applied to cities, specifically in relation to the generation of policy and resolution of the environmental conflicts which can sometimes result.

The intention throughout is to utilize techniques that will give serious consideration to the balance of environmental quality both now and in the future; wherever possible to maintain or enhance the quality and diversity of environment which current generations have inherited; and finally to seek to improve the quality of life of the current generation of city dwellers. There is no doubt that this is an ambitious agenda. It requires careful consideration and an acceptance by all parties and agencies involved in decision making that the process can be aided by the application of those methodologies. Environmental standards and thresholds based on high quality scientific research, clear objectives and up to date environmental data, and agreed processes for the valuation of environmental goods are all fundamental to this process. So too is the acceptance of a democratic, objective and unbiased assessment of the potential effects of new developments.

Many developing countries demonstrate surprisingly high activity rates in respect of some of the techniques discussed. Project level EIA and CBA incorporating various valuation methods are not uncommon. A good deal of this activity however stems from the action of aid agencies. The marked lack of suitably trained local personnel needs to be addressed if progress is to be maintained. Also this review suggests that most activity is confined to the level of projects. SEA and environmental audit are rarely practised and yet remain vital to the overall analysis of environmental factors described above. Future progress thus depends on greater involvement of all concerned groups, not just aid agencies and governments, and it requires investment in environmental training and an acceptance of the need for policy analysis as well as continued project level concern.

All the techniques should be applied carefully, and the most appropriate technique to the prevailing circumstances chosen in each case. Abuse, obfuscation or the perversion of methodologies in the interests of particular political or financial ends sometimes occurs but is unacceptable and will undermine their rational use for the environmental cause. But neither should we see these various methodologies as of peripheral relevance in themselves or treat them as mechanistic ways of arriving at solutions. We suggest they have a value in furthering the sustainability of cities, but they are tools to be used in that process, not formulae to be blindly applied and adhered to in the pursuit of a more sustainable world. They have to be related to programmes and policies, including such things as health-related effects, infrastructure improvement and other spheres featured in other chapters in this volume.

References

Bateman, I (1995) 'Environmental and Economic Appraisal', in T O'Riordan (ed) *Environmental Science for Environmental Management*, Longman, Harlow

Clawson, M (1959) *Methods of Measuring the Demand for and Value of Outdoor Recreation*, Reprint No 10, Resources for the Future, Washington DC

Clawson, M and J L Knetch (1966) *Economics of Outdoor Recreation*, Resources for the Future and Johns Hopkins University Press, Baltimore, MD

Corley, M, M Smith and S Varadurajan (1991) 'A Network Approach to Enhanced Environmental Management', *Project Appraisal*, 6 (2), pp 66–74

Cuff, J (1994) 'SEA: Evaluating the Policies EIA Cannot Reach', *Town and Country Planning*, February, pp 45–7

DoE (1993) *The Environmental Appraisal of Development Plans: A Good Practice Guide*, HMSO, London

Fortlage, C (1990) *Environmental Assessment: A Practical Guide*, Gower Technical, Aldershot

Glasson, J, R Therivel and A Chadwick (1994) *Introduction to Environmental Impact Assessment*, UCL Press, London

Goode D (1990) 'A Green Renaissance', in D Gordon (ed) *Green Cities, Ecologically Sound Approaches to Urban Space*, Black Rose Books, Montreal

Grandstaff, Dixon and Eutrirak (1986) in J Dixon, Hofschmidt and M Maynard (eds) *Economic Valuation Techniques for the Environment: A Case Study Workbook*, John Hopkins University Press, Baltimore MD and London

Haque, M M (1991) 'Sustainable Development and the Environment: A Challenge to Technology Choice Decision Making', *Project Appraisal*, 6 (3), pp 149–58

HM Treasury (1991) *Economic Appraisal in Central Government: A Technical Guide for Government Departments*, HMSO, London

Holdgate, M W (1979) *A Perspective of Environmental Pollution*, Cambridge University Press, Cambridge

Hyman, E L (1990) 'An Assessment of World Bank and AID Activities and Procedures Affecting Urban Environmental Quality', *Project Appraisal*, 5 (4), pp 198–212

Lee, N and C Wood (1987) *Environmental Impact Assessment: Five Training Case Studies*, Occasional Paper No 19, Department of Planning and Landscape, University of Manchester, Manchester

Morris D (1990) 'The Ecological City as a Self-Reliant City', in D Gordon (ed), *Green Cities: Ecologically Sound Approaches to Urban Space*, Black Rose Books, Montreal

Morris, P and R Therivel (eds) (1994) *Methods of Environmental Impact Assessment*, UCL Press, London

Munasinghe M (1993) *Environmental Economics and Sustainable Development*, World Bank Environment Paper No 3, World Bank, Washington DC

Nelson, Jon P (1982) 'Highway Noise and Property Values', *Journal of Transport Economics and Policy*, 16 (2), pp117–37

Panayatou, T and C Sussangkarn (1991) 'The Debt Crisis, Structural Adjustment and the Environment: The Case of Thailand', Paper prepared for the World Wildlife Fund Project on the Impact of Macroeconomic Adjustment on the Environment, Washington DC

Pearce, D W (ed) (1991) *Blueprint 2: Greening the Global Economy*, Earthscan London

Ranasinghe, M (1994) Extended Benefit-Cost Analysis: Quantifying some Environmental Impacts in a Hydropower Project, *Project Appraisal*, 9 (4), pp 243–52

Therivel, R et al (1992) *Strategic Environmental Assessment*, Earthscan, London

Tietenberg T (1992) *Environmental and Natural Resource Economics*, Harper Collins, New York

Verocai Moreira (1988) 'EIA in Latin America', in P Wathern (ed) *Environmental Impact Assessment: Theory and Practice*, Unwin Hyman, London

Wathern, P (1988) *Environmental Impact Assessment: Theory and Practice*, Unwin Hyman, London

Winpenny, J T (1991) *Values for the Environment*, HMSO, London

Wood, C and M Dejeddour (1992) 'Strategic Environmental Assessment: EA of Policies, Plans and Programmes', *Impact Assessment Bulletin*, 10 (1), pp 3–22

World Bank (1993) *The World Bank's Role in the Electric Power Sector*, A World Bank Policy Paper, World Bank, Washington DC

Chapter Eight

Conclusions

Cedric Pugh

Although some characteristics of the literature on sustainable development can be traced to the 1970s, it has been since the late 1980s that thematic positions have deepened along the lines that 'economic growth' and 'sustainability' are not necessarily detrimental to each other. As some of the chapters in this book demonstrate, in application to urban sustainable development there are significant gaps between a prescription for growth and sustainability on the one hand and the realities of the world on the other. Insanitary conditions in low-income living areas lead to significant disease and death, consequently retarding both sustainability and economic development. Principles of comprehensiveness in the pursuit of 'healthy cities' can be explicated, but the scope and experience in implementing city-wide policies and programmes is currently very limited. Among the poor there is much to be said for linking sustainability, economic improvement, and some aspects of policy development with the participation and empowerment of the poor. But the necessary processes in this can cut across established patterns of political and professional power, and additionally community development is often slow, relying upon 'learning by doing'. Even though the improvement of infrastructure and utilities can be brought within affordability and appropriate technology, again various professional, political and social impediments can slow down progress.

Similar problems arise in broader scale issues. Many cities are experiencing structural economic change that disturbs inherited power structures and redistributes winners and losers. The application of a prescriptive sustainable development is bound to have variability in effectiveness with mixed success and failure. Some cities and towns will be progressive and others retarded by what one author terms 'sclerosis'. Some aspects of progress will depend upon installing institutional arrangements for analysing, appraising and monitoring development and environmental impact. As with other necessary elements, again questions are raised about leadership, capacities for reform, and supplying adequate education and training in the requisite knowledge and skills. From the international perspective it is clear that important roles and influences reside with the World Bank, UNDP, UNEP, UNCHS and WHO. However, just as questions arise on the institutional and organizational capacity of national and local governments, so too do these questions have relevance for the potential (in)effectiveness of international organizations. As indicated in the book, international organizations require some reform and some 'learning by doing'. Overall, it is seen that progress in sustainable development in cities is closely associated with appropriate policy and institutional reform. Although some exemplars exist, success depends upon particular conditions which are not always readily replicable. More than this, the notion of 'sustainable development' itself changes as knowledge and social structures develop and become more complex. It has been shown that such changes have been occurring since the 1992 Earth Summit. The development of knowledge merits some attention.

KNOWLEDGE: CREATION, DESTRUCTION AND DEVELOPMENT

The subject 'urban sustainable development' is in its infancy, with prospects for strong growth and future maturity. Knowledge can be created, destroyed (i e the elimination of error) and developed in more or less adequate ways. What does the philosophy of science and social science suggest as good development of knowledge? It would have fertile cumulative qualities. The range would include theory, concepts, principles, empirical findings, new techniques and concerns for developing vertically from the detailed picture, through problem solving, to the big picture. It would draw upon theory and findings in basic science and social science, relating these to urban sustainable development, and the new field would also assume some of its own unique characteristics. Research would also range from interest in the 'grand issues' of political economy to applied micro-studies of socioeconomic and physical conditions in urban environments. The new subject would develop some mainstreams and orthodoxies, but be open to epistemologically useful heterodox ideas.

It is also appropriate to be aware that inadequacies and distortions can occur in the development of knowledge. For example, Meier (1994) an eminent American development economist, was commissioned to undertake a review of development studies research in Britain in the period 1980 to 1994. He found some good work but also some significant inadequacies, including meagre theoretical development, excessive ideological idioms, only modest multidisciplinary work, and detrimental conflicts between contract funded and scholarship research. He also noted that there were few examples of collaborated research programmes drawing together expertise in industrialized and developing countries, especially for long-term empirical and theoretical work. Over time, in research the inadequacies can become just as embedded and consolidated as the good qualities. All of this signifies that research fields should themselves be evaluated, and even in their infancy new subjects should set out upon some useful lines of development.

In indicative outline, the collection of writings in this book offer some of the following contributions in the development of knowledge. Various authors have entered discourse on the concept and meaning of 'sustainability', 'sustainable development' and the way these can be related to economics, to society and to ecology. They do not have agreed and unified conclusions, but add understanding and concepts. Some aspects of this subject can be clarified. The term 'sustainable development' refers to some definite patterns of development, these being characterized as being influenced by deliberated environmental considerations. Urban relevance is added in various conceptual perspectives. For example, 'health' can be understood as a state of wellbeing which expresses physical, social and mental attributes. This is brought into relationship with 'sustainability', therefore informing meaning, interpretation and programmatic possibilities in urban sustainability. Or, in another perspective, the idea of 'urban income' can establish economic welfare as comprising take-home pay, the net value of environmental amenities and disamenities, and social income, including intra household transfers. Obviously, for some the net value of environmental amenities and disamenities will be negative and subtract from other components of income. This may press the significance of policy development, including for example the incremental improvement of infrastructure services.

Some chapters in the book advance the progress of knowledge in micro-studies, including collaboration between researchers in industrial and developing countries. An example is the detailing of living conditions in low-income living areas of São Paulo, Jakarta and Accra. This research has also led to establishing principles and concepts in urban development. The idea of the 'environmental transition' relates such things as insanitary conditions, air pollution from industrial particulates, and greenhouse gases to levels of aggregate income and stage of development. The idea is intellectually useful and it can readily be applied to the formulation of policies in environmentalism. But the book also suggests that opportunity and constraint in policy formulation can be influenced by the very processes of urban economic development. Spatial–structural change in cities is not uniform either within any city through medium-term periods or between different cities. Economic change places demands upon the reform of policies, of institutions and of the urban professions. Responses to these demands will themselves be variable in timing, in appropriate perception and in their effectiveness. Again, it is seen that the way developmental and environmental change is elaborated and understood has both epistemic (ie knowledge creating) and social (ie policy) worth.

As suggested earlier, the subject of urban sustainable development is in its infancy. It is not at the stage when a systematic set of core theories and principles can be identified. This book clearly offers only some formative and incremental ideas and principles, related to early stages of subject development. The new subject occupies a place within general development studies. And it should be appreciated that like urban sustainable development, general development studies have adopted environmentalism only comparatively recently. Specialists in urban sustainable development will need to have awareness of environmentalism in general development studies. This section finishes with some indications of the current progress of knowledge creation in the idea of sustainability in general development studies.

As reasoned by Goldin and Winters (1995) it is necessary to bring theory, technique and empiricism to the forefront in the intellectualism of sustainability. Also, there is much to be said for securing the sustainability debate upon economic foundations, though, as this book reveals, other relevant foundations include selections from physical sciences, from studies of institutions and from sociopolitical structure. In the economics of development the emerging (controversial) conclusions that have relevance to sustainability are as follows:

- First, owing to the significance of the 'whole picture' in environmentalism, major conceptual and analytical attention should be given to macroeconomics and development economics, with supporting microeconomic studies. Orthodox economics can achieve progress, along with some acceptance of heterodoxy. Studies to date indicate that it is erroneous to assume that people are basically inclined to invest just for themselves rather than for futures.
- Second, the position of developing countries is significant, not only for their own standards of living, but also for their impacts upon global warming. As indicated in the introductory chapter, develop-

ing countries are going through important 'demographic', 'wage and poverty', and 'environmental' transitions. Increases in particulate and greenhouse gas pollutions will very much be related to these transitions with interdependent cause and consequence relationships between pollution, mass poverty, and progress with economic development. Overall it is useful to think of an international development period in the next 50 years or so characterized by a 'pollution hump'. Empirical evidence in industrial countries shows that abatement in particulate and greenhouse gas pollution occurs with higher levels of income, this abatement following medium-term increases during the transition from poor to middle-income country status. However, there is nothing natural about this eventual abatement process: it depends upon social choices and environmental policies. But, as shown in this book, in their insanitary living environments the poor place priority upon improved sanitation rather than on more remote issues such as global warming. This does not, of course, in itself mean that attention to global warming should be relegated. All of this has implications in research and policy perspectives. For research, some emphasis should be given to comparative air pollution and abatement in urban areas. For policy, with the current and imminent high volume of industrial growth in China and India some collaborated international attention should be given to ways in which the pollution intensities of output can be reduced without intolerable adversity to economic competitiveness. More generally in policy, priority should be given to reducing the length of the explosive phases in the transitional 'pollution hump'.

• Third, contrary to much populist opinion and purist causes for 'ecologism', some centrally important economic findings give little support for an overriding general pessimism. The economic costs of maintaining physical, human, environmental and other assets are not unduly high, though they have to be brought within appropriate accounting and policy frameworks. Environmental policies are unlikely to have any significant adversity upon prospects for long-term growth. In pursuing environmentalism, economic liberalism has a significant role as well as do selective and appropriate regulation. Environmental problems need to be approached on a wide front rather than within occasional and narrowly based programmes. Some international aspects of environmentalism can be attended to by inter-country bargaining and negotiation, especially where there may be gaps in internationally imposed regulations. One current example is in Mexico where some industrial countries have assisted in developing fluorescent lamps to replace oil-burning lamps: the World Bank acted as coordinator and participating industrial countries could account the abatement of pollution as credits in the post-Earth Summit agreements.

The foregoing reveals that some useful knowledge creation is being achieved in development economics. As mentioned previously, the subject matter of this book, urban sustainable development, is only in its formative stages. A research future which brought together general development studies, urban economic development, and environmental studies would have much to commend and justify it. Urban development is a major contributor to macroeconomic growth, to changes in human well-being, and to the characteristic state of the environment. However, within the existing intellectual development of the literatures urban and development studies are largely separated. The environmental connection may draw these studies more closely into interdependence. The discussions above also reveal that knowledge creation sometimes has relevance for the formulation and monitoring of policy. This raises issues that centre upon 'political economy' and something can be said about the political economy of sustainable development.

POLITICAL ECONOMY

The theory and practice of 'sustainable development' is inherently embedded in political economy. This is so for a number of reasons. Questions of economic development and policies for the environment are at the interface of state–market relationships, and programme development sometimes includes state and market relationships with NGOs, CBOs, firms and households. The late twentieth-century brown agenda issues range through the politics and economics of international organizations such as the World Bank, various UN agencies, then to action plans by national governments, and to localized development of slum upgrading and the expression of city–regional 'Agenda 21' development, derived from the authority of the 1992 Earth Summit. Liberalized markets can be variously and simultaneously pro environmentalism but also adverse to sustainability to the extent that they generate social costs such as traffic congestion and air pollution. At the same time, state interventions and government agencies may achieve mixtures of success and failure in their environmental impacts, either through policies or in their economic activities that impinge upon the environment and development. At all levels of policy and programme application there are situational complexities in endeavouring to balance economic efficiency, the operation of markets, regard for the public goods and economic externality aspects of the environment, and attention to issues affecting poverty and social justice. In most instances, the balancing and reconciling has to be custom-made and specific because situational complexity precludes the application of ready-made and easily replicable solutions. In more general perspective, as indicated in the Introduction, the political economy of environmentalism stands in contrast to that of ecologism. Some advocates of ecologism call for fundamental state intervention and a return to localized self-sufficient economic organization. All the foregoing is indicative of the deep and extensive presence of political economy in sustainable development.

The authors in this book have included attention to issues of political economy in more or less direct and indirect ways. Examples can be recalled. Discussions were undertaken on the relative position of environmentalism and ecologism, on the capacity of international organizations, on the role of institutional reform and development. Reference was made to the context of 'enablement liberalism' in the late twentieth century themes of economic development, this influencing the way sustainability has been interpreted. Some authors have deliberated upon the positive contributions community development, participation and empowerment can make among the poor in environmental improvement projects. In dealing with sanitary and utility improvements in the living areas of the poor in cities such as São Paulo, Jakarta and Accra, Gordon McGranahan and his coauthors argued that pragmatic and appropriate political economies at localized levels had the sort of complexities that meant that resolutions could not be achieved simply by making shifts along the spectrum of more or less government or market involvement. Often it was a case of improving, changing and increasing both market and government involvements. Other authors demonstrated that the agenda of issues, the significance of various environmental elements and the opportunities for market and state reform are subject to subtle and important changes in the economic dynamics of modern urban development. The chapter on methods of environmental appraisal revealed that the selection and application of techniques require judgement, creative thinking and adaptability to changing conditions. Overall, policy agendas for state activity have been seen to be enormously wide ranging, covering regulations, taxes, property rights, institutional reform, education and the association of sustainable development to social, health and economic policies.

From the foregoing it is clear that sustainable development is varietal in the principle and application of political economy. Nevertheless, it is appropriate to press the point that approaches to the political economy of sustainable development can vary in quality and relevance. This statement has historical and situational significance. Discussions in the previous section of this chapter made reference to Meier's recent review of research in development studies in Britain (Meier, 1994). Meier discovered that research developments can be negligent of theory and technical application, excessively ideological and political, and lacking a useful cumulative creation of knowledge. Thus, it is appropriate to have some caution and wariness in the nature of how political economy might develop in the theory and practice of urban sustainable development. Although political economy should not be compressed into monolithic approaches, it is possible to set out some relevant guidelines and appreciation.

The term 'political economy' has been used in a rather generalized and ill-defined way in the urban literature. For example, various economists, political scientists, historians, geographers, sociologists and others describe themselves as 'political economists'. Consequently, 'political economy' comes in a variety of versions, some with the intention to separate orthodox (neoclassical) economics from 'political economy'. However, the idea of sustainable development is associated with 'development economics' a specialization in economics which, although including neoclassical economics, ranges more widely. Development and growth economics was central in 'classical economics' which occupied the period 1775 to 1870, preceding neoclassical economics which established itself as mainstream economics after 1870. In more modern times, that is after the Second World War, development economics was revived and its development has been characterized with competing theory, empiricism and evaluation. In consequence, sustainability and environmentalism has potential association to various theories, concepts and techniques. As discussed in the Introduction, the idea of sustainability came to the fore in the late 1980s, a period which has been deeply influenced by the economics and politics of 'enablement liberalism'.

'Enablement liberalism' has some of its roots in the new political economy (NPE). The NPE endeavours to explore the relationships between economics and politics, including the analysis of what governments do and why they do what they do. It also takes some of its characteristics from orthodox economics, accepting significant market roles. All of this raises the question of the potential role and influence of alternatives such as radical sociopolitical approaches. In the period 1970 to the mid-1980s radical political economy was expressed in neo-Marxism and dependency theory, deriving its basis from ideas of class, surplus, and exploitation. These ideas had some influence in the urban and housing literature, especially in the writings of Burgess (see Pugh, 1994). Since the demise of state socialism after 1988 there has been less interest in the intellectual development of neo-Marxist and dependency theory for the interpretation of urbanization in developing countries. Moreover, controversially, authors such as Booth (1985) have argued that the radical political economy of the 1970–85 period had reached a conceptual, theoretical and empirical impasse. He argued that concepts were inconclusive, empirical work arid and repetitive, and large, significant areas were undertheorized and under-researched. Neglected areas included the environment, and environmental performance under state socialism was bad. For future prospect, political economy could usefully be developed from the basis of strength in economics and by developing a theory of governmental reforms for environmentalism.

The term 'political economy' was originally coined by the French author Antoine de Montchetien in the seventeenth century, and he used it to argue that governments should have a proper regard for economics in running a country. Adam Smith subsequently took the idea further, elaborating economic principles in a wider consideration for history, institutions, public policy, moral philosophy and the (then) major public issues of the time in the late eighteenth century. Economics has always been developed as 'political economy', though some elements in orthodoxy tend to hide this in a penchant of some authors for technocratic approaches. Perhaps urban sustainable development will develop 'strong' and 'weak' versions of political economy. In the 'strong' versions authors would have knowledge of the social science of the environment, of urban economic issues, and of ideas and theories from development economics. Weaker versions will be self limiting in confining the scope to rather generalized commentary on economic and political issues. Economics, politics, the environment and urban studies are actually full of substance in theory, technique, concepts and findings. Political economy thus has the potential for appreciation in intellectual depth and width. It can also be pursued circumspectly. For example, the post-1950 record of markets and governments reveals mixed achievement: there are examples of market success and failure and of state success and failure. Advocates for the superiority of the market, or alternatively for the state, are often arguing from ideological preconception rather than from an overall review of the evidence which, as argued above, reveals various mixtures of success and failure. Also, some chapters in this book indicate the relevance of multi-institutional approaches in environmental programmes. The main needs from political economy perspectives are to improve the performances of states, markets, NGOs, CBOs and households, acting separately and in partnerships. All of this has relevance in social science research and in policy making.

URBAN SUSTAINABLE DEVELOPMENT

Most of the chapters in this book make reference to the notion of urban sustainable development, though the authors sometimes use different words to describe and evaluate the idea. It is appropriate to give a summarized perspective on what has been said on this topic and to extend meaning and interpretation. In the summarized perspective, here is what authors have stated and reasoned:

- First, the idea of urban sustainable development does not mean a city–regional self-sufficiency in the use of environmental resources or in economic functioning. Environmental interdependency runs through a geographical spectrum from the localized to the globalized. Furthermore, economic and human development depends upon national and international trade. In the perspective of actual conditions, economic development falls within the globalization of finance, technology, management practices and so on, with variations in the degrees of progressiveness and 'sclerosis'.

- Second, urban sustainable development has varying localized expression, depending upon situational geography, level of community affluence, stage of development, and the application of (in)effective environmental and related social and economic policies. This can be given illustrative general exampling. At conceptual levels, the 'environmental transition' proceeds from significance upon neighbourhood sanitary and health conditions, through particulate air pollution, to greenhouse gases in air pollution. However, in some city–regions these will be occurring simultaneously and with all expressions increasing in volume. At policy development levels, infrastructure and other improvements can be introduced incrementally within affordability and feasibility. Also, technical analyses and appraisals can be developed gradually over the medium term. The scope and content of appraisal and monitoring can themselves be changed through time: for example, localized environmental and health indicators can be integrated.

- Third, with appreciation that conceptual dilemmas exist, it is clear that 'sustainability' has simultaneous reference to the ecological, the economic, the social and the institutional. But the appreciation is not to be confined to the conceptual. Interdependence links the ecological, the economic, the social and the institutional through cause–consequence relationships in operating economies, cities and social processes. Examples are many and varied. Some significant examples include the ways poverty can lead to economic and environmental degradation, and simultaneously the ways in which bad urban environments can increase the volume of poverty and change the nature of poverty. Thus, issues of social equity are always embedded in the cause for improved urban environments. Complex interdependence has further implications in society, including issues of governance. Issues of governance include policy formulation, institutional reform, transparency, probity and participation. Finally, it is not possible to be effective in policy by confining environmental causes to policies that are in their own right explicitly for improving physical environments. Most economic, social, health and educational policies have environmental relevance. The 'environmental' is multifaceted, multi-institutional and set within multiple objectives.

The foregoing is not a comprehensive portrayal of what constitutes 'urban sustainable development', but it provides some basic indicative principles. From this basis a few points can be developed further by posing some relevant questions. Is it possible to reconcile the subject of urban sustainable development with approaches in the conventional literature? In what ways do the patterns of development in fast growing cities in developing countries enhance or retard environmental improvement? Is it possible to conceive of patterns of urban development that meet some prescriptively good principles in urban sustainable development?

Three approaches in the conventional literature can be discerned. First, town planning has been primarily concerned with the theory and practice of land use and development control. In application to developing countries it had dilemmas of appropriateness and effectiveness (Devas and Rakodi, 1993). And, sustainable development has been added in a somewhat fragmentary and occasional way. Sustainable development has not been incorporated or pursued from the basis of theory, concept and professional operation in town planning. In some expressions town planning has been conservationist and detached from economic development, leading to applications in some developing countries that ignore the realities of mass poverty in urban conditions. Second, the idea of 'urban management' has become more significant since the mid-1980s. Although urban management has not yet been developed to a stage where there is widespread professional and intellectual agreement of what constitutes its core principles and content, some ideas have been presented. For example, various perspectives engage the attention of authors in the book edited by Davey and his coauthors (1996). With reference to developing countries, the early literature is pursuing public and general administrative principles in such spheres as budgeting, central-local government relations and structures of urban governance. Environmental and developmental aspects are again included in fragmented and occasional ways. Third, human geography has brought environmental issues into its study and research programmes. This is developing in an eclectic way. One example is the book edited by Main and Williams (1994). The contributing authors focus upon some environmental catastrophes which impact upon the poor, including earthquakes, the Bhopal chemical explosion and unstable self-built housing on steep hillslopes. Again, the approach has not been much concerned with the theoretical, conceptual and policy issues of 'sustainability' and 'urban' development in fast growing cities.

Some of the discussions in the Introduction reviewed the nature of urban development in fast growing cities in developing countries. Research indicates that large cities grow with both intensive economic activity in central areas and with decentralization and lateral spread in the expanding suburbs. The form and pattern of macro-spatial development leads to growing demands for transport which adds to energy costs and some greenhouse gas pollution (Mohan, 1994). Urban land is often in concentrated ownership and land values increase with rapid demographic and economic growth. In effect, the growth transfers wealth and income to landowners, this including some 'unearned increments'. Moreover, because the decentralization of economic activities often occurs haphazardly rather than with strong (multiple) urban centres, the pattern of development adds to transport demands and has some inconvenience for residents. Better patterns of macro-spatial development could occur, but they would be dependent upon specific land policies and planning for settlements.

Multi-centred patterns of urban development have been conceived and reasoned from the basis of theory and first principles. The key authors have all been in a situational and policy context of rapid demographic and economic growth in developing societies (Marshall, 1884; Coase, 1960; Currie, 1976; Stretton, 1970; Neutze, 1965 and 1973; Pugh, 1980). Taking all the authors together, the theory and advocacy would run along the following lines. Multi-centred urban development can reduce arbitrary inequality, can improve price-access to urban services, can economize upon transport and rationalize some energy uses, and can control some unearned increments in land, returning them to the general community. It is possible to find a land policy basis in this that is not unacceptably confiscatory in land and that is free of excessive bureaucracy. The prescriptive aims are to concentrate some economic activities, to satisfy some social needs and to enhance environmentalism. Policy requirements are for land acquisition at (non speculative) use values by joint venture public and private corporations or by statutory land commissions that compete with private developers. The public sector does not engage in direct production, but rather facilitates private and social property rights among participants in land development and use. Scale of land acquisition is important: it has to be sufficient to create integrated development, sometimes using housing programmes in conjunction with land policies. Essentially, what is done is that land acquisition and disposal operate in managed markets (i e 'enablement') to bring economic externalities, monopoly elements and other market imperfections into accountability. It does not require nationalization or universal leasehold to achieve the ends of policy. Private locational investments can be stimulated by reducing unproductive risks which occur in uncoordinated urban development. Development plans are devised to create concentrated activities in multiple centres which are linked by major modes of transport. Examples of good practice occur in Singapore (Pugh, 1995a; 1995b; 1996), in South Australia (Stretton, 1970), in Sweden and Norway (Pugh, 1980), and in the extension of Singaporean practices into the People's Republic of China at Suzhou (Pugh, 1995b). Thus, it is possible to practise good principle, but caution should be added. The foregoing land policies require skilled public administration and political acceptance, and these appropriate conditions are not always present.

The managed markets approach to macro-spatial urbanization adds principle and practice dimensions to the idea of 'urban sustainable development'. It reveals urban sustainable development at the intersection of economic growth and development, environmentalism and urban spatial-economic development. As suggested in earlier sections, these ideas put elements of theory and principle into an infant subject which has its own sets of theoretical relevance. These are not those of conventional town planning, though the fields clearly overlap. In application, it has been seen that the new subject sphere has much to do with fast growing cities. Some cities have 'mega' size status, including Mexico City, São Paulo, Bombay, and others. Large cities pose special considerations in urban sustainable development, including servicing, governance and environmental degradation. Explicit policies to curb growth of such cities have not been effective. However, as indicated above, there are ways to formulate policies to improve macro-spatial development. Even where the full policy set cannot be implemented it is possible to take opportunities to enhance suburban centring. Also, with the transition from import substitution to export-led development policies, 'mega' city growth is likely to slow down. Protected markets encourage entrepreneurs to locate in large cities, whereas export emphasis places competitive premiums upon smaller cities with lower land and property costs.

FINAL WORD

Sustainability and environmental improvement are inherently long term. They depend upon securing suitable and stable policy frameworks, laws and political commitments. Stability and subtle adjustment are quite obviously adversely affected by wars, ethnic conflicts, severe international economic cyclicality, and the persistence of social tensions related to mass poverty. Accordingly, the cause for environmentalism and improved urbanization depends upon the broad development of social, economic and political cooperation. Although environmentalism has implications for future generations, it is the world's millions in the current and next generations whose lives and welfare are significantly tied up with improvement in the environment and in social cooperation.

The drama of millions is already being played out in the demographic and economic transitions in the developing countries. It is a drama in varied scenes and with widening results in welfare. Here are two contrasting family careers and lives since the early 1960s. Carmen Garcia's family migrated to Mexico City in the late 1950s, building a meagre self-help hutment in the western suburbs. In childhood some of her friends died from enteritis. She married and over the years with her family established her self-help house, improved over time. Eventually the local authorities installed sanitation and infrastructure. In the 1990s, for over six months of each year Mexico City is highly polluted from photosynthetic smog. The World Bank has provided a substantial loan programme to improve air quality in Mexico City, but other problems are increasing. The population of over 20 million are using water at high rates, leading to a lowering of the aquifer and dependence on costly distant supplies. Sim Sok Lee was born in Singapore and her parents once lived in a crowded shophouse close to the foetid river basin in the central city area. The family then moved to a new apartment built by the government's housing agency, the Housing and Development Board. By the 1990s over 85 per cent of Singaporeans were living in the board's modern housing. In the wider city context, government had restricted motor vehicle use, developed modern public transport and introduced environmental improvements. The Singaporean economy grew impressively and Singapore became a 'garden city' with widespread economic and social benefits. 'Sustainable development' is worth pursuing, but development in the coming decades is likely to have varied environmental results, with major consequences upon the lives of hundreds of millions.

References

Booth, D (1985) 'Marxism and Development Sociology: Interpreting the Impasse', *World Development*, 13 (7), pp 761–87

Coase, R (1960) 'The Problem of Social Cost', *Journal of Law and Economics*, 3 (1), pp 1–44

Currie, L (1976) *Taming the Megagopolis*, Pergamon, Oxford

Davey, K et al (1996) *Urban Management: The Challenge of Growth*, Avebury, Aldershot

Devas, N and C Rakodi (eds) (1993) *Managing Fast Growing Cities*, Longman, Harlow

Goldin, I and L Winters (eds) (1995) *The Economics of Sustainable Development*, Cambridge University Press, Cambridge

Main, H and H Williams (eds) (1994) *Environment and Housing in Third World Cities*, Wiley, Chichester

Marshall, A (1884) 'The Housing of the London Poor: Where to House Them', *Contemporary Review*, February

Meier, G (1994) 'Review of Development Research in the UK: Report to the Development Studies Association', *Journal of International Development*, 6 (5), pp 465–517

Mohan, R (1994) *Understanding the Developing Metropolis: Lessons from the City Study of Bogatá and Cali*, Colombia, Oxford University Press, Oxford

Neutze, G (1965) *Economic Policy and the Size of Cities*, Australian National University, Canberra

— (1973) *The Price of Land and Land Use Planning: Policy Instruments in the Urban Land Market*, OECD, Paris

Pugh, C (1980) *Housing in Capitalist Societies*, Gower, Aldershot

— (1994) 'Housing Policy in Developing Countries: The World Bank and Internationalization, 1972–93', *Cities*, 11 (3), pp 159–80

— (1995a) 'International Structural Adjustment and Its Sectoral and Spatial Impacts', *Urban Studies*, 32 (2), pp 261–85

— (1995b) 'Reply: Issues of Interpretation, Adverse Selection and Political Economy', *Cities*, 12 (6), pp 413–24

— (1996) '"Urban Bias" and the Theory and Practice of Development in Developing Countries', *Urban Studies*, 33 (7), forthcoming

Stretton, H (1970) *Ideas for Australian Cities*, Georgian House, Melbourne

Acronyms and Abbreviations

ADAB	Association of the Development Agencies of Bangladesh
AIDS	acquired immune deficiency syndrome
BMA	Bangkok Metropolitan Administration
CBA	Cost-benefit analysis
CBO	community-based organization
CCC	Chittagong City Corporation
CVM	contingent valuation method
DANIDA	Danish International Development Assistance Agency
DCF	discounted cash flow
EA	Environmental Audit
ECBA	Environmental cost benefit analysis
EIA	Environmental Impact Assessment
EU	European Union
GATT	General Agreement on Tariffs and Trade
GDP	gross domestic product
GEF	global environment facility
GSS	Global Strategy for Shelter
HCP	Healthy Cities Project
ICMA	International City County Management Association
IDA	International Development Association
IDEA	Industrial Development for Environmental Action
IIED	International Institute for Environment and Development
ILO	International Labour Organization
IMF	International Monetary Fund
MHP	municipal health plan
MOH	Ministry of Health
NAFTA	North American Free Trade Agreement
NGO	non-governmental organization
NIE	new institutional economics
NPE	new political economy
NPV	net present value
NUV	non-use value

OECD	Organization for Economic Cooperation and Development
OIE	old institutional economics
OPEC	Organization of Petroleum Exporting Countries
OPP	Orangi Pilot Project
PPP	purchasing power parity
SEA	Strategic Environmental Assessment
TCM	travel cost method
TEV	total economic value
UMP	Urban Management Programme
UN	United Nations
UNCED	United Nations Conference on Environment and Development
UNCHS	United Nations Centre for Human Settlements
UNDP	United Nations Development Programme
UNEP	United Nations Environment Programme
UNICEF	United Nations Children's Fund
UPP	Urban Poverty Programme
USAID	United States Agency for International Development
UV	use value
WCED	World Commission on Environment and Development
WHO	World Health Organization
WICE	World Industry Council for the Environment
WTO	World Trade Organization
wtp	willingness to pay

Index

CPSIA information can be obtained at www.ICGtesting.com
Printed in the USA
LVOW03s1406240914

405667LV00003B/12/P